A

TREATISE ON PAINTING

BY

LEONARDO DA VINCI.

TRANSLATED FROM THE ITALIAN BY

JOHN FRANCIS RIGAUD, R.A.

———

WITH A LIFE OF LEONARDO AND AN ACCOUNT OF

HIS WORKS BY JOHN WILLIAM BROWN.

———

LONDON

GEORGE BELL & SONS

1897

ARS EST HABITUS QUIDAM FACIENDI VERA CUM RATIONE.

ARISTOT. *Ethic.* lib. 6

Leonardo da Vinci

Engraved by H. B. Worthington

London; G. Bell & Sons. York Street. Covent Garden.

PREFACE

———◦◦◦———

WHEN Leonardo da Vinci made his will, nine days before his death—which took place on the 2nd of May, 1519, at his château at Clos-Lucé (Cloux), near Amboise—he bequeathed all his manuscripts and drawings to Messer Francesco da Melzi, gentleman, of Milan, "in remuneration of grateful services done to the testator." Melzi transted his treasures to his residence at Vaprio, where, years afterwards, he died. His heirs set little store the writings of the great painter, and suffered thirteen d volumes and the "drawings in the garret" to be away as valueless. Some of these drawings fell into hands of the Earl of Arundel, and are now in the al Collection at Windsor. Many of the others, after quent changes of proprietorship, were presented to the nbrosian Library at Milan.

At the close of the eighteenth century, there were in this library thirteen volumes of Leonardo's, including the celebrated "Codice Atlantico," a book of huge size, containing 1750 sketches which had been collected by the sculptor Pompeo Leoni of Arezzo.*

In 1796, Bonaparte seized these books and sent them to Paris, where they were placed in the Bibliothèque de l'Institut. After the Peace, in 1815, the "Codice Atlantico" was returned to the Ambrosian Library. The other twelve volumes still remain in Paris.

In the year 1651, a selection from these manuscripts of such passages as relate to the Art of Painting, came into the possession of Raphael du Fresne, who published them in the original Italian, under the title of "Trattato della Pittura," accompanied by a series of engravings from outline drawings by Nicholas Poussin (to which shadows and backgrounds were added by Errard), and a set of geometrical designs by Alberti. In the same year, the work was translated into French by Roland Fréard, Sieur de Chambray, and issued with the same plates.

In 1721, a translation into English—it is not known by whom—was published in London, and in 1796 another edition was printed, which was soon exhausted; for in the year 1802, Mr. John Francis Rigaud, a member of the Royal Academy, undertook to translate the work afresh, and to re-arrange the whole book so as to make it easier of reference; careful indexes were given, and the plates were re-engraved. This edition lasted till 1835, when a new

* From an inscription in the Ambrosian Library, we learn that a King of England (probably Charles I.) offered 3000 gold doubloons of Spain for this work.

Sorry:
The defect on the previous page was that way in the original book we reproduced.

one was issued by Messrs. Nichols and Son, to which was added a Life of Leonardo by Mr. John William Brown. This gentleman had the privilege of constant admittance not only to the private library of his Imperial and Royal Highness the Grand Duke of Tuscany, but also to his most rare and valuable collection of Manuscripts in the Palazzo Pitti, where he was permitted to copy from the original documents and correspondence whatever he conceived useful to his subject. He was enabled to produce what was *then* the most trustworthy Life of Leonardo that had ever appeared. Since that time many new biographies of Leonardo have been written, of which one of the most important is that by Signor Gustavo Uzielli.

The 1835 edition of the "Treatise on Painting" has long been scarce. It is now reprinted, and the more recent facts which have been discovered concerning the life of Leonardo, and a full account of his manuscripts and his acknowledged paintings have been added.

Nicholas Poussin's drawings and Alberti's designs are reproduced, and great pains have been taken to make Leonardo's work as useful as possible to students of Art.

John Francis Rigaud, the translator of the "Trattato della Pittura," was born of French parents at Turin, in 1742. His father, who was a merchant, intended his son to follow his profession; but young Rigaud evinced so strong a talent for painting, that he was allowed to follow his own desires. After he had received good instruction in art from Chevalier Beaumont, principal painter to the King of Sardinia, Rigaud travelled much in Italy, and stayed more especially in Rome, Parma, and in Bologna, where, in 1766, he was elected a member of the Clementine Academy. In 1772, Rigaud left Italy and went to Paris, where he remained but a short time. He then came to England, and gained much praise for his picture of *Hercules.* In the November of the year of his arrival, he was elected an Associate of the Royal Academy, and in 1784 he became a full member. With the exception of a journey on the Continent, Rigaud spent the rest of his life in England. He died in 1810, at Packington, in Warwickshire, the seat of the Earl of Aylesford, his chief patron.

In the parish church at Packington is an altar-piece painted by Rigaud for the Earl of Aylesford—noteworthy from the circumstance that it is supposed to be the first work executed in fresco in this country.

Among other honours in art, Rigaud was made a Member of the Royal Academy of Stockholm, and Historical Painter to the King of Sweden.

CONTENTS.

THE LIFE OF

LEONARDO DA VINCI.

——◦◦◦——

AMONG the many distinguished individuals who flourished in
Italy during the early part of the sixteenth century, whether
we consider his splendid and almost universal talents, or the
excellence of his character, there is none more worthy of com-
memoration than Leonardo da Vinci. Through a long and active
life his mind was zealously devoted to the revival of the arts,
to which he contributed in a greater degree, perhaps, than any
single individual of ancient or modern times. The arts of poetry,
music, and especially painting, were embraced by him with an
enthusiasm which awakened that of others, and gave a mighty
impulse to the mental energies, not only of his contemporaries
and countrymen, but of distant nations and posterity.

Every incident in the life of such a man must be full of
interest to the lovers of biography: the more so from the very
remarkable fact, that in no language have those incidents been
properly collected, though abundant and authentic sources of
information exist on which such a work might be founded. To
supply in some degree this deficiency, is the object of the
following pages.*

Leonardo da Vinci was born in the year 1452, at Vinci, in the
Val d'Arno Inferiore, on the confines of the Pistoiese territory,
not far from the lake of Fucecchio. He was the natural son of
Ser Piero Antonio da Vinci, who, in the year 1484, was Notary
to the Seignory of Florence. It is said that his mother was a

* This Life of Leonardo was first published in 1828.

servant * in his father's family ; but this must remain uncertain, from the length of time that has since elapsed, and the numerous reports that contradict each other, not only in what relates to his origin, but even to the year of his birth, in which there is a difference of no less than seven years.† It is, however, certain, that he was entirely brought up in his father's family ; a fact attested by an old and well-authenticated register, found among the ancient archives of Florence by Signore Dei, who has written largely on the subject of Leonardo's genealogy. It is a matter of some regret, that, amidst all his learned and elaborate researches, that gentleman has not been able to procure any documents to prove that Da Vinci was subsequently declared legitimate, which from various circumstances appears to be extremely probable. If we may believe the register, and there is no better authority, Leonardo was seventeen years old when his father was forty ; so that he must have been born when Piero was a young man, and most likely before his marriage.

His father had four wives, Albiera di Giovanni da Zenobi Amadori, Francesca di Ser Giuliano Lanfredini, Margherita di Francesco, and Lucrezia di Guglielmo Cortigiani ; and a proof that Leonardo still formed a part of his family after his third marriage, is afforded by a passage in one of Belincionni's sonnets, addressed to Madonna Lucrezia da Vinci, which begins

" A Fiesole con Piero e Leonardo ; "

and relates the pleasures he enjoyed at their villa near Florence. It is hardly probable that he would have received such unvarying attentions, had he been considered merely as a natural child. Moreover, we find from several documents in the " Codice Atlantico," that his family were at all times proud of his relationship, and his uncle Francesco da Vinci left him an equal share of his property with his brothers and sisters.

Leonardo was gifted with one of the finest forms that can be imagined, in which strength and symmetry were beautifully combined ; his face was strongly expressive of his ardent mind,

---

* Her name was Caterina. She afterwards married a certain Accatabriga di Piero del Vacca, di Vinci.—*Uzielli.*

† Vasari says he was born in 1445.

and of the frankness and energy of his character. He would, it
may be presumed, have distinguished himself in the literary
world while in his youth, had he not been as unsteady as he
was enthusiastic in his various pursuits.   He made such
wonderful progress in arithmetic, that when a child he frequently proposed questions which his master himself was unable
to resolve.   He next attached himself to music as a science, and
soon arrived at such perfection in playing on the lyre, which
was his favourite instrument, as to compose extemporaneous
accompaniments to his own poetical effusions.   The following
sonnet is one of the very few which are extant:—

> " Chi non può quel che vuol, quel che può voglia :
>   Che quel che non si può folle è il volere.
>   Adunque saggio è l'uomo da tenere
>   Che da quel che non può suo voler toglia.
> Pero che ogni diletto nostro e doglia
>   Stà in si e no, saper voler potere,
>   Adunque quel solpuò che è col dovere,
>   Ne trae la ragion fuor di sua soglia.
> Ne sempre è da voler quel che l'uom pòte,
>   Spesso par dolce quel che torna amaro
>   Piansi già quel che io volsi, poiche io l'ebbi.
> Adunque tu, lettor di queste note,
>   Se a te vuoi esser buono, e ad altri caro,
>   Vogli sempre poter quel che tu debbi."

But, although an ardent admirer of the arts in general,
painting appeared to be his favourite pursuit, to which he
more particularly applied himself in all its different branches;
and in which he soon attained great excellence, as well as in the
art of forming models and designs.

Cimabue, Giotto, and Masaccio had already begun to revive
the art of painting in Italy, and more particularly in Tuscany,
where, from the powerful patronage of Lorenzo de' Medici, so
justly styled " the Magnificent," the arts were most certain to
find protection and encouragement.   His liberality had already
acquired for his native Florence the honourable appellation of
the " Modern Athens ;" and his taste for literature and the fine
arts considerably influenced the state of public opinion among
his countrymen.

The Signore Piero, perceiving that his son's abilities and inclinations might lead to future wealth and fame, determined to show the productions of his self-cultivated talents to Andrea Verocchio, one of the most celebrated painters, sculptors, and architects of that age.* Messer Andrea, surprised at the strong indications of original talent and hope of future excellence which these early productions evinced, gladly consented to receive the young Leonardo into his "studio," convinced that a pupil of so much merit could not fail of increasing his master's celebrity; but he soon found that his scholar had little need of his instructions, and that he would ere long surpass him in his own works.

It happened about this time that Messer Andrea was employed to paint a picture of St. John baptizing our Saviour; and anxious to stimulate his young pupil to greater exertion, he desired his assistance in this composition. Leonardo executed the part assigned him with such extraordinary skill, that, as Vasari relates, the angel painted by him greatly excelled all the rest of Andrea's picture, which, he says, "was the occasion of Messer Andrea's leaving off painting, enraged that a child should know more than himself." †

Having thus early given proof of wonderful abilities, Leonardo employed himself in studying the different branches of the art to which he now intended more particularly to devote his attention. But the natural inconstancy of his disposition frequently impelled him to desert his studio, and indulge in imaginary speculations. His time, however, was never unemployed; and though his occupations were always various, and sometimes inconsistent, he nevertheless most assiduously cultivated whatever was calculated to adorn his mind or increase his accomplishments. He must also have worked very diligently at his profession, as his father could not have afforded him much money for his amuse-

---

* Andrea del Verocchio, or Verrocchio, a Florentine painter, architect, and jeweller, died at Venice in 1488, where he was employed in forming the equestrian statue of Bartolomeo Coglioni-in-bronze. He was more celebrated as an architect and sculptor-than as a painter.—See his life by *Vasari.*

† This statement must be received with some qualification. Leonardo remained with Verocchio till 1477, when he was twenty-five years of age.

ments; and he is known, if we may believe his contemporaries, to have led rather a gay life. The delight of society wherever he went, and an extraordinary favourite with the fair sex, he became too fond of dress and parade; he maintained a numerous retinue of servants, a sumptuous equipage, and purchased the most spirited horses that could be procured. These extravagances were, however, extremely pardonable in a young man flushed with success and conscious of his superior acquirements, particularly as they could only be supported by the produce of his own industry, and must therefore have greatly tended to stimulate his exertions.

Like most people who are endowed with great natural talents, he undertook much more than he was able to accomplish; and we find him continually changing his occupations: at one time diligently employing himself in astronomical observations, to ascertain the motion of the heavenly bodies; at another, intently pursuing the study of natural history and botany; yet, with all his versatility of talent and inconstancy of disposition, never permitting himself to neglect his favourite pursuit. With the utmost perseverance he sought every possible means of improving himself in painting, from the time he left the studio of Andrea Verocchio and became his own master.

The numerous works on scientific subjects that Leonardo has left to posterity, sufficiently prove how well he must have employed his youth, though very little is to be found in the writings of his contemporaries to give us any information of the occurrences of his every-day life. Both Vasari and Lomazzo relate that he invented various machines for lifting great weights, penetrating mountains, conducting water from one place to another, and innumerable models for watches, windmills, and presses. Two of the many projects which he had in contemplation, some of which were almost too wild for belief, deserve to be particularly noticed. One of them was to lift up the Cathedral of San Lorenzo *en masse*, by means of immense levers, and in such a manner that he pretended the edifice would not receive the slightest injury. The other, which was more feasible, was to form the Arno into a canal as far as Pisa, and which would have been extremely beneficial to the commerce of Tuscany.

That Leonardo continued to reside at Florence, or at least in its neighbourhood, is confirmed by the story Vasari relates of the *Rotella del Fico*, which was a round piece of wood cut from the largest fig-tree on his father's estate. Signore Piero was very fond of field sports and country amusements; and one of his " contadini " who was particularly useful to him on these occasions, brought him a piece of wood, requesting him to have something painted on it as an ornament for his cottage. Willing to gratify his favourite, he desired his son to do as the man wished; and Leonardo, determined to paint something that should astonish his father by the great progress he had made in his art. This piece of wood must have been roughly made and badly put together, as our young artist was obliged to have it planed off and the interstices filled up with stucco, so as to leave a surface sufficiently smooth for his purpose. He then considered for some time what he should represent, and at length determined on painting a monster that should have the effect of Medusa's head on all beholders. For this purpose he collected every kind of reptile—vipers, adders, lizards, toads, serpents, and other poisonous or noxious animals, and formed a monster so wonderfully designed, that it appeared to flash fire from its eyes, and also to infect the air with its breath. When he had succeeded to his wishes in this horrible composition, he called his father to try its effect upon him; who, not expecting what he was to see, started back with horror and affright, and was just going to run out of the room, when Leonardo stopped him by assuring him it was the work of his own hands, exclaiming, that he was quite satisfied, as his picture had the effect he anticipated. Signore Piero was, of course, too much delighted with his son's performance to think of giving it to his " contadino," for whom he procured an ordinary painting, and sold Leonardo's to a merchant of Florence for one hundred ducats. This was a very large sum to give for a picture, when the value of money at the time is remembered; but it was soon after sold to the Duke of Milan for three times the original cost.

The life of a painter, however celebrated, cannot be expected to furnish the same variety of incidents as that of a warrior or a statesman, though the civil virtues and splendid talents of Leonardo da Vinci were probably more useful to his country than the warlike qualifications of his more ambitious contemporaries, which were usually accompanied by violence and followed by remorse.

Leonardo da Vinci had now reached his thirty-first year, and was most indefatigable in the study of whatever might tend to his improvement or increase his knowledge in the art of painting, to which he almost exclusively devoted himself. One of his first undertakings was the celebrated cartoon (pasteboard, or rather, thick paper), which he designed, by order of the King of Portugal, for a piece of tapestry that was to be worked in Flanders for that monarch. This drawing represented the *Story of Adam and Eve* when first tempted to sin, and surpassed everything which had been seen of the kind.

One of his first pictures was a painting of the *Madonna*, in which he introduced, among other accessories, a vase of flowers, so inimitably executed that the dew seemed glittering on the leaves. This production became afterwards the property of Pope Clement the Seventh, who purchased it at an immense price. For his friend Antonio Segni he formed a design of *Neptune*, drawn in his car by sea-horses through the ocean, surrounded by tritons, mermaids, and all the other attributes of that deity which his fertile imagination could invent. It was some time after presented by Segni's son, Fabio, to Messer Giovanni Gaddi, with this epigram:—

> " Pinxit Virgilius Neptunum : pinxit Homerus
> Dum maris undisoni per vada flectit equos :
> Mente quidem vates illum conspexit uterque;
> Vincius est oculis, jureque vincit eos."

Da Vinci always took great pleasure in delineating the most grotesque figures and extraordinary faces, so that, if he met a man in the street with any peculiarity of ugliness or deformity of countenance, he would follow him until he had a correct idea of his face, and would then draw the person, on his return home, from memory, as well as if he had been present. He not only studied to perfect himself in giving the mere beauty or deformity of the likenesses he painted, but he sought to give the very air, manner, and expression of the persons represented. He at all times preferred studying from nature to following rules that were then but imperfectly understood; and he was in the habit of inviting the contadini, and people of the lower orders, to sup with him, telling them the most ridiculous stories, that he might delineate the natural expressions of rude delight undisguised by the refinements of good breeding. He would then show them their own likenesses, which no one could possibly behold without laughter at the ridiculous faces which he had caricatured, but with so much truth that the originals could not be mistaken.* He was so indefatigable in pursuing the object of his ambition, that he neglected no means of procuring fresh studies for his pencil. He would sometimes put himself to the pain of accompanying criminals to the place of execution, and would remain with them in their last moments, that he might catch the expression of their countenances, and delineate the agony of their sufferings. In short, there was no branch of his art which he considered unworthy of his attention, aware that perfection in anything is only to be attained by unwearied industry and application.

We find from Vasari, that it was about this time that he painted a picture for the Grand Duke Cosimo the First, representing an *Angel* in strong light and shade, which was placed by that prince in the collection of the Palazzo Vecchio, from whence it has been missing for upwards of a century. Most probably it was turned out of its place from the oversight or carelessness of the directors, who had condemned it to be put aside with a quantity of rubbish, old furniture, and frames, which are occasionally sold by order of the Duke's guardaroba. It was not long since bought by a "rivenditore" for twenty-one quatrini, about three-pence, and resold to its present possessor, the Signore Fineschi, a drawing-master of Florence, for five pauls—two shillings and sixpence. There is no doubt of the originality of this painting, both from the particular style of colouring Leonardo made use of, and the sort of stucco with which it is covered behind, a chemical composition which he is well known to have used to preserve his pictures from the worms when they were painted on wood. It is also most accurately described in Vasari's Life of Leonardo, in these

* The best of these caricatures were published by Clarke, in 1786, from drawings by Wenceslaus Hollar taken from the Portland Museum.

words:—" Among the best things in the Duke Cosimo's palace is the head of an Angel, with one arm lifted up in the air, shortened off about the elbow, and the other with the hand on the bosom. It is a very extraordinary thing that this great genius was in the habit of seeking for the very darkest blacks, in order to effect a sort of chiaroscuro, which added more brilliancy to his pictures, and gave them more the appearance of night than the clearness of day; but this was in order to increase the relief, and so improve the art of painting."

The celebrated picture of the *Medusa's Head*, which is now in the Public Gallery at Florence, was executed about this time, but, as it was a work that required great labour, it, like too many of his undertakings, is in an unfinished state. It is a most extraordinary subject, and the snakes are interwoven and grouped together instead of hair with such wonderful skill, that it excites almost as much disgust as admiration.

The fame of Leonardo's extraordinary abilities spread through Italy, and he was invited by several princes to reside at their courts, and enrich their palaces with his works. The example of the great Lorenzo had raised an emulation among the princes of Italy for the encouragement of literary men; and whoever was distinguished by talent was sure not only of wealth and preferment, but was flattered and caressed by all his superiors. The unusual tranquility Italy enjoyed from the wise precautions and conciliatory policy of Lorenzo de' Medici, left her turbulent rulers at leisure to cultivate the arts of peace. Their habitual restlessness required employment; and reduced to inaction by the temporary cessation of their petty wars and intrigues, their ambition consisted in drawing to their respective courts the greatest men of that luminous period. Lorenzo may therefore be justly styled, not only the Mæcenas of Florence, which he governed, but of the age in which he lived, as his politics so materially influenced the revival of literature and the progress of general civilization.

Anxious to secure to himself a certain provision for his expensive style of living, Leonardo addressed a letter to Ludovico Sforza, surnamed *Il Moro*, offering his services to that prince, who governed Milan during his nephew's minority, and whom he knew to be most desirous of attracting to his court all

the *literati* of the age, under the pretence of assisting him in
the young Duke's education.* None of the writers of that period
have given any reason why Leonardo preferred the patronage
of Ludovico to that of the house of Medici, particularly as the
latter were distinguished by their liberal encouragement of the
arts. Perhaps Lorenzo might have sent him to Il Moro, with
whom he was in strict alliance; or Leonardo might himself have
preferred Milan, where he would have hoped to have found a
more extensive field for the exercise of his talents, and less
competition than he must have had to contend with at Florence
The uncertainty of his birth perhaps influenced so high-minded
a man; and he probably wished to establish his own fortunes at
a strange court, where he was only known as an illustrious
Florentine, distinguished by his sovereign for the superiority of
his talents and acquirements. Whatever might have been Da
Vinci's motive, it is certain that he entered the service of the
Duke of Milan, and consented to receive an annual salary of
five hundred scudi, which was then by no means a contemptible
sum. He was, moreover, entitled to various privileges and
immunities, and permitted to appropriate to his own use the
produce of such of his paintings as were not executed by the
Duke's order.

It is important to the history of Leonardo da Vinci to fix, as
nearly as possible, the period of his arrival at Milan. From the
most authentic sources it appears that he must have taken up
his residence there previous to the year 1487; for we find in an
old treatise entitled "Della Luce e dell' Ombra," in his own
hand-writing, the following observation: "A dì 23 d' Aprile 1490,
chominciai questo libro, e richominciai il Cavallo." † In this
memorandum he no doubt alludes to the equestrian statue of
Francesco Sforza the First, which, if he recommenced in 1490, he

---

* It is a curious fact, that Leonardo da Vinci frequently wrote
from right to left, like the Persians, for which no one has been able
to account. It was most probably from a love of singularity; and,
although it increases the difficulty of deciphering his manuscripts, it
also serves to place their identity beyond dispute. This singularity
is supposed by many of his biographers to have arisen from the fact
that he was left-handed.

† "On the 23rd of April, 1490, I began this book and recommenced
the horse."

must have begun long before, as it must have consumed much time to form the necessary moulds and designs. Moreover, he is alluded to by Belincionni, a Florentine poet, who resided at the court of Ludovico il Moro, and celebrated most of the principal events of that period, under the name of the "Appelle Fiorentino:"

> "Quì come l' ape al miel viene ogni dotto,
> Di virtuosi ha la sua corte piena:
> Da Fiorenza un Apelle ha qui condotto;" *

and the editor Tantio, or Tanzi, has added in the margin, fearing it might not be understood, "Magistro Leonardo da Vinci."

There is also another authority not less respectable than the former, in the Ricordi of Monsignore Sabba da Castiglione, which dates his coming to Milan as far back as 1483, from the circumstance of his having been an eye-witness to the destruction of this unfinished equestrian statue, when the French under Charles the Eighth took possession of Milan, in 1499. There is no evidence to confirm the assertion of this noble Milanese writer that his contemporary Leonardo had worked at this model for sixteen years; but there is no reason to disbelieve him when he declares he saw the bowmen of Gascony make use of this magnificent production as a target.

Ludovico il Moro, at whose request Leonardo went to the court of Milan, although only nominally Regent, governed that state with absolute authority; for his nephew Giovan-Galeazzo possessed merely the title, and enjoyed the pageantry of sovereignty, without the slightest power.

Ludovico Sforza, surnamed "Il Moro," not from his darkness of complexion, as is erroneously stated by Gibbon, but from his having taken a mulberry-tree, in Italian *Moro*, for his device,† was a prince of great talents, and one of the first

---

* " Like bees to hive, here flocks each learned sage,
   With all that's great and good his court is throng'd:
   From Florence fair hath an Apelles come."

† "The Signore Ludovico Sforza, Duke of Milan, adopted a mulberry-tree, *Moro*, as his device, from its being considered wiser than all other trees, as it buds later, and does not flower until it has

politicians of the age. Although the more noble qualities of his mind were obscured by ambition, he was greatly beloved by all who were about his person and admitted to his intimate society. He was frank and pleasing in his manners, easy of access, and liberal even to profusion to those who possessed his confidence. To a very handsome and prepossessing exterior, he united the most powerful eloquence. He successfully cultivated the arts of peace, and lost no opportunity of drawing to his court those who had most distinguished themselves in the arts and sciences. It was his opinion that much more might be done by council than by arms; and that the pen was frequently of more weight than the sword; he was therefore averse to warlike enterprises, and always preferred obtaining his object by overreaching his adversaries in politics and intrigue. To such a man Leonardo da Vinci must have been invaluable. His various talents, to a prince who so well knew how to appreciate them, were of the greatest importance, and he was received at his court with every possible demonstration of favour and affection. It would far exceed the limits of this work to enumerate all the celebrated men whom Ludovico had drawn around him under the laudable pretence of his nephew's instruction and amusement. The poet Belincionni has enumerated them in his various compositions; and Leonardo is also mentioned in most honourable terms.

> "Del Vinci e suoi pennelli e suoi colori,
> I moderni e gli antichi hanno paura." *

The Padre Luca Paciolo, who was the friend and companion of Leonardo and the great restorer of mathematics in Italy, places our hero before all his contemporaries, and makes the following playful allusion to his name "Il Vince in scoltura, getto, e pittura, con ciascuna il nome verifica." †

escaped the injuries of winter, when it immediately bears fruit: thereby demonstrating itself of a nature to do nothing hastily, but rather maturely to reflect, and then promptly execute. This wise prince made use of this device as emblematic of a similarity of disposition."—See *Giovio, Vite d'Uomini Illustri.*

* " Vinci and his pencils and his colours, both moderns and ancients have in dread."

† " In sculpture, casts, and painting, Vinci verifies his name in all."

Vasari is greatly mistaken in supposing that Ludovico sent for Da Vinci merely to amuse him with his musical talents;* for it appears very improbable that this prince, who was so well aware of Leonardo's knowledge and taste for the fine arts, from having the famous *Rotella del Fico* in his possession, which was painted by him when a young man, should have considered him in the light of a musician. Whatever reputation he might have gained for playing on the lyre, it is evident that he himself considered that accomplishment a mere pastime, as he never makes the slightest mention of his musical abilities in the celebrated letter addressed by him to the Duke of Milan : and if the enlightened politics and vast ideas of Ludovico il Moro are considered, it will be readily conceived that Leonardo was sent for with the view of giving instruction to others as well as of working himself, by instituting an academy of arts and sciences, of which he was to have the chief direction. We know also, from the best historians of the period, that this wary prince, from the moment of his brother Galeazzo Maria's assassination, had formed the plan of usurping his throne, and therefore was particularly anxious to draw over to his party the most celebrated men in Italy; as the protection and patronage of such eminent persons could not fail to increase his reputation and strengthen his power. The advantage of such a mode of proceeding had been already seen in the popularity of the Medici at Florence, and of his own ancestors the Visconti at Milan. That painting was never neglected in Lombardy, is shown by the Abbate Lanzi, in his " Storia Pittorica," in which he observes, that " while the whole of Europe was obscured by the grossest ignorance, Lombardy still preserved the use, and cultivated a general taste for, the art of painting, of which there

* " It is true that he was an excellent musician and a particularly good performer on the lyre ; so much so, that Lommazo reputes him superior to every one in that art. A note is to be seen in his Codex marked Q. R. p. 28, where a new viola is mentioned of his construction ; and in another place there is a drawing by him for a lyre. Vasari speaks of a lyre which belonged to him in the form of a horse's head, the greatest part of which was silver ; and I saw his portrait done with a guitar in his hand for the frontispiece of an old parchment manuscript dedicated to Cardinal Ascanio Sforza."—See *Ammoretti.*

are several monuments still existing; amongst others the church of Galiano, about six miles to the south of Como, painted in the year 1007."

When Giotto came to Milan, which undoubtedly was previous to 1334, to paint the Visconti palace, that art assumed a superior character, and created a school which has produced many great men, whose works are still preserved in some of the ancient churches and in the private collections of several individuals. There is a lasting monument of the revival of sculpture in the church of San Francesco, done in the year 1316, representing the transit of the Blessed Virgin, in marble, and two other monuments, the work of Giovanni da Pisa, finished in 1339. The improvement of architecture may be dated from the time when Gian Galeazzo Visconti invited the first masters to Milan in order to construct the cathedral; but they had not then abandoned the Gothic style. The Abbate Lanzi's work just cited, will show the progress made in the arts and sciences until the arrival of Leonardo; but a great deal is to be gathered from the inedited Memoirs of the Painters, Sculptors, and Architects of Milan, by the late Antonio Albuzzi.

At the court of Il Moro, Leonardo found himself in possession of what was then considered an affluent fortune, which relieved his mind from the consideration of being obliged to provide for his own support. He found Ludovico an easy patron, and was much delighted with his situation. Caressed and flattered by the whole court, he entered with all the energy of his character into the pleasures and amusements of the gay world, and made almost daily progress in the confidence and good opinion of Ludovico, by flattering his wishes and sharing his amusements. By turns a poet, a painter, a musician, and always a most accomplished courtier, he completely gained Il Moro's favour, who, although a crafty politician and a man of sense, was, nevertheless, open to flattery, and unable to resist the fascinations of such versatile talents. Ludovico was a great lover of pleasure, and was almost as much distinguished by the dissolute intrigues and lascivious amours of his private life, as by the sagacity and steadiness of his public conduct; and whilst Da Vinci assisted at his councils, and adorned the city with public buildings, he likewise painted his mistresses, and diverted his leisure hours with music and poetry; in short, he was always ready either for his patron's service or pleasure.

The first public work in which Leonardo was employed after his arrival at Milan, was the celebrated equestrian statue of Francesco Sforza the First, which, if we may believe the authority before cited of Monsignore Sabba da Castiglione, he began in 1483. According to the poet Taccone, it would have been sooner commenced had any one been found capable of undertaking it :—

> " E se più presto non s' è principiato,
> La voglia del Signore fu sempre pronta :
> Non s'era un Leonardo ancor travato,
> Che di presente tanto ben l'impronta," etc.*

From the high opinion entertained of his taste, Leonardo was made director of all the public fêtes and entertainments either given by the sovereign, or to him by the lords of his court; of which Belincionni has preserved the recollection in the poems written by him on these occasions; and if Tantio, who collected and published them, has observed a proper chronological order. we may date the two representations in praise of Patience and Labour, given by the Sanseverini family in honour of the nuptials of Isabella and Beatrice, to the first year of his residence at Milan. To this period we may also refer Leonardo's celebrated portraits of Ludovico's two favourites, Cecilia Gallerani and Lucrezia Crevelli, so frequently celebrated by the poets of that age.

Belincionni's sonnet on the picture of the former does more honour to the painter than the poet :—

> " Di che t' adiri, a chi invidia hai Natura !
> Al Vinci che ha ritratto una tua stella.
> Cecilia sì, bellissima, oggi è quella
> Che a' suoi begli occhi, il sol par ombra oscura.
> L' onor é tuo, sebben con sua pittura
> La fa che par che ascolti, e non favella.

---

* " And if this work was not sooner begun,
  The sovereign's will was always ready,
  But a Leonardo had not then been found,
  Who at this time so well undertakes it."

Pensa quanto sarà più viva e bella,
Più a te fia gloria nell' età futura.
Ringraziar dunque Ludovico, or puoi,
E l' ingegno e la mano di Leonardo
Che a' posteri di lei voglion far parte.
Che lei vedra così, benchè sia tardo,
Vederla viva dirà: basti à noi
Comprender or quella, ch' è natura ed arte."

This portrait was at Milan at the end of the last century, in the
Marchese Bonesana's collection, and there is a fine old copy in
the Public Gallery. The Gallerani married Count Ludovico
Pergamino; she was a lady of very great talents, and a poetess.
Da Vinci painted one of his best pictures for her, representing
the Virgin and Child in the act of blessing one of those roses
usually called *Rosa della Madonna*; and this picture was in the
possession of a wine-merchant at Milan when the French occupied that city during the late war. It is framed in the fashion
of those times, with a scroll bearing this inscription:—

" Per Cecilia qual te orna, lauda, e adora
E'l tuo unico figlio, o beata Vergine exora! "

The portrait of Lucrezia Crevelli, which was not less celebrated
and admired than that of her fair contemporary, is now in the
Louvre at Paris.

The greatest proof of the esteem and consideration in which
Il Moro must have held Leonardo, not only as a painter,
sculptor, and mechanic, but also as a man well versed in all the
arts and sciences, is his having chosen him to be the founder and
director of the academy he caused to be established. The Padre
Luca Paciolo informs us, that that prince had long been desirous
of forming a union of learned men and skilful artists, who might
reciprocally communicate their knowledge, and forward the progress of literature and the arts. That such an academy existed
at Milan, the first that was ever known in that city, and to which
Leonardo gave his name, is proved by the testimony of Vasari,
and by several manuscripts still existing in the Ambrosian
Library, and also by six engravings representing several ingenious devices, in the centre of which is inscribed " Academia
Leonardi Vinci."

It is most probable, that for the use of this academy, and for the purpose of argument with his colleagues and instruction to his pupils, Leonardo wrote all those treatises which are to be found, not only in his "Trattato della Pittura," but in several manuscript volumes which are now preserved in the Public Gallery at Milan. This would easily explain his reasons for undertaking so many and such various arguments; and would also account for the number of unconnected ideas, unfinished sketches, memoranda, and materials for the composition of future works, as well as several complete and highly finished discourses. Among the latter, his "Trattato della Pittura," is generally considered as one of his best and most useful compositions; so much so that the Count Algarotti has not hesitated to declare, that even in the present day he should not desire any better elementary work on the art of painting; an opinion entertained by many other distinguished writers.

Although it is now almost impossible to fix the exact epoch of the foundation of the Vinci Academy, it must have been about the year 1485 or 1486, as, previous to that time, we know that Leonardo was engaged in forming the model of the equestrian statue of Francesco Sforza, and afterwards in painting the two portraits of Ludovico's mistresses which have been mentioned.

In 1489 we find Da Vinci occupied, by his patron's orders, in preparing a grand fête which was to be given in celebration of the young Duke Giovan-Galeazzo's marriage with Isabella of Arragon. For this entertainment he invented a moving representation of the planets, which, as they approached the royal party in their evolutions, opened of themselves and discovered a person dressed to represent the deity attributed to each planet, who recited verses composed by Belincionni in honour of the occasion.* We also learn from an old manuscript, in which there is a memorandum in his hand-writing, that he invented and directed a sort of joust, or tournament, given by Messer Galeazzo da Sanseverino to the Duke and his court; this he incidentally mentions from the circumstance of his servant Jachomo having committed a theft on the occasion.

* The reader will find an account of these fêtes in the Ricordi if Monsignore da Castiglione : and Belincionni's verses are included on his works, collected and published by Tantio, at Milan, in 1495, which are now extremely scarce.

In 1492, Il Moro having formed a plan to turn the waters of the Ticino, in order to fertilize the country to the right of that river, had recourse to Leonardo's knowledge of hydraulics to carry his intentions into execution. We know from his notes, that about that time he visited Sesto Calende, Varal Pombio, and Vegevano, where " ai 20 di Marzo del 1492," he observes that " nella vernata le vigne si sotterano."

In this manner Ludovico continued to avail himself of Da Vinci's various talents, and kept him constantly employed, not only as a painter, but also in superintending the magnificent entertainments given either by himself or his nobles, in directing the public works, and in ornamenting his palaces.*

It is supposed by some writers that Leonardo first introduced the art of engraving on wood and copper, and that the designs of several old plates, representing the most celebrated literary men at Ludovico's court, were of his composition. It is also said that these were the first examples of an author's portrait being prefixed to his works, unless we credit Pliny's account that the Romans were accustomed to make use of engravings on wood. His beautiful picture of *The Virgin and Child with St. John and St. Michael*, now in possession of Count San Vitale, of Parma, is dated, and—what is almost without example in his works—is inscribed, " Leonardo Vinci fece, 1492."

About the end of the autumn in 1494, Charles the Eighth invaded Italy, and repaired to Pavia, where Il Moro had prepared the most magnificent fêtes and entertainments for his reception, the arrangement of the whole being entrusted to the elegant taste of Leonardo da Vinci.

* To give some idea of the manner in which the Hall of the Castle of Milan was painted, and of the prices in those days, the following note is transcribed, viz.:—

" The narrow border round the top of the room, 30 lire. The moulding underneath, each square separately, 7 do. ; and the expense of blue, gold, bistre, indigo and gum, 3 do. Three day's labour.— Pictures under the panels, 12 lire each. Each of the arches, 7 lire. The cornice under the windows, 6 soldi the brace. For 24 stories from the Roman History, 10 lire. An ounce of blue 10 soldi. Gold, 15 soldi. Black, 2½ do. Five days' labour in the composition," etc. etc.

The Italian lira is about 8½d. English, and the soldo is as nearly as possible a French sous.

During his residence at Pavia, Leonardo, who never permitted any opportunity to escape him by which he could acquire information, determined to employ his time in studying the anatomy of the human frame under the instructions of Marc' Antonio della Torre, a learned Genoese, and one of the most celebrated professors of that university. These two great men were equally pleased with each other; the professor deriving much benefit from the correct drawings Leonardo executed to illustrate their studies, and the latter being greatly improved by the thorough knowledge of the human frame which he thus acquired.

It was always Da Vinci's opinion that a perfect acquaintance with anatomy was essentially necessary to a painter, and that without it he could not hope to attain any excellence in his art —a doctrine which he has enforced in a manuscript now existing in the Ambrosian Library at Milan. "It is necessary that a painter should be a good anatomist, that in his attitudes and gestures he may be able to design the naked parts of the human frame, according to the just rules of the anatomy of the nerves, bones, and muscles; and that in his different positions he may know what particular nerve or muscle is the cause of such a particular movement, in order that he may make that only marked and apparent, and not all the rest, as many artists are in the habit of doing; who, that they may appear great designers, make the naked limbs stiff and without grace, so that they have more the appearance of a bag of nuts than the human superficies, or rather more like a bundle of radishes than naked muscles."

In this manner Leonardo and his learned instructor pursued their studies together, deriving equal advantage from the exertion of their respective talents. Da Vinci used to draw the naked parts of the human frame in red chalk; while his friend described them with such admirable skill, that Vasari declares he was the first who brought the science of anatomy into general repute, by rendering it plain to all. Some of these drawings are preserved in the Royal Library in London. The celebrated Dr. Hunter, in his course of Anatomical Lectures published in 1784, mentions having seen them, and greatly admires the precision with which they are executed, particularly the most minute parts of the muscles.

From Pavia Charles, still accompanied by Ludovico and his court, repaired to Piacenza, and there soon after received intelligence of Giovan-Galeazzo's death. This occasioned Il Moro's immediate return to Milan; when the Ducal Council, privately suborned, decreed that the crown should be confirmed to him in preference to Giovan-Galeazzo's infant children, as they considered it necessary to the general good to place the government in the hands of a powerful prince, who could defend the state and provide for its security amidst the broils and misfortunes which threatened the tranquility of Italy.

In the mean time Leonardo had returned to Milan from Pavia, where he left his friend Marc' Antonio della Torre, and recommenced his exertions for his patron Ludovico, who, now firmly established as Duke of Milan by the voice of the people, the connivance of the French King, and the Emperor's grant, had greater leisure for the cultivation of the fine arts. He was a prince of quiet habits, mild in his manners, and particularly averse to bloodshed—so much so, that we may doubt his having been at all concerned in his nephew's death. In order to gain the favour of the people, he amused them with continual entertainments, and collected around him the greatest men from all parts of Italy, who by their talents and accomplishments might contribute to the embellishment of his city, or the refinements of his court. The poet, the historian, and the painter, equally shared his patronage, and were equally zealous in their demonstrations of gratitude. The court of Milan became what that of Florence had ceased to be; the latter being desolated by internal broils, the arts of peace fled to a more congenial soil, and Ludovico was now the great patron of the fine arts, and the restorer of literature in Italy.

Shortly after his return to Milan, Leonardo was called upon to celebrate the Duke's virtues, and designed a picture of which we find a description in his own writing: " Il Moro representing Fortune, with flowing hair and his hands extended, and Messer Gualtiere in the act of doing homage to him in the foreground ; Poverty, in frightful guise, is pursuing a youth whom Il Moro is sheltering under his robe, while with his golden rod he menaces the monster, and warns him not to approach."

From several memoranda and remarks which are to be found

among his manuscripts, such as, " A dì 24 Marzo 1494, venne Galeazzo a stare meco, con il patto di dare 5 lire il mese, pagando ogni 14 dì del mese. Datemi da suo padre fiorini due di Reno;" and a little lower down, "A dì 14 di Luglio ebbe da Galeazzo fiorini 2 di Reno,"—it is evident he was in the habit of receiving scholars who paid him for the benefit they derived from his instructions, and the information they gained by frequenting his studio.

In the year 1495 there is no mention of any particular work having been undertaken by Leonardo. It is most probable that he was occupied in perfecting the Vincian Academy; as it is supposed he wrote his famous Treatise addressed to the Duke about this time, in which he examines the respective merits of the two arts, painting and sculpture. It is much to be lamented that this book is no longer extant, as it would have been highly interesting to know the opinion of one so capable of forming a proper judgment from his extensive knowledge of the fine arts. Leonardo's treatise was composed for the use of the Academy, and is even now held in general estimation. In the collection of his works lately published at Paris, there are several tracts comparing the different merits of the sister arts, both considered relatively and individually, which prove that this treatise really existed; and it is moreover frequently alluded to in the " Trattato della Pittura," written by Lomazzo, who was his friend and scholar.

Leonardo's pencil was not, however, unemployed during this year, as the Duke ordered him to paint his own and the Duchess's portraits on each side of a large picture representing Mount Calvary, which Montorfano had painted on the wall of the refectory in the Convento delle Grazie. This task he very unwillingly undertook, if we may believe Padre Gattico, a Dominican friar, who has left an account of this convent in manuscript, in which he says: " Quelle pitture si sono infradiciate per essere dipinte all' olio, perchè l' olio non si conserva in pitture fatte sopra mure e pietra."* About the end

* " These pictures have mouldered away in consequence of their being painted in oil; oil does not keep in paintings made upon walls and stone."

of this year there was printed, at Milan, a curious work on music, by Franchino Gaforio, which was preceded by an engraving, supposed to have been done by Leonardo, or by one of his scholars under his direction and with his assistance.

In the year 1496, Da Vinci derived much pleasure from the arrival of his friend and countryman the Padre Luca Paciolo, who has been before mentioned in these pages. As they had studied together, and were equally well versed in mechanics, mathematics, and architecture, they were mutually delighted with each other's society, and Leonardo had sufficient influence with the Duke to persuade him to receive his friend into his service. Engaged in the same pursuits, they lived in the same house, shared the same studies and amusements, and assisted each other in their separate undertakings. Paciolo prevailed on his friend to draw all the geometrical figures for his Treatise on Architecture, as he well knew there was no one capable of executing them with the same precision; and he acknowledges this assistance in the following well-merited eulogium: "As in the disposition of the regular bodies, you will observe those which are done by that most worthy painter, architect, musician, and universally endowed Leonardo da Vinci, a Florentine, at the city of Milan, when we were both in the pay of the most excellent Duke Ludovico Maria Sforza, in the year of our salvation 1496."

A little further on he mentions the drawings which Leonardo made for his work on the "Divina Proportione," which he dedicated in manuscript to the Duke Ludovico. They were sixty in number, and were published in 1509, with a new dedication to Pietro Soderini, Gonfaloniere of Florence, to whom he writes: "Libellum . . . . Ludovico Sportiæ nuncupavi tanto ardore, quoque sua Vincii nostri Lionardi manibus scalpta," etc.

To this period also belong the drawings, or rather illustrations, of the celebrated "Codice Triulziano," which was written by the Duke's eldest son, Maximilian, when a child studying the Latin language. This manuscript forms a small quarto volume, written on parchment, which, besides being ornamented with numerous highly finished devices and heraldic emblazonments, is enriched with several pictures relating to the youth and occupations of the young prince, who then possessed the title of Count of Pavia. Among these there are two which are generally considered the production of Leonardo's pencil: one representing the Count in the act of doing homage to his cousin the Emperor Maximilian; and the other, of the same prince amusing himself catching birds, while his tutor, Count Secco di Borella, is advising him to leave off his diversions and attend to his studies. This manuscript is held in the greatest estimation, and is still preserved at Milan.

About the end of this year Ludovico il Moro went to Pavia, attended by all his court, to meet the Emperor Maximilian, whom he had invited into Italy. Triumphal arches were prepared everywhere on his road, and most magnificent fêtes awaited his arrival wherever he stopped; as Ludovico disguised his true reason for this conference under the pretence of merely doing homage to his feudal lord. Leonardo, who accompanied his patron on this occasion, had no doubt a principal share in arranging these festivities. That he was not forgotten by the Duke is proved by his having ordered him to paint a picture of *The Nativity*, which he presented to the Emperor in honour of the occasion, and which is now in the Imperial cabinet at Vienna.

Leonardo's residence at the court of Milan, although extremely agreeable to himself, was highly detrimental to his fame as a painter; as he was so constantly occupied in different works for the good of the state and the amusement of the court, that he could not devote so much of his time to painting as his admirers wish. A number of those pictures which are really his own, are left in an unfinished state, from the extreme nicety of his taste. His imagination went so far beyond what it is in the power of man to execute, that he was seldom or ever contented with his own works, and he would frequently lay aside a picture altogether, if it did not equal his ideas of the subject. At other times he would hastily abandon an undertaking, if his design did not embrace all that his imagination had preconceived. Hence there remain so few pictures by this inimitable artist; but these few are so very highly finished, that no one since has been supposed to have surpassed him. Many of the pictures which are shown in Italy as Leonardo's paintings, are falsely considered so, particularly in Milan, where they are generally the work of some of his scholars, with the advantage of receiving the last touches from himself.

There could have been no part of Da Vinci's life more pleasant to himself than the time he spent at Milan previous to the misfortunes of the house of Sforza. In the full enjoyment of his princely patron's confidence and favour, he lived in the most splendid manner, beloved and respected by everybody. Free from all care for present wants, and too little accustomed to consider the future, he passed his time in the gratification of his favourite pursuits, and devoted his leisure to the entertainment of his friends. Expensive in his habits, he kept a most liberal table; his house was always open to those who were distinguished in any way for talents or accomplishments; and he drew around him the best society in Milan during that brilliant period. He sought for merit wherever it was to be found, for the rust of envy never corroded his noble heart, and the poorest artist was always welcome to a seat at his board and a share of his purse.

His principal object in life was the encouragement of literature and the arts, in all their various branches; and, enthusiastically desirous of promoting what he most loved, he assisted the poor, encouraged the weak, and brought forward the unknown. It is only to be regretted that his means did not equal his inclinations; for his profuse liberality rendered him but ill qualified to give assistance to others; and unfortunately his friend and patron Ludovico il Moro had exactly the same propensities. He also undertook more than he was capable of finishing; his ideas were too much enlarged for his situation, which impoverished his treasury, diminished his revenues, and became the principal cause of his ultimate ruin. A proper attention to his expenditure is as necessary to a prince as to an individual, without which, even with the very best intentions, neither can be certain of remaining honest. The one must oppress his subjects, the other must defraud his equals; and both must risk the loss of that claim to assistance in the hour of need which both may occasionally require. Upon no one was this truth more severely impressed than on Ludovico il Moro, who, although he had exhausted his finances in beautifying his city and encouraging the arts, was neglected by his subjects when

they found he had exhausted his resources; and they left him
to pay the forfeit of his imprudence and ambition with the loss
of his dominions and his life.

On his return to Milan from Pavia, the Duke was desirous of
enriching his capital with some great work that should be considered worthy of Da Vinci's talents, and that might serve to
perpetuate the fame of the artist and the liberality of the prince.
With this idea Ludovico desired Leonardo to paint his celebrated
picture of *The Last Supper*, on the walls of the refectory in the
Dominican Convent of the "Madonna delle Grazie."

It was almost impossible to have selected a subject more
adapted to Leonardo's taste and genius, and he had certainly
never before undertaken so interesting a work. He proposed
to represent the moment when our Saviour exclaims "Amen,
dico vobis quia unus vestrûm me traditurus est." This gave
him an opportunity of exercising his peculiar talent, of representing the different passions that agitate the human frame, and
of giving to each individual of his picture the merit and interest
of a separate composition, without disturbing the harmony of the
whole.

It is not exactly known when he commenced this picture, but
from various circumstances it appears that it must have been
about the year 1497, as Bottari tells us there is a rude engraving
bearing that date, and supposed to be Leonardo's own work.
The Padre Luca Paciolo mentions, in one of his manuscripts,
that in 1498 Leonardo had already considerably advanced in
drawing the outlines of this composition; and whoever observes
it now, at least as much as is spared to us from the ravages of
time and the attacks of ignorance, will easily perceive that three
or even four years are very little to have employed on such an
undertaking; the more so when we consider Leonardo's extreme
difficulty in being satisfied with his own productions. It is also
to be remembered, that he was obliged to form a cartoon of the
same size as his picture.

The general disposition of this admirable work is considered
extremely simple, and therefore the more appropriate to the
subject. Our Saviour is represented seated in the middle, which
is the place of honour: his attitude is tranquil and majestic, a
kind of noble serenity appears to pervade his countenance and

action, which impresses respect. The Apostles, on the contrary, are in extreme agitation, and their attitudes and countenances are expressive of various emotions. Fear, love, anxiety, and a desire to penetrate the full extent of our Saviour's meaning, are easily distinguishable in their looks and gestures. But when Leonardo wished to pourtray the character of the divinity on the figure and countenance of our Lord, his hand was too weak to represent the conceptions of his mind, and whatever he executed was still very far from satisfying the sublimity and delicacy of his ideas. At length, despairing of success, he unburthened his mind to his friend Bernardo Zenale,* who, not believing that he could surpass what he had already done, advised him to leave the head of Christ unfinished. Leonardo, after much consideration, resolved to follow his friend's counsel: in imitation of Timanthes, of whom it is related, that in his picture of *The Sacrifice of Iphigenia*, having employed every possible expression of grief in the attendants, he conceived he could not do more justice to the father's feelings, who was to behold the sacrifice of his own child, than by covering his face with his mantle, and leaving the effect to the beholder's imagination.†

Nothing can be more impressive than the idea of the impossibility of representing our Saviour's countenance by human means; and this very imperfection becomes a greater beauty in a country where one is too much accustomed to see the Deity represented, or rather misrepresented, in all sorts of extraordinary and fantastic forms, in the old frescoes and mosaics.‡

Having settled this difficulty, he found himself speedily embarrassed by another, which was to find a countenance sufficiently

---

* This painter and architect was a native of Treviso, and was working at the same time as Leonardo in the Convent of the "Madonna delle Grazie." Lomazzo mentions him as the author of a treatise on Perspective, of which he had a thorough knowledge.—See Lomazzo, *Idea del Tempio della Pittura*, book 5, chap. 21.

† Pliny, lib. 35, cap. 10.

‡ As an example of the paintings alluded to, it is sufficient to mention an old picture on wood of the *Annunciation*, in which the Almighty is represented as an old man looking in at the window, while the angel is delivering the divine message to the Virgin.

wicked to convey an idea of the man who was about to betray his divine master. This feeling, to one who was always in the habit of long reflection before he attempted anything of consequence, greatly delayed his work, and gave rise to the story Vasari tells of the Prior of the Dominicans, who became impatient whenever he saw Leonardo in contemplation instead of continuing his picture; he being one of those who imagine that a painter must be neglecting his work whenever his hands are not actually employed on it. He therefore complained of Leonardo's indolence to the Duke, who, in order to satisfy him, inquired about the picture, and found that the artist never passed a day without working at it at least for two hours. Still, however, its progress did not keep pace with the Prior's impatience, who continued to persecute the Duke with his complaints until he prevailed on him to send for Da Vinci, and remonstrate with him on his delay. But Ludovico did this with so much kindness and affability that Leonardo was quite charmed with the prince's condescension, and willingly explained to him, that a man of genius is, in fact, never less idle than when he appears to be entirely so, particularly in painting, where so much depends on a just and proper conception of the subject. He concluded by telling the Duke, " There remain, Sir, only two heads unfinished in the whole picture. That of Christ I have long despaired of ever being able to complete, as I am quite convinced of the utter impossibility of finding a model on earth capable of representing the union of divinity with humanity, and much less can I hope to supply the deficiency from my own imagination. Nothing, therefore, is wanting but to express the character of Judas, and I have for some time sought without success, among your prisons and the very refuse of the people, for a countenance such as I require; but if your Excellency is so impatient that the picture should be finished, I can take the likeness of the Dominican Prior, who richly deserves it for the impertinence of his interference." The Duke could not avoid laughing heartily at this sally, and being fully convinced how much labour and judgment Leonardo bestowed on each individual, was only impressed with a still greater respect for his talents. It may also be easily supposed that the fear of being handed down to posterity as Judas, effectually silenced the Prior's impor-

d

tunities.* Da Vinci, however, was a man of too much honour to have had any idea of putting his threat in execution, as has been erroneously asserted; besides which, the Prior of the Dominicans is described by the writers of that period as having too noble an appearance for such a purpose. Some little time after, Leonardo found a face such as he required, so that by adding something from his imagination, he finished the head of Judas, completed his picture, and excelled all his former productions.

In this wonderful composition, which was then considered almost a miracle of human perfection, Leonardo derived the greatest assistance from his previous studies. These he found a perfect treasure of intelligence to him; and, whenever he was at a loss for any particular trait of countenance, he had recourse to his tablets, and there found ample reason to applaud his former industry; for, as has before been observed, he never lost an opportunity of drawing every remarkable countenance that he could meet with. This he considered to be of such utility, that he always carried a small sketch-book in his girdle, in which he drew whatever made the most impression on his imagination; and he advised all artists to do the same. It was his opinion that nature was the best teacher; and for that reason he obliged his scholars to delineate the most extraordinary as well as the most beautiful features they could meet with, which he considered the best means of taking good likenesses. Had he entertained any doubt of the usefulness of this system, the assistance he derived from it in his great work of *The Last Supper*, where he had so many different feelings and passions to pourtray, would have been sufficient to confirm his opinion.

This inimitable picture has been so frequently described, and so universally eulogised, that there is little which is new to be said upon the subject, and any description of that painting would be superfluous after the beautiful engraving made from it by the Chevalier Raphael Morghen. It therefore only remains to join in the general regret excited by its too speedy decay, which has deprived the world of what formed the glory of Da Vinci, and

---

* This story is to be found in Bottari's "Lettere Pittoriche," and is also told by Vasari and several of Leonardo da Vinci's contemporaries.

the wonder of the age in which he lived. As far back as the middle of the sixteenth century, Armenini speaks of this picture as half destroyed: if we may believe Da Vinci's friend and scholar Lomazzo, who frequently mentions it in his Treatise, the colours soon disappeared, so that the outlines only remained to indicate the excellence of the drawing. In the early part of the seventeenth century, both Cardinal Borromeo and Padre Gattico, who resided some time in the Dominican Convent at Milan, agree in saying of this picture, "che del Cenacolo vedeansi solo le reliquie;" and that from its continually mouldering away, copies had been taken of it in all sizes by most of the celebrated artists of that time. These are now dispersed throughout Italy.* In 1624, Bartolomeo Sanese, who saw both the original and the famous copy in the Chartreuse Convent of Pavia, by Marco Oggione, declared that more praise was due to the Chartreuse than the Dominicans; as, while Leonardo's own work was so much destroyed by age and damp as to be scarcely discernible, the copy would be the means of handing it down to the admiration of posterity.. The picture became gradually so much worse, that Scannelli, who saw it in 1642, observes, that "There are but few vestiges remaining of the figures; and the naked parts, such as heads, hands, and feet,

* The following is the most authentic list of the ancient copies still extant:—
1. In the Franciscan Convent at Milan, by Lomazzo, in 1561.
2. In St. Barnabas, a small copy by Marco Oggione.
3. At St. Peters, a copy by Santagostino.
4. In the Grand Monastery, by Lomazzo.
5. In the Public Library, done by order of Cardinal Borromeo.
6. In the Monastery of the Jesuits, two miles from Milan, by Oggione.
7. In the Grand Chartreuse at Pavia, by Marco Oggione in 1510, now in the possession of the Royal Academy of Arts. During the Revolution this copy passed into France. It was afterwards, in 1815, offered for sale in London, and, it is said, was bought by the Royal Academy for £600.
8. At St. Benedetto, at Mantua, by Monsignori.
9. At Lugano, by Bernardino Luini.
10. In Spain, at the Escurial, by Luini.
11. In France, at St. Germain's, painted by Luini, by order of Francis the First.
12. At Ecoens; painter unknown.

are almost entirely annihilated." This is the only excuse the
Dominicans could possibly have had for cutting off the feet of our
Saviour and several of the Apostles near him, in order to enlarge
their entrance into the refectory. Nothing but the extreme
decay of the picture itself could palliate so senseless an act;
and it is most probable that it remained in this neglected state
until 1726, when the painter, Bellotti, succeeded in cleaning and
restoring it so well that it appeared to revive, and almost to
regain its former beauty. Many writers assert that Bellotti
simply repainted it on Da Vinci's outlines; but this is denied
by his contemporaries, and Padre Pino assures us that he
" made the picture revive by some secret of his own, retouching
with the point of his brush only those places where the colour
was quite peeled off."

Notwithstanding Bellotti's labours to preserve this painting, it
soon began to lose its newly acquired beauty, and to peel off and
moulder away in such a manner that the Abbate Luigi Lanzi, in
his celebrated work of the " Storia Pittorica dell' Italia," observes,
that there were only three heads in the whole picture that could
be considered as Leonardo's painting. However, it remained
tolerably discernible until the Dominicans themselves were
driven out of their Convent when the French army invaded
Italy under Napoleon. The Convent was then used as a
cavalry depôt, and the refectory turned into a stable; so that
the brutality of the soldiery soon completed what the ignorance
of the priesthood and the ravages of time had commenced.
With a spirit of destruction scarcely to be accounted for, the
troops of republican France had no hesitation in firing at our
Saviour and all the Apostles, leaving more proofs of their skill
as marksmen than of their feelings as Christians or civilized
beings.

It is now so much destroyed that it is even a matter of dispute
whether it was originally painted in oil, fresco, or tempera.
That it was done in oil is most probable, from it always having
been said so in the earliest engravings, and spoken of as such in
contemporaneous writings, and also from its speedy decay, there
being rarely an instance of the durability of oil painting upon
walls. Many authors pretend that the colours faded so soon
from Da Vinci's having made use of some particular varnish

or chemical preparation, as he was always considered too fond
of experiments. Had Leonardo been merely a painter, he would
have been contented with the usual methods of painting; but
his lofty genius and love of new inventions tended on this, as on
many other occasions, to eclipse his fame; for, had it been otherwise, this great work might have been spared to the present age.
Much of the destruction which this picture has suffered must
doubtless be attributed to bad restoration; and considerable
allowances should be made for the envy of his contemporaries.

We may endeavour to trace the progress of its decay, as the
only consolation which remains to us for such a loss; and when
we consider the time at which it was executed, it must be allowed
to have been one of the greatest works of art ever undertaken.
Raphael's "School of Athens," is considered by some as a work
of greater merit; but it should be recollected that a number of
years had elapsed between the painting of these two pictures,
and that great progress had been made in the arts during that
period. Besides, it is scarcely just to Leonardo da Vinci that
Raphael should claim superiority from having profited by the
improvements which his predecessor had introduced. It is a
curious coincidence that the two invasions of Italy by the French
should have been equally detrimental to Da Vinci's two great
works, although so many centuries intervened between them.
Monsignore Sabba da Castiglione, a noble Milanese, tells us
in his "Ricordi," that "he saw the bowmen of Gascony make
use of Da Vinci's model for the colossal statue of Francesco
Sforza as a target," and many noble Milanese of the present day
could tell us in their "ricordi," that they saw the troops of
republican France make a somewhat similar use of his magnificent picture of *The Last Supper*.

In 1497, Ludovico's wife, Beatrice of Este, died after a short
illness, and the Duke honoured her memory, according to Corio,
with a "stupendissime ossequie." From several notes in his
tablets we find that these were directed by Leonardo, which
affords an additional proof of his patron's confidence.

It was about this time that he became acquainted with Andrea
Salaj'no, whom he received into his studio, and soon admitted to
his intimate friendship. He had the greatest regard for this
young man, and took great pleasure in teaching him everything

relating to painting; in which he acquired such proficiency, that some of his works in Milan have been falsely attributed to Leonardo. The probability is, that some of them were corrected by him, or had the advantage of receiving his finishing touches. Salaj'no was so gratefully attached to his master, that he never quitted him from that period, and was the constant companion and sharer of his fortunes.

Da Vinci's principal occupation during this year was the navigation of the Adda, between Brizzio and Frezzo. This was a most difficult undertaking, from the rapidity of the stream, and the numerous shoals which impeded its progress. From different circumstances we may believe that he formed plans to overcome all these difficulties, though it does not appear that they were carried into effect at that period, as the political troubles which embarrassed his patron obliged him to put a sudden termination to many of the works which he had previously undertaken. There is proof, however, that he invented new lock-gates, and in many ways improved the navigation of the Martesana canal.

It is not known that Leonardo painted anything of consequence subsequent to his grand work of *The Last Supper*, before the misfortunes of the house of Sforza obliged him to return to his own country, except another portrait of the beautiful Cecilia Gallerani, on wood, which is at present in the possession of the Palavicini family at San Calocero.

The greatest mortification to Leonardo was his being obliged to abandon all idea of finishing the equestrian statue of Francesco Sforza, which was to have been cast in bronze, and had already occupied him so many years. His mould was prepared, and nothing was wanting but the metal, which the Duke was no longer able to furnish, as, according to Luca Paciolo's calculation, it would have taken 200,000 pounds weight of bronze. In vain did Leonardo solicit his friends to use their utmost influence with the Duke; in vain did the poets of the court endeavour to flatter him into acquiescence with Da Vinci's wishes; Ludovico no longer had it in his power to expend money on the fine arts, but was obliged to employ the little that remained in his own defence.

Da Vinci's situation must now have been extremely unpleasant, as it appears, from a fragment of one of his own letters, that the Duke owed him more than two years' salary. He must have been in great pecuniary embarrassment before his pride would have permitted him to have written " that he was no longer able to continue his works at his own expense, as he had not the means either of paying his workmen or purchasing his materials." It must have been a most bitter disappointment to him to have found his time so thrown away, as he could no longer entertain any hope of making his cast of this statue, on which he had bestowed so much labour, and from which he had expected to have derived so much fame. His enemies assert that his design was too grand and speculative to have been ever carried into effect; but great allowances should be made for the envy excited by his talents and success at the court of Milan.

It appears, however, from several memoranda in his own handwriting, that Leonardo himself not only considered it possible, but had made his calculations with the greatest nicety, and would have, no doubt, succeeded in his undertaking, had not the political events of the times put it entirely out of his power.

In the following year, 1495, the Duke gave Leonardo a proof of his friendship and generosity, by making him a present of a small estate near the Porta Vercellina, with full power to bequeath it to whom he pleased, or to dispose of it in any way he thought proper.* Whether this land was given as a compensation for the arrears that were justly his due, or as a gift for services received by the state, is immaterial; most probably the Duke wished to avert as much as possible the want and misery to which he feared Da Vinci would be exposed in the event of his own ruin, as he had been exclusively employed for the benefit of the house of Sforza and the government of Milan. It is a proof, however, of Il Moro's goodness of heart, that

---

* This gift is registered in the public office at Milan as follows:—
"1429, 26 Aprilis, Ludovicus Maria Sfortia, dux Mediolani, dono dedit D. Leonardo Quintio (*sic*) Florentio, pictori celeberrimo, pert. n. 16 soli seu fundi ejus vineæ quam ab Abate seu Monasterio S. Victoris in suburbano portæ Vercellinæ proxime acquisierat, ut in eo spatio soli pro ejus arbitrio ædificare, colere hortos, et quicquid ei vel posteris ejus, vel quibus dederit ut supra, libuerit, facere et disponere possit."—Copied verbatim from the Register.

he could remember the wants of his friends when pursued on all sides by his enemies. Shortly after, he was forced to fly from the city.

The flight of his patron, and the subsequent change in the government of Milan must have caused the greatest regret to Da Vinci and his friends, who had equal reason to lament his fate as a prince and an individual, as they were all obliged to him for the means of continuing their studies and exercising their talents. He had been their patron and friend; and although his enemies accuse him of having encouraged the fine arts solely from ostentation, the greatest praise is due to him for the manner in which he promoted general knowledge. His worth must have also been more appreciated by his literary friends when brought into comparison with their new masters; for Louis the Twelfth, after he had made his grand entry into Milan, thought of nothing but fêtes and entertainments during the time he remained there; and the French in general were extremely indifferent to the progress of literature and the arts. They destroyed a magnificent building which Leonardo had designed for Galeazzo da San Severino, and wantonly broke up his model for the equestrian statue, both of which must have caused him great mortification.*

Finding his talents neglected, himself unrewarded, and his works no longer esteemed, without any immediate prospect of his former patron's re-establishment in Milan, Leonardo determined to leave a city where his finances were so much reduced, and his situation so unpleasantly altered. It appears, however, that he delayed his departure until the year 1500, and that he waited the issue of Il Moro's return to Milan at the request of his faithless subjects, when they revolted against the French. Hoping to maintain himself by force, the ex-Duke raised a body of Swiss mercenaries, who, instead of fighting in his defence, basely sold him to his enemies, by whom he was taken in

---

* The destruction of this model has always been supposed to have taken place when the French entered Milan in 1499, but recently discovered evidence has shown that it was still in existence, though not perhaps in a perfect state of preservation, in 1501.—See Campori. "Nouveaux documents sur Leonard de Vinci." *Gazette des Beaux-Arts*, 1866.

disguise with his brother the Cardinal Ascanio, and several of his followers. Il Mora was imprisoned in the castle of Loches, in France, where, after ten years' confinement, he died of a broken heart at the unhappy issue of all his wild dreams or ambition.

During the uncertainty of this revolution, while awaiting the result of his patron's last struggle for power, Da Vinci remained at Vaprio * to be out of the way of the cabals and disturbances of the capital. This would have given him an opportunity of studying the source of the Adda, which had always been a favourite object of his researches. Or perhaps he lingered behind in hopes of seeing Milan again restored to tranquility, and the love for the arts revived in a place where he had so highly distinguished himself. He must also have been extremely unwilling to lose the fruits of his long services to this state, as he considered himself attached to the court of Milan, whatever sovereign might be at the head of that government. But, perceiving at length that the French thought of nothing but their amusements, he made up his mind to return to his own country; and shortly after, accompanied by his friends Salaj'no and Luca Paciolo, set out for Florence, where he resolved to take up his residence, and hoped to find employment.

In the meantime the government of Florence had passed into other hands, and had undergone an almost entire change. Disgusted with the arrogance and imbecility of Pietro de' Medici's conduct, his fellow-citizens had revolted from his sway, and banished him and his whole family, declaring them enemies to the state. They had elected Pietro Soderini, one of their principal citizens, as their Lord, with the title of " Gonfaloniere Perpetuo," and the city was now enjoying more tranquility than it had experienced since the death of Lorenzo the Magnificent. The immense wealth produced by their extensive commerce enabled the Florentines to cultivate the fine arts, and adorn their city with public buildings, notwithstanding the miseries and disturbances occasioned by the perpetual struggles of contending

* The Melzi Villa, at Vaprio, is half-way between Milan and Bergamo, on the canal of the Martesana. The situation was extremely pleasant, and this place was a great favourite with Da Vinci, who frequently retired there.

parties to obtain a preponderance in the government of the state. Their patriotism and public spirit overcame every difficulty, and the pride of all was interested in enriching their country with works of art, and in giving employment to the first artists of the age.

Leonardo da Vinci was received with every distinction by the Gonfaloniere, who immediately enrolled him in the list of those artists who were employed by the government, and assigned him a sufficient pension to provide for his subsistence, which enabled him to form a tolerably comfortable establishment, with his friend Paciolo and his scholar Salaj'no. On the subject of this pension, Vasari relates the following anecdote :—

" Leonardo was very high-minded, and extremely generous in all his actions. It is said that, going one day to the bank for the monthly provision that he was accustomed to receive from Pietro Soderini, the cashier wanted to give him some bundles of halfpence, which he refused, saying, ' I am not a halfpenny painter.' " *

It is a great pity that Da Vinci allowed his pride to have so much ascendency over his better judgment. His irritable sensibility was his greatest enemy through life, and was the occasion of his losing many friends, who had both the power and inclination to assist him. This prevailing foible was also extremely detrimental to his fame in his profession, as it frequently blinded him to the difficulties of executing the vast conceptions of his all-comprehensive mind. His brilliant imagination made him suppose that everything must give way to his abilities, and led him into errors which have deprived posterity of some of his best works. His ideas were too gigantic for the age in which he lived, and it would have been much better for his reputation as a painter if he had been a less universally accomplished man.

After his return to Florence, he pursued his studies with unremitting assiduity, and diligently worked at his profession, which he was the more obliged to attend to from no longer

---

* " Io non sono un dipintore per quatrini." The quatrino is trans-lated in the text as a halfpenny, to make it the more intelligible ; its real value is the fifth part of a grazia, which is the eighth of a franc, valued at 6¼d. English.

having the advantage of so good a salary as he had enjoyed at Milan. Instead of the luxuries and extravagances of Il Moro's splendid court, he had now to accommodate himself to the more prudent restrictions of a republic, whose sumptuary laws were enacted in a spirit of economy quite different to what he had seen at Milan.

The first work of consequence in which he was engaged, was an altar-piece for the church of the "Annunziata." Unfortunately, however, he only formed the design of this picture, which is generally called the Cartoon of Santa Anna, which was so exquisitely finished, that Vasari says, "not only all the artists, but the whole city, men and women, young and old, flocked to see it in such crowds, that for two days it had almost the appearance of a public festival." The same author describes the artist's having successfully expressed in the countenance of the Virgin Mary "all the grace which simplicity and beauty could possibly give to the mother of Christ, anxious to show the modesty, humility, and thankfulness, which she might be supposed to feel in contemplating the beauty of her child, which she is supporting in her lap; while she is looking down at St. John, a little boy playing with a kid, encouraged by the smiles of Santa Anna, who is delighted to see her terrestrial progeny thus become almost celestial." "A consideration," he further observes, "truly worthy of Leonardo's talents and genius." This picture was carried to France in the time of Francis the First; but it must have found its way back to Italy, as it belonged to Aurelio Luini when Lomazzo wrote his Treatise on Painting.*

About this time Da Vinci applied himself more particularly to portraits, and painted two of the most celebrated beauties of Florence—the Lady Ginevra, wife of Amerigo Benci, which, according to Vasari, was "una cosa bellissima," and the Madonna Lisa, wife of Francesco del Giocondo, which all the artists and writers of that period considered as the perfection of portrait-painting. Vasari describes this picture in so very minute and lively a manner, that it is impossible to give a more accurate description of it than by making use of his own words, written

* This cartoon is now in the possession of the Royal Academy.

on the spot shortly after it was finished : "In this head the beholder may observe how nearly it is possible for art to approach nature. The eyes have the lustre and expression of life. The nose, and more particularly the mouth, have more the appearance of real flesh and blood than painting, from the beautiful contrast of the vermillion of the lips with the clear red and white of the complexion. Whoever attentively looks at the throat, can almost see the beating of the pulse. As the Madonna Lisa was a very beautiful woman, Leonardo studied all possible means of making her picture surpass everything that had been then seen of the sort. He was in the habit of having music, singing, and all kinds of diversions to make her laugh and remove the air or melancholy so frequently to be observed in portrait-painting ; which produced so pleasing an effect in this picture, that it gave to the canvas an almost superhuman expression, and the only wonder seemed to be that it was not alive."

Francis the First bought this picture for his collection at Fontainbleau, and paid 4000 gold crowns to the family for whom it was painted, a sum that would be equal to 45,000 francs in the present day. It is now in the Louvre, and is considered one of the finest specimens of Leonardo's painting extant : it is called "La belle Joconde ;" there is a landscape in the back-ground.

After remaining two years at Florence, Da Vinci travelled over the greater part of Italy, and made notes and drawings of what-ever he found instructive and amusing. It would have been highly interesting to have had an opportunity of collecting the remarks of a traveller so perfectly capable of describing what-ever he saw, and who united in himself the different qualifications of a painter, mechanic, and architect, with the philosophical feelings of a liberal-minded man. He must have visited the whole of the Romagna, as we find from his notes that he was at Urbino on the 30th July, 1502, where he designed the fortress. He went to Pesaro, Rinucci, and Cesena, where he remarks " the picturesque manner in which the vines were suspended in festoons." It would have been difficult to have assigned a reason for his having consumed his time and money in travelling, if it were not sufficiently explained by the fact of the Duca Valentino's having appointed him his surveyor and engineer-general. This naturally obliged him to visit all the strong places, of which the Duke had usurped the dominion as Gonfaloniere or Captain-General of the ecclesiastical army. The immoderate ambition of the house of Borgia was, in this instance, of material service to Leonardo, enabling him to see more of his country than he had hitherto done, without any expense to himself; as it is well known that, whatever were Valentino's vices, he was, either from policy or ostentation, liberal even to excess to those who were in his service. Pope Alexander the Sixth died 18th August, 1503, in the seventy-first year of his age, a victim, it is supposed, to his own treacherous intrigues, as he is said to have taken a goblet of poisoned wine which he had prepared for one of his guests. This circumstance destroyed all the brilliant projects of the house of Borgia, and occasioned the sudden downfall of Valentino and his dependents. He was succeeded by Julius the Second, whose wisdom and integrity partly indemnified Christendom for the profligate enormities by which his predecessor had disgraced the pontificate. The Pope's death also speedily terminated Da Vinci's commission, as in 1503 we find him returned to Florence, and engaged to paint one side of the council-hall in the Palazzo Vecchio, by the desire of the Gonfaloniere Pietro Soderini.

This was the origin of all the jealousies and disputes between Leonardo da Vinci and Michael Angelo Buonarroti, who had also been employed to make designs for the same purpose; and hence arose a rivalry between these two great men which caused them to exert their utmost abilities in the cartoons they respectively executed. As these paintings were intended as a sort of national monument, it was necessary to select some trait in the Florentine history which might at once serve to commemorate the glory of the republic and the fame of the painter. From a long memorandum in Leonardo's handwriting, we find that he chose for his subject the defeat of Nicolo Picinino, the Milanese General, near Anghiari, in Tuscany, and that he had collected every circumstance of this battle, either real or fictitious, in order to delineate it properly. We can easily perceive from his remarks the labour he must have bestowed on collecting materials for this picture, which, it is much to be regretted, was never executed, as Vasari relates that having tried his preparations on the wall, for painting it in oil, he found it did not succeed, and therefore abandoned the undertaking altogether. Here is another instance of his versatility of talent interfering with his fame as a painter; for, had he been entirely ignorant of chemistry, he would necessarily have been obliged to content himself with the ordinary rules of fresco painting, and he might again have left a work that would have immortalized his name.

As these cartoons no longer exist, a description of them may prove interesting. Vasari tells us that Leonardo represented a combat of horsemen fighting for a standard, which group was only intended as a part of the historical design just alluded to. It was so wonderfully executed, that the horses themselves seemed agitated with the same fury as their riders, and were fighting as hard with their teeth as their riders with their swords, to obtain possession of the contested flag. "Neither is it possible," continues Vasari, "to describe Leonardo's designs, in the soldiers' dresses so beautifully varied, as well as in the incredible skill he showed in the forms and attitudes of the horses, as no other artist could delineate the muscles and actions of the horse with such uncommon beauty and fidelity."[*] Michael Angelo's cartoon represented a troop of soldiers suddenly called to arms when bathing, and the scene of his picture was the siege of Pisa by the Florentines, and has been so fully described by Mr. Duppa[†] in his Life of that great artist, that it need not be here repeated. Both these cartoons were shown in the Medici palace until the death of the Duke Giuliano, when they disappeared without any person being able to account for it. Vasari says that Michael Angelo's was torn in pieces, and that in his time there was a small piece, remaining in the hands of a dilettante at Mantua. It may be supposed in what esteem they must have been held, when their fame was sufficient to induce Raphael to come to Florence for the sole purpose of studying them. He was so much surprised and

[*] One part of Leonardo's cartoon was engraved by Marc Antonio, the other by Agostino Veneziano. The former is called "Les Grimpeurs," and both are exceedingly rare. An engraving by Gerard Edelinck of the "Battle of the Standard," is well known. It is said to have been taken from a drawing by Rubens.

[†] And more recently by Mr. Heath Wilson, in his "Life and Works of Michael Angelo Buonarroti, 1876."

delighted at their freedom of manner and boldness of execution, that from that moment he is said to have resolved to abandon the stiffness and poverty of his master Pietro Perugino's style.

During his stay in Tuscany, Leonardo renewed his former friendship with Giovan Francesco Rustici,* who had been his fellow-student with Andrea Verocchio when they were both young men. Rustici was a man of good family, and more an artist from inclination than necessity. He had the good taste to listen to Da Vinci's criticism, to whom he was particularly attached; and was also well acquainted with the worth of his observations. He was esteemed a good sculptor and architect by his contemporaries, as well as by his friend Leonardo; and the three statues which he cast in bronze for the baptistery at Florence, remain to this day memorials of his fame.

In 1504, Leonardo da Vinci lost his father, with whom he had always continued on the most affectionate terms. Whatever might have been his birth, he had made a point of keeping up a constant correspondence and perfectly good understanding with his family. It appears that soon after the Signore Piero's death, he placed a considerable sum of money at interest with the chamberlain of Santa Maria Nuova, as there are several memoranda among his papers of his having received small payments at different times from this person, and he afterwards disposed of this particular property in his will. From this we may suppose that some of his works had been very liberally rewarded, as this money could only have been acquired by his own exertions. It is Ammoretti's opinion that he visited France in 1506, but there is not sufficient proof of his having undertaken that journey in the several memoranda on which this gentleman hazards his assertion; for they might have as easily referred to his subsequent residence in that country, although he certainly considered himself in the service of the King of France as sovereign of Milan. In whatever way he employed the intermediate time, it is certain that Leonardo was again in Lombardy in 1507, as there is the following memorandum in his own hand-

* Giovan Francesco Rustici was a man of a very extraordinary turn of mind; he became the founder of a society or club called the Pajuolo, of which the account, given by Vasari, is very illustrative of the manners of the times.

writing: "Canonica di Vaprio, a dì 5 Luglio 1507, cara mia diletta Madre et mia Sorella et mia Cognata avvissovi come sono sano per la grazia di Dio," etc.; which sufficiently proves the fact of his having been staying at that time with his friends the Melzi. That he was frequently in the habit of residing with them, not only at their house at Canonica, but also at their palace at Vaprio, there remains a proof as glorious to the artist's feelings as to his generous patrons', in the picture of the *Madonna and Child* which he painted on the wall of his apartment in their palace. The head of the Madonna is six palms in height, and that of the Child four. This painting suffered considerably in 1796, by some soldiers having made a fire close to the wall on which it is executed; but the faces are still in tolerable preservation.

In 1507, Louis the Twelfth of France, finding himself continually disturbed in the possession of his Lombard dominions by the Venetians and the States of the Church, joined the famous league of Cambray, that he might be at more liberty to invade Italy with a sufficient force to establish his affairs on a firmer basis of political security. At Agnadello, near the Adda, the King gained a complete victory over the Venetians, and returned to Milan to celebrate his triumphs and revive the drooping spirits of its inhabitants by the presence of his splendid court. These fêtes and entertainments must have again called forth Leonardo's exertions, for they are described with great pomp by Arluno, in a manuscript now in the Ambrosian Library, who talks of the triumphal arches and paintings executed by the first masters in honour of the occasion. Although he does not mention Leonardo da Vinci's name, he evidently alludes to him by his making use of the phrase " pitture mollissime," which that author was accustomed to apply to him alone. Besides which, it is well known that he was in great favour with his Majesty at that time, as he appointed him painter to the court of France, and gave him twelve ounces of water from the canal of the Martesana, which was a sort of right of property extremely valuable to its possessor. As far as this gift can be at present understood, it appears that he was entitled to as much water as could be drawn off by a tunnel that measured one foot in diameter, which is equal to twelve ounces; and that he had the right of applying this to whatever purpose he pleased. To an engineer of his talents this was of the greatest value, as he might have either applied it to hydraulical purposes or sold it to the proprietors of the neighbouring lands to enrich the cultivation of their soil by its irrigations. By his letters from Florence it would appear that he intended making the former use of it, but the latter would also have yielded him a handsome revenue. It is not likely that he ever realized this property, but he showed that he considered it belonged to him, by disposing of it in his will. While in attendance on the French court at Milan, he painted the portrait of Gian Jacopo Triulzio, which is mentioned by Lomazzo, and is now in the Public Gallery at Dresden.*

The death of his uncle, Messer Francesco da Vinci, a share in whose inheritance his brothers contested with him, on the ground of his illegitimacy, determined him to go to Florence to settle the dispute. It is not known how the affair was determined between them, but we may be allowed to conjecture that it must have been in an amicable manner, from the circumstance of his leaving his property in and near Florence to be equally divided between his brothers at his death. In 1512 he returned to Milan, where he principally employed himself in hydraulical researches, in order to perfect the canal by which he had brought the Adda to the walls of the city. But he was again destined to be interrupted in his professional occupations; for he had scarcely time to see his friends, and get settled in his habitation, before the new government of Milan was broken up, and the tranquility of Lombardy so much destroyed, that he was again obliged to seek refuge in a more peaceful quarter.

The Princes of Italy, jealous of the presence of a foreign army, whose power might become inimical to their interests, concluded a league with the Emperor to replace the house of Sforza on the throne of Lombardy. In a short time Maximilian, the eldest son of Il Moro, returned in triumph to take undisputed possession of his paternal inheritance, escorted by the same. Swiss mercenaries who had so shortly before betrayed his father He was received with acclamations and rejoicings by the inhabitants of Milan. Leonardo himself, although belonging, as he

* This is now known to be a portrait by Holbein, of Moreit, jeweller to Henry VIII.

conceived, to the court of France, was sufficiently attached to the remembrance of his old patron, to paint two portraits of the young Duke Maximilian, one of which is now in the Gallery of Milan, and the other in the private collection of the Melzi family. But the situation of Milan, and the disturbed state of politics in Italy, were so extremely detrimental to Da Vinci's projects, that he was almost unable to procure a subsistence by his profession. Between the two governments he had already lost what he considered as a provision for his old age, as he was now more than sixty, and no longer possessed that buoyant feeling and ardent disposition that carried him through everything in youth. It was quite in vain for Leonardo, or any of his followers and companions in the Academy, to think of remaining in a place where nothing was to be expected but tumults and revenge. Literature and the fine arts are nurtured by peace and tranquility alone; where these cease to exist, the artist who desires to increase his reputation had better depart also. Accordingly, we find, by the following memorandum, that Leonardo at last set out for Rome, accompanied by his principal friends and scholars: " Partii da Milano per Roma ad dì 24 di Settembre 1514, con Giovanni, Francesco Melzi, Salaj, Lorenzo ed il Fanfoia." [*]

Leonardo arrived in safety at Florence, where he found the power of the house of Medici restored by the election of the Cardinal Giovanni to the pontificate, under the name of Leo the Tenth, after the decease of Julius the Second. The Pope's brother, Giuliano de' Medici received him into his household and took him to Rome. Every individual possessed of either talents or reputation was then hastening to that capital to recommend himself to the notice of Leo the Tenth; a pontiff whose name must ever be respected in the annals of literature and the arts, and whose princely liberality, by completing the restoration of learning, made Rome once more mistress of the civilized world.

Although advanced in years, and the ardour of feeling con-

---

[*] Probably this Giovanni means " Il Beltraffio," but there is no mention of any person called Fanfoia, unless it is a mistake for Fojano, who is frequently spoken of by Lomazzo and others in their manuscripts.

siderably abated by the experience which can only be acquired from a knowledge of the world and its disappointments, Da Vinci yet hoped to distinguish himself amongst those who contended for the Pope's favour.

On his arrival he was well received by Leo, both from the high reputation he enjoyed, and the circumstance of his being presented to the Pontiff by his brother Giuliano, whose favour da Vinci had completely gained. But his talents excited the envy of all those who surrounded his Holiness's person and had already secured his confidence, as they considered his approach as a sort of invasion of what they had appropriated to themselves as a right: so seldom can men of genius bear with any sort of competition. No one was more free from this unworthy feeling of envy than Leonardo himself; no one more anxious to do ample justice to the merits of others; but, most deservedly, accustomed to hold the first place at Milan, and conscious that many of the improvements in the arts which he now saw brought into use, were owing to his own inventions and to the improvements which he himself had introduced, he could not avoid feeling most acutely that he no longer possessed the same superiority over others which he had done in his youth. If he had given himself time to think, he would have been consoled by the reflection that this was the natural consequence of the progress of the arts, to which he, more than any other person, had eminently contributed. Instead of feeling mortified at the practice of the theory which he himself had first propagated, he ought to have rejoiced at its having met with the success which he had originally contemplated. But his bodily health was no longer equal to the energy of his mind, and his increasing infirmities made him more than usually irritable, for he had naturally too much pride to indulge any feelings of vanity.

Under these circumstances it was not to be expected that Da Vinci could have felt himself happily situated at Rome. Harassed by disappointments, his genius was overcast by the praises he heard on all sides bestowed on others, whom he could not have considered in any way superior to himself. But they enjoyed a greater share of his Holiness's favour, and kept Leonardo in the back-ground by persuading the Pope that he embraced too many branches of science to be able to succeed in any, and that he was become much too speculative in his ideas to execute any work of importance. By these and similar calumnies, unworthy of their own fame, and prompted solely by jealousy, they contrived to keep Da Vinci without any employment worthy of his talents.

Of all the celebrated persons who at that time ornamented the court of Rome, Raffaelle enjoyed the greatest share of the Pope's confidence and esteem, although he was more considerably indebted to his predecessor Pope Julius the Second. This Pontiff first brought him into notice at the recommendation of his kinsman, Bramante da Urbino, who was then in his service, and employed him to paint a suite of rooms in the Vatican. He executed this commission with such extraordinary taste and skill, that the frescoes he then painted are generally considered superior to any of his subsequent productions under the reign of Leo the Tenth.

The great Michael Angelo, who was also at Rome at this period, had not the good fortune to be so much distinguished by Leo as he had been by Julius, who was his friend and patron; and it ought to be observed, in justice to the latter, that many of the great works, the whole praise of which has been unthinkingly bestowed on Leo, more properly belonged to his predecessor, he having originally undertaken them, though Leo had the liberality and generosity to carry them into effect. If Leonardo da Vinci had enjoyed the advantage of the protection of Julius the Second, he would, no doubt, have been in a much better situation; and had he employed that time in his service which he lost during the disturbances at Milan, he would not only have been at the head of his profession as an artist, but his knowledge of military tactics, and his talents as an engineer, would have made him an invaluable acquisition to that warlike Pontiff.

The reign of Leo the Tenth forms so striking an era in Italian literature, that one is too apt to confound him personally with the age in which he lived. Without at all wishing to deteriorate the good qualities which this magnificent Pontiff undoubtedly possessed, it appears from the history of those times, that the age contributed more to his elevation, than he did individually to the advancement of learning. Had Julius lived a few years longer, we should have talked of the Julian age of Rome, instead of "the golden days of Leo," and the advantages to mankind would have been much the same. The ruling principle of Leo's policy was the aggrandizement of the house of Medici; and by simply following the taste of the age, and acting up to the spirit of the times, he could most easily attain his object, while he gratified his own taste for splendour by becoming the liberal patron of men of letters. It is easy to be generous, even to profusion, with what does not belong to us; and few of St. Peter's representatives have ever made a freer use of his patrimony. Circumstances made Leo what he was, and unless he had abandoned the pontificate altogether he must have been talked and flattered into virtues which he might not have otherwise possessed. It is certainly no proof of his discernment or good taste, that he either could not or did not appreciate the talents of Leonardo da Vinci sufficiently to fix him near his person; while it is well known that he neglected those of Michael Angelo Buonarroti.

Leonardo, however, during his short stay in Rome was not altogether unemployed, as he painted a picture for Messer Baldassare da Pescia, the Pope's datario (almoner), who seems to have had more feeling for the artist's merits than his master. This picture was painted on wood, and represented a Holy Family, consisting of the Virgin and Child, with St. Joseph and St. John behind, in which group was a portrait of a young lady in full length, of singular beauty and noble features. De Pagave, in speaking of this picture, observes that, "although the Vincian style is perfectly discernible, it is evident that he had imitated Raffaelle in this composition;" and for this reason he probably chose to distinguish it by the monogram of his own name, that it might not be taken for the work of any other artist. The beautiful lady whose portrait he introduced in this picture, is supposed to be the Pope's sister-in-law, as it is very natural that Leonardo should have paid this compliment to his patron's wife, Giuliano de' Medici having just married Filiberta of Savoy. Whoever the lady might have been, the picture was so wonderfully executed that it attracted the Pope's attention and occasioned him to employ Da Vinci, old as he was, in preference to Raffaelle and Michael Angelo, in the execution of a work which afterwards became the cause of his disgrace and of his departure from Rome. Vasari relates the story, that Leonardo, with his usual love of experiments, began to distil different herbs and oils to make a particular kind of varnish, and that some ill-natured persons told this to the Pope, who exclaimed, "Oh! this man will never do anything, for he begins to think of the end of his work, before the commencement." This hasty remark was immediately repeated to Leonardo, who, already disgusted with his Holiness for having sent for Michael Angelo to Rome, with whom he was on bad terms, determined on leaving it.

It is not to be wondered at, that so high-minded a man as Leonardo should have been offended at such an observation. Conscious of his own merits, and indignant at the neglect with which he had been treated during his residence at the papal court, he could not do otherwise than resolve to quit a place where he had met with so many vexations, and seek another patron in spite of his age and infirmities. There is nothing to be collected, either from his notes or the manuscripts in the Ambrosian Library, to prove that he undertook anything more of consequence at Rome, except some improvements he introduced in the mint for purifying and embellishing the Roman coin. Before his misunderstanding with the Pope, he had most likely painted the fresco of the Virgin on the walls of St. Onofrio, of which nothing now remains; as well as several other pictures for various individuals, who still cherished his name, and were anxious to possess some specimen of his abilities.

It was most unworthy of Leo's character, as the great Mæcenas of the whole Christian world, to have treated Leonardo da Vinci with so little consideration. If for no other reasons but his former works, long experience, and great reputation, he should have received him with kindness. The extreme amiability of his manners towards all might have at least blunted the shafts of envy and ill-nature. That he was himself superior to such meanness, he had given a proof in the last picture he painted, where he had, in a great measure, adopted the ease of Raffaelle's style, in addition to the exquisite softness and minute finishing of his own. It was no small compliment to Raffaelle that Leonardo, even in his old age, should have condescended to imitate him; for in such a man it was condescension to alter his style in imitation of any one. Although it would be impossible to deny that Raffaelle excelled Da Vinci in painting nearly as much as Michael Angelo did in sculpture, still it must be generally allowed, that, if they were the greater artists, he was the greater man, without derogating from the high character of either. When we consider the state in which Leonardo da Vinci found the arts when he first engaged in painting as a profession, the improvements which he introduced, the scholars whom he educated, and the prejudices which he annihilated, we are all lost in admiration of his various merits. Even Michael Angelo and Raffaelle are obliged to him for a part of their glory; because they first became the great men they were from studying his works. Raffaelle borrowed from him that almost divine grace, which Leonardo so well knew how to impart to the countenances he painted; Michael Angelo took from him that daring style of drawing by which he astonished mankind; and if afterwards both surpassed him, they were nevertheless infinitely indebted to the advantages they derived from his original inventions. Yet, such is the ungrateful reward of talent in all times, this man was obliged to expatriate himself when more than seventy years of age!

The politics of Italy were now again becoming embroiled. King Louis the Twelfth of France died on the first day of the year 1515, and he was succeeded by Francis the First. It was not to be supposed that a young King of only twenty-one years of age would feel inclined to submit quietly to the loss of his Italian dominions, particularly as he had assumed the title of Duke of Milan on his accession to the throne, both in right of his predecessor and of the Emperor's concession of that duchy at the league of Cambray. Having concluded an advantageous peace with the King of England and the Archduke of Austria, afterwards Charles V., the young monarch advanced towards Italy, determined to make light of every difficulty. His successes induced Leo to incline towards an accommodation. Francis was already in possession of Pavia; and his armies were proceeding with rapid strides to reconquer the whole of Lombardy.

These political events no sooner became public than Leonardo da Vinci resolved to profit by the successes of his former patrons, the French, in whose service he still considered himself. He therefore set out for Pavia, where he was received by Francis with every mark of friendship. He soon became a great favourite with his Majesty, who delighted in his society and conversation; and Da Vinci's spirits began to revive at again finding himself in a situation where all his excellent qualities were duly appreciated. He felt himself of the same consequence he had formerly been; and presiding over the revels and entertainments of a magnificent court, he exerted his utmost taste and skill to please his chivalrous patron and his nobles.

It is supposed that the Lion, spoken of by Lomazzo, was contrived by Leonardo on this occasion to increase the pomp of some of the fêtes given in honour of the King's successes. This piece of mechanism was so admirably contrived, that the lion walked of itself up to the King's throne, and threw open its body, which was filled with *fleurs de lis*, in compliment to his Majesty. This pageant is frequently mentioned by the writers of that period, when it was, no doubt, considered as a most wonderful invention.

Both the Pope and the King of France were extremely desirous of an interview, and Bologna was fixed upon as the place where the congress should be held. The King came attended with very little pomp, and only a small part of his brilliant court, but among them was Leonardo da Vinci,* who must have been highly gratified in being able to show himself to the Pope's followers as the friend and favourite of a powerful monarch, after having been almost compelled to quit Rome. To the young King his experience was doubtless of the greatest use in treating with so wary a politician as Leo; and his general knowledge of Italy, both in politics and literature, must have increased his favour with Francis, to whose interest he was now most firmly attached, and from that time Leonardo considered himself as belonging to the French court. Conscious of his own deserts, Leonardo da

---

* Among Leonardo's papers was found a design for the portrait of Siguore Artus, under which is written, in his own handwriting, "Ritratto di M. Artus, Maestro di Camera del Rò Francesco primo, nella Giunta con Papa Leon decimo," which fully proves that Da Vinci was present on that occasion.

Vinci felt as an insult what was merely the effect of an envious cabal; but his sensitive mind was so deeply wounded, that he determined to abandon his country for ever, and establish himself at the Court of France for the rest of his days. If his pride could have submitted to prove his superior merit by his works, instead of showing that he was offended by leaving the court of Rome, there is every probability that he must have triumphed over his enemies and regained the Pontiff's favour. But most likely he considered himself too old to begin the struggle anew, and he was perhaps too proud to submit to a competition for fame in a country where he had for so many years held the first place, and which was so much indebted to his exertions for many of the advantages which she possessed in the fine arts. Another reason that must have naturally influenced him at his time of life, was the instability of the Italian courts, the disadvantages of which he had sufficiently experienced in the downfall of the house of Sforza, and the continual changes of the government of Milan. By these circumstances he had lost all the fruits of his long services to that state during the best part of his life; and even his reputation had considerably suffered by it, in the destruction of his works. The equestrian statue of Francesco Sforza, which he was to have cast in bronze, and by which he hoped to have established his fame as a sculptor, never proceeded any further than the model, and even that was destroyed by the brutality of the soldiery. The evils of war and the miseries of civil dissension had dispersed his friends and scholars, and nothing remained of the Academy which he had founded, but the effects which it produced on the arts in laying a foundation for the improvement of painting, by which all subsequent artists have more or less benefited. The friends of his brighter days were all either dead or no longer able to struggle against the misfortunes which they had met with from the unsettled state of their country; so that it was not to be wondered at that Da Vinci should have preferred sheltering himself under the protection of a powerful monarch who promised to provide most generously for the rest of his life, to the precarious subsistence which Italy could afford him.

Previous to his departure from Milan, the King tried every means in his power to remove the painting of *The Last Supper,* in order to send it to France. Everything was done to deprive Milan of this magnificent work which she has so badly taken care of; but it was found impracticable, although Francis would have spared no expense to have succeeded in his designs, and Leonardo did all in his power to gratify his new patron. However, all their efforts were ineffectual, and, as Vasari says, "the picture having been done immediately on the wall, his Majesty was obliged to depart with his wish ungratified, and leave the painting to the Milanese."

About the end of January 1516 Leonardo accompanied Francis the First to Paris, as painter to the court of France, with an annual salary of 700 crowns, and a liberal provision for all his wants; where he met with a reception equal to his merits. The King treated him with distinguished favour, and the courtiers vied with each other in following his Majesty's example.

From the time of his arrival in France, his health began to deteriorate, so much so, that he was incapable of applying himself to anything of consequence. It is known from the direction of a letter found among his papers, "A Monsieur Lyonard Peintre, par Amboise," that he must have been at that place; as also from the circumstance of his will being dated from thence, in which he speaks of the furniture and valuables he possessed at "Du Cloux," about a mile from Amboise, where he most likely resided.

It does not appear probable that he painted anything in France, as Vasari tells us that the King himself could not prevail on him to finish his cartoon of Santa Anna,* which he had brought from Italy, and which was afterwards painted by some of his scholars on his outlines. It is also most likely that Leonardo, finding himself growing old, and much oppressed with sickness, would not have wished to undertake any work that he no longer felt himself able to complete without almost compromising his former reputation. We may therefore suppose that the painting of Francis's mistress, "La belle Ferronnière," is the work of some of his scholars.†

---

* Now in the Library of the Royal Academy.

† It is now surmised that the portrait known as "La belle Ferronnière" is that of Isabel d'Este, Marchioness of Mantua, whom

Towards the latter end of his life, Leonardo's health was so much broken, that his infirmities no longer permitted him to take any part in the pleasures of the world, and he began to prepare himself for that awful change which he expected to be soon called upon to make. Vasari tells us, that believing himself near death, Da Vinci devoted the remainder of his days to a more strict observance of the precepts of the Catholic religion; which would almost imply that he had lived the greater part of his life without any. But this inference is strongly contradicted by the morality and propriety of his general conduct. For although his person, talents, and accomplishments would have given him every probability of success, particularly when united with the example of a most libertine court, it is well known there was no man of his time less addicted to gallantry and intrigue. His writings, also, are all of a more serious nature than could have been expected from the vivacity of his disposition in early life. And even his paintings are entirely free from any sort of lascivious or indecent ideas. He seldom painted naked figures; but whenever he did undertake such subjects, they were always remarkable for the purity and modesty of their attitudes; as in the Leda, which is mentioned by Lomazzo, where he painted the eyes cast down from shame. Vasari must, therefore, have intended to express a total abandonment of the present to fix his mind exclusively on the future, rather than to insinuate any want of religion in his youth. Naturally enthusiastic in his feelings, he turned his thoughts to his Maker with the same ardour which had distinguished him in all his actions; and his death was as glorious as his life had been virtuous and useful. Having accompanied the court to Fontainbleau, he is stated by Vasari to have expired in the arms of Francis the First, who came to visit him during his illness, and happened by accident to be with him when he was seized with a mortal paroxysm that speedily terminated his existence. What a triumph to the arts! and what an honour to the King! who had the pleasing remembrance of having comforted the last moments of one of the greatest artists that had then enlightened the world; and

Leonardo is known to have painted in 1500.—See "Academy," vol. i., page 123, " Two lost years in the life of Leonardo da Vinci." .

Francis must have looked back with more real satisfaction and self-approbation, to the recollection of his having supported and soothed Leonardo da Vinci in the hour of death, than to many of the more brilliant events of his reign. If at such a moment, when all artificial distinctions are at an end, Leonardo could have entertained one worldly thought, it must have alleviated his sufferings and encouraged his hopes, to know that he breathed out his soul in the arms of one of the greatest monarchs in Europe, who, while living, regarded him with the warmest admiration, and when dying lamented him with the sincerest regret.

Such was the enviable fate of Leonardo da Vinci, who died at the age of seventy-five (on the 2nd of May, 1519), universally esteemed and as universally regretted. His whole life was spent in advancing the happiness of his fellow-creatures by furthering the progress of science. Few men have done more good in the world : a generous patron, an affectionate friend, and a liberal-minded man, he was as ready to promote the views of others as he was to acknowledge their merit; and he had scarcely a wish beyond the advancement of general knowledge and the encouragement of the fine arts.

Several authors, and among others Ammoretti, attempt to deprive Leonardo of the honour of having died in the arms of Francis, which they treat as a fictitious story invented to amuse the lovers of the marvellous ; but it is too well confirmed by contemporary writers and general tradition to be destroyed by these sceptics. We have, moreover, the testimony of Vasari, who relates the circumstance in these words :—" At length, seeing himself near death, he confessed himself with much contrition; and although he was unable to stand, he desired his friends and servants to support him, that he might receive the holy sacrament out of bed in a more reverent posture. When fatigued with this exertion the King came to visit him, and Leonardo, raising himself up in his bed out of respect to his Majesty, began to relate the circumstances of his illness, and the wrongs he had done both to God and man, by not making better use of his talents. In the midst of this conversation he was seized with a paroxysm, which proved the messenger of death; on seeing which, the King hastened to assist him, and supported him in his bed, in order to alleviate his sufferings. But his divine spirit, knowing he could not receive greater honour, expired in the King's arms in the seventy-fifth year of his age."*

Leonardo's having made his will at Amboise is no proof of his having died at Cloux, particularly as it was written some months † before his death. And as it is well known that Fontainbleau was the favourite residence of Francis, there is every reason to suppose that he would have desired Leonardo's assistance in the embellishment of that place. As he was also attached to the court and to the King personally, he would in all probability have been wherever his master was. Another reason Ammoretti gives for discrediting this anecdote, is the circum-

* "This circumstantial narrative, like many others related by Vasari, has been found to be open to considerable doubt. In the first place it has been proved that Leonardo died at Cloux on the 2nd of May, 1519 (nine days after he had made his will), while Francis I. was, it would appear, at St. Germain-en-Laye at that date, awaiting the accouchement of the Queen. It is true that the ordinance signed by the King at St. Germain on the 1st of May, and quoted by Venturi as a proof of his presence there on that day, is not conclusive, for it appears that such ordinances might be signed in the absence of the King by the secretary; but a journal of the time of Francis I., preserved in the 'Bibliotheque Nationale' at Paris, makes no mention of any journey of the King at this date, and etiquette, it is known, demanded his presence at that particular time at the court of St. Germain. Moreover, Melzi, in his letter, announcing the death of Leonardo to his brothers, does not allude to the circumstance of his dying in the King's arms, which he would most likely have done had such been the case; and Lomazzo, who also must have known something of the matter, expressly states that 'Francis, King of France, *wept* when he heard *from Melzi* that Da Vinci was dead, who had painted *The Last Supper* in Milan, a work beyond all others.'

"All these small facts combined form a strong argument against Vasari, and have led to an almost universal disbelief in this pretty story, especially as the hypothesis started by Dupresne, and adopted by several writers, that Leonardo died at Fontainbleau, was proved untenable. This mistake probably arose from a Flemish painter of the name of Leonard being employed by Il Rosso when he was decorating the palace of Fontainbleau in 1530. In Leonardo's time Fontainbleau was a mere hunting-box."—"Life of Leonardo da Vinci," by Mrs. Charles Heaton.

† This is an error. Leonardo died nine days after he had made his will.

stance of Francesco Melzi's having written from Amboise to inform Da Vinci's brothers of his death. But is it not possible, and even probable, that Melzi, as his executor, should have gone to the place where his effects were, and of which he had also to give an account? At any rate, this story is too pleasing a fiction, if it be one, to be slightly discredited; and few would wish to disbelieve what tradition has handed down to us, what all the poets and painters who have since touched on the subject have confirmed, and what is, besides, as glorious to Leonardo as it is creditable to Francis.*

To a noble presence and beautiful countenance, Da Vinci united uncommon strength both of body and mind. His eloquence was so persuasive, that Vasari says, "Con le parole sue volgeva al sì e al no ogn' indurata intentione;" and his physical force was so great, that he could bend a horseshoe as if it were lead. He was very magnificent in his attire, and rather too fond of adorning his person in early life; but these foibles were more than counterbalanced by the hospitality and liberality of his disposition. The founder of an academy over which he presided for some years, he may be supposed to have left a great many literary works, which are most of them in manuscript, and preserved in different public libraries throughout Europe. Among these are a treatise on Hydraulics, with designs, another on Anatomy, and another on the Anatomy of the Horse, which is noticed by Vasari, Borghini, and Lomazzo; and a treatise on Perspective and on Light and Shade. But his best-known work is the "Trattato della Pittura," of which there are several editions; an old one with etchings by Stefano della Bella, and a more recent one printed at Paris by Du Fresne in 1651, with figures by Nicolas Poussin. This was translated into English and published in London by John Senex in 1721. The ensuing translation, by Rigaud, was first published in London in 1802.

As an engineer, the canal of the Martesana, by which he

* In the year 1863, M. Arsène Houssaye instituted a search for the tomb of Leonardo at Cloux, and found two stones, one bearing the letters LEO—the other INC—which M. Houssaye thinks are conclusive evidence that they formed part of the inscription, LEO-NARDO DA VINCI.

conducted the waters of the Adda to the walls of Milan, a distance of nearly two hundred miles, would have been alone sufficient to establish his reputation.* In this great work he obliged the impediments of nature to give way to the efforts of genius, and he succeeded to the admiration of all Italy.

As a painter, Leonardo da Vinci may be considered the first who reconciled minute finishing with grandeur of design and harmony of expression. His was the very poetry of painting. His exquisite taste, by continually making him dissatisfied with his works, urged him on to a nearer approach to perfection than had ever been attained. For this reason his scholars were superior to those of any other master, as he exacted from them the same profound attention to nature, and laborious minuteness of style, which distinguished himself.

It is to be remembered, to the immortal honour of Leonardo da Vinci, that he first dissipated the film of ignorance which impeded the progress of the arts; and if Raffaelle and Michael Angelo afterwards surpassed him in his own line, it is to him that justly belongs the merit of having first pointed out the road which they so successfully followed. It is easier to improve than to invent; but to him who had the talents to imagine and the courage to overcome the prejudices of ages, ought to belong the gratitude of posterity, more than to those who, by following his precepts, increased their own reputation. To no one, in short, are the arts more largely indebted than to Leonardo da Vinci, whose virtues endeared him to all who knew him, and whose exertions so mainly contributed to the refinement and civilization of future ages.

* The canal of Martesana was executed in the time of Francesco Sforza, the father of Il Moro, long before Leonardo's arrival in Milan. He probably, however, repaired and made improvements in it.

A TREATISE ON PAINTING.

DRAWING.

PROPORTION.

1.—What the young Student in Painting ought in the first place to learn.

THE young student should, in the first place, acquire a knowledge of perspective, to enable him to give to every object its proper dimensions: after which, it is requisite that he be under the care of an able master, to accustom him, by degrees, to a good style of drawing the parts. Next, he must study Nature, in order to confirm and fix in his mind the reason of those precepts which he has learnt. He must also bestow some time in viewing the works of various old masters, to form his eye and judgment, in order that he may be able to put in practice all that he has been taught.*

* This passage has been by some persons much misunderstood, and supposed to require, that the student should be a deep proficient in perspective before he commences the study of painting; but it is a knowledge of the leading principles only of perspective that the author here means, and without such a knowledge, which is easily to be acquired, the student will inevitably fall into errors, as gross as those humorously pointed out by Hogarth, in his Frontispiece to Kirby's Perspective.

2.—*Rule for a young Student in Painting.*

The organ of sight is one of the quickest, and takes in at a single glance an infinite variety of forms; notwithstanding which, it cannot perfectly comprehend more than one object at a time. For example, the reader, at one look over this page, immediately perceives it full of different characters; but he cannot at the same moment distinguish each letter, much less can he comprehend their meaning. He must consider it word by word, and line by line, if he be desirous of forming a just notion of these characters. In like manner, if we wish to ascend to the top of an edifice, we must be content to advance step by step, otherwise we shall never be able to attain it.

A young man, who has a natural inclination to the study of this art, I would advise to act thus: In order to acquire a true notion of the form of things, he must begin by studying the parts which compose them, and not pass to a second till he has well stored his memory, and sufficiently practised the first; otherwise he loses his time, and will most certainly protract his studies. And let him remember to acquire accuracy before he attempts quickness.

3.—*How to discover a young Man's Disposition for Painting.*

Many are very desirous of learning to draw, and are very fond of it, who are, notwithstanding, void of a proper disposition for it. This may be known by their want of perseverance; like boys, who draw everything in a hurry, never finishing, or shadowing.

4.—*Of Painting, and its Divisions.*

Painting is divided into two principal parts. The first is the figure; that is, the lines which distinguish the forms of bodies and their component parts. The second is the colour contained within those limits.

5.—*Division of the Figure.*

The form of bodies is divided into two parts; that is, the proportion of the members to each other, which must correspond with the whole; and the motion, expressive of what passes in the mind of the living figure.

6.—*Proportion of Members.*

The proportion of members is again divided into two parts, viz., equality, and motion. By equality is meant (besides the measure corresponding with the whole), that you do not confound the members of a young subject with those of old age, nor plump ones with those that are lean; and that, moreover, you do not blend the robust and firm muscles of man with feminine softness; that the attitudes and motions of old age be not expressed with the quickness and alacrity of youth, nor those of a female figure like those of a vigorous young man. The motions and members of a strong man should be such as to express his perfect state of health.

7.—*Of Dimensions in general.*

In general, the dimensions of the human body are to be considered in the length, and not in the breadth; because in the wonderful works of Nature, which we endeavour to imitate, we cannot in any species find any one part in one model precisely similar to the same part in another. Let us be attentive, therefore, to the variation of forms, and avoid all monstrosities of proportion; such as long legs united to short bodies, and narrow chests with long arms. Observe also attentively the measure of joints, in which Nature is apt to vary considerably; and imitate her example by doing the same.

8.—*Motion, Changes, and Proportion of Members.*

The measures of the human body vary in each member, according as it is more or less bent, or seen in different views, increasing on one side as much as they diminish on the other.

9.—*The Difference of Proportion between Children and grown Men.*

In men and children I find a great difference between the joints of the one and the other, in the length of the bones. A man has the length of two heads from the extremity of one shoulder to the other, the same from the shoulder to the elbow, and from the elbow to the fingers; but the child has only one, because Nature gives the proper size first to the seat of the intellect, and afterwards to the other parts.

10.—*The Alterations in the Proportion of the human Body from Infancy to full Age.*

A man, in his infancy, has the breadth of his shoulders equal to the length of the face, and to the length of the arm from the shoulder to the elbow, when the arm is bent.* It is the same again from the lower belly to the knee, and from the knee to the foot. But, when a man is arrived at the period of his full growth, every one of these dimensions becomes double in length, except the face, which, with the top of the head, undergoes but very little alteration in length. A well-proportioned and full-grown man, therefore, is ten times the length of his face; the breadth of his shoulders will be two faces, and in like manner all the above lengths will be double. The rest will be explained in the general measurement of the human body.†

11.—*Of the Proportion of Members.*

All the parts of any animal whatever must be correspondent with the whole. So that, if the body be short and thick, all the members belonging to it must be the

---

* See chap. 351.   † Not to be found in this work.

same. One that is long and thin must have its parts of the same kind; and so of the middle size. Something of the same may be observed in plants, when uninjured by men or tempests: for, when thus injured, they bud and grow again, making young shoots from old plants, and by those means destroying their natural symmetry.

12.—*That every Part be proportioned to its Whole.*

If a man be short and thick, be careful that all his members be of the same nature, viz., short arms and thick, large hands, short fingers, with broad joints; and so of the rest.

13.—*Of the Proportion of the Members.*

Measure upon yourself the proportion of the parts, and, if you find any of them defective, note it down, and be very careful to avoid it in drawing your own compositions. For this is reckoned a common fault in painters, to delight in the imitation of themselves.

14.—*The Danger of forming an erroneous Judgment in regard to the Proportion and Beauty of the Parts.*

If the painter has clumsy hands, he will be apt to introduce them into his works, and so of any other part of his person, which may not happen to be so beautiful as it ought to be. He must, therefore, guard particularly against that self-love, or too good opinion of his own person, and study by every means to acquire the knowledge of what is most beautiful, and of his own defects, that he may adopt the one and avoid the other.

15.—*Another Precept.*

The young painter must, in the first instance, accustom his hand to copying the drawings of good masters; and when his hand is thus formed and ready, he should, with the advice of his director, use himself also to draw from relievos; according to the rules we shall point out in the treatise on drawing from relievos.*

16.—*The Manner of drawing from Relievos, and rendering Paper fit for it.*

When you draw from relievos, tinge your paper of some darkish demi-tint. And after you have made your outline, put in the darkest shadows, and, last of all, the principal lights, but sparingly, especially the smaller ones; because those are easily lost to the eye at a very moderate distance.†

17.—*Of drawing from Casts or Nature.*

In drawing from relievo, the draftsman must place him-self in such a manner, as that the eye of the figure to be drawn be level with his own.‡

* From this, and many other similar passages, it is evident, that the author intended at some future time to arrange his manuscript collections, and to publish them as separate treatises. That he did not do so is well known; but it is also a fact, that, in selecting from the whole mass of his collections the chapters of which the present work consists, great care appears in general to have been taken to extract also those to which there was any reference from any of the chapters intended for this work, or which from their subject were necessarily connected with them. Accordingly, the reader will find, in the notes to this translation, that all such chapters in any other part of the present work are uniformly pointed out, as have any relation to the respective passages in the text. This, which has never before been done, though indispensably necessary, will be found of singular use, and it was thought proper here, once for all, to notice it.

In the present instance the chapters, referring to the subject in the text, are Chap. 15, 17, 18, 19, 20, 26; and though these do not afford complete information, yet it is to be remembered, that drawing from relievos is subject to the very same rules as drawing from Nature; and that, therefore, what is elsewhere said on that subject is also equally applicable to this.

† The meaning of this is, that the last touches of light, such as the shining parts (which are always narrow), must be given sparingly. In short, that the drawing must be kept in broad masses as much as possible.

‡ This is not an absolute rule, but it is a very good one for drawing of portraits.

18. —*To draw Figures from Nature.*

Accustom yourself to hold a plummet in your hand, that you may judge of the bearing of the parts.

19 —*Of drawing from Nature.*

When you draw from Nature, you must be at the distance of three times the height of the object; and when you begin to draw, form in your own mind a certain principal line (suppose a perpendicular); observe well the bearing of the parts towards that line; whether they intersect it, are parallel to it, or oblique.

20.—*Of drawing Academy Figures.*

When you draw from a naked model, always sketch in the whole of the figure, suiting all the members well to each other; and though you finish only that part which appears the best, have a regard to the rest, that, whenever you make use of such studies, all the parts may hang together.

In composing your attitudes, take care not to turn the head on the same side as the breast, nor let the arm go in a line with the leg.* If the head turn towards the right shoulder, the parts must be lower on the left side than on the other: but if the chest come forward, and the head turn towards the left, the parts on the right side are to be the highest.

21.—*Of studying in the Dark, on first waking in the Morning, and before going to sleep.*

I have experienced no small benefit, when in the dark and in bed, by retracing in my mind the outlines of those forms which I had previously studied, particularly such

* See chap. 101.

as had appeared the most difficult to comprehend and retain; by this method they will be confirmed and treasured up in the memory.

22.—*Observations on drawing Portraits.*

The cartilage, which raises the nose in the middle of the face, varies in eight different ways. It is equally straight, equally concave, or equally convex,—which is the first sort. Or, secondly, unequally straight, concave, or convex. Or, thirdly, straight in the upper part, and concave in the under. Or, fourthly, straight again in the upper part, and convex in those below. Or, fifthly, it may be concave above, and straight beneath. Or, sixthly, concave above, and convex below. Or, seventhly, it may be convex in the upper part, and straight in the lower. And in the eighth and last place, convex above, and concave beneath. The uniting of the nose with the brows is in two ways: either it is straight, or concave. The forehead has three different forms. It is straight, concave, or round. The first is divided into two parts, viz., it is either convex in the upper part, or in the lower, sometimes both; or else flat above and below.

23.—*The Method of retaining in the Memory the Likeness of a Man, so as to draw his Profile, after having seen him only once.*

You must observe and remember well the variations of the four principal features in the profile; the nose, mouth, chin, and forehead. And first of the nose, of which there are three different sorts,* straight, concave, and convex. Of the straight there are but four variations, short or long, high at the end, or low. Of the concave there are three sorts; some have the concavity above, some in the middle, and some at the end. The convex noses also vary three ways; some project in the upper part, some in the middle,

* See the preceding chapter.

and others at the bottom. Nature, which seems to delight
in infinite variety, gives again three changes to those noses
which have a projection in the middle; for some have it
straight, some concave, and some convex.

24.—*How to remember the Form of a Face.*

If you wish to retain with facility the general look of a
face, you must first learn how to draw well several faces,
mouths, eyes, noses, chins, throats, necks, and shoulders;
in short, all those principal parts which distinguish one man
from another. For instance, noses are of ten different sorts: *
straight, bunched, concave, some raised above, some below
the middle, aquiline, flat, round, and sharp. These affect
the profile. In the front view there are eleven different
sorts. Even, thick in the middle, thin in the middle, thick
at the tip, thin at the beginning, thin at the tip, and thick
at the beginning. Broad, narrow, high, and low nostrils;
some with a large opening, and some more shut towards
the tip.

The same variety will be found in the other parts of the
face, which must be drawn from Nature, and retained in
the memory. Or else, when you mean to draw a likeness
from memory, take with you a pocket-book, in which you
have marked all these variations of features, and after
having given a look at the face you mean to draw, retire
a little aside, and note down in your book which of the
features are similar to it; that you may put it all together
at home.

25.--*That a Painter should take Pleasure in the Opinion of everybody.*

A painter ought not certainly to refuse listening to the
opinion of any one; for we know that, although a man
be not a painter, he may have just notions of the forms
of men—whether a man has a hump on his back, a thick

* See the two preceding chapters.

leg, or a large hand; whether he be lame, or have any other defect. Now, if we know that men are able to judge of the works of Nature, should we not think them more able to detect our errors?

—— ——————

ANATOMY.

26.—*What is principally to be observed in Figures.*

THE principal and most important consideration required in drawing figures, is to set the head well upon the shoulders, the chest upon the hips, the hips and shoulders upon the feet.

27.—*Mode of Studying.*

Study the science first, and then follow the practice which results from that science. Pursue method in your study, and do not quit one part till it be perfectly engraven in the memory; and observe what difference there is between the members of animals and their joints.*

28.—*Of being universal.*

It is an easy matter for a man who is well versed in the principles of his art, to become universal in the practice of it, since all animals have a similarity of members, that is, muscles, tendons, bones, etc. These only vary in length or thickness, as will be demonstrated in the Anatomy.†

* Man being the highest of the animal creation, ought to be the chief object of study.

† An intended treatise, as it seems, on anatomy, which, however, never was published; but there are several chapters in the present work on the subject of anatomy, most of which will be found under the present head of Anatomy; and of such as could not be placed there, because they also related to some other branch, the following is a list by which they may be found: chapters 6, 7, 10, 11, 34, 35, 36, 37, 38, 39, 40, 41, 42, 43, 44, 45, 46, 48, 49, 50, 51, 52, 129.

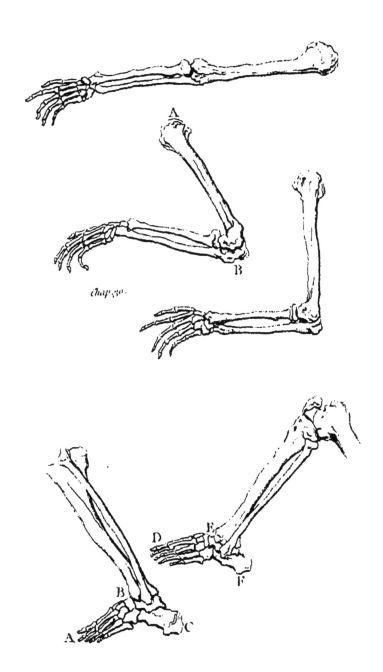

chap. 36.

chap. 37.

As for aquatic animals, of which there is great variety, I shall not persuade the painter to take them as a rule, having no connection with our purpose.

29.—*A Precept for the Painter.*

It reflects no great honour on a painter to be able to execute only one thing well, such as a head, an academy figure, or draperies, animals, landscape, or the like, confining himself to some particular object of study; because there is scarcely a person so void of genius as to fail of success, if he apply earnestly to one branch of study, and practise it continually.

30.—*Of the Measures of the human Body, and the bending of Members.*

It is very necessary that painters should have a knowledge of the bones which support the flesh by which they are covered, but particularly of the joints, which increase and diminish the length of them in their appearance. As in the arm, which does not measure the same when bent, as when extended; its difference between the greatest extension and bending, is about one eighth of its length. The increase and diminution of the arm is effected by the bone projecting out of its socket at the elbow; which, as is seen in figure A B, *Plate I.*, is lengthened from the shoulder to the elbow; the angle it forms being less than a right angle. It will appear longer as that angle becomes more acute, and will shorten in proportion as it becomes more open or obtuse.

31.—*Of the small Bones in several Joints of the human Body.*

There are in the joints of the human body certain small bones, fixed in the middle of the tendons which connect several of the joints. Such are the patellas of the knees and the joints of the shoulders, and those of the feet. They are eight in number—one at each shoulder, one at each knee, and two at each foot under the first joint of the great toe towards the heel.   These grow extremely hard as a man advances in years.

32.—*Memorandum to be observed by the Painter.*

Note down which muscles and tendons are brought into action by the motion of any member, and when they are hidden.   Remember that these remarks are of the greatest importance to painters and sculptors, who profess to study anatomy, and the science of the muscles.   Do the same with children, following the different gradations of age from their birth even to decrepitude, describing the changes which the members, and particularly the joints, undergo ; which of them grow fat, and which lean.

33.—*The Shoulders.*

The joints of the shoulders, and other parts which bend, shall be noticed in their places in the Treatise on Anatomy, where the cause of the motions of all the parts which compose the human body shall be explained.*

34.—*The Difference of Joints between Children and grown Men.*

Young children have all their joints small, but they are thick and plump in the spaces between them ; because there is nothing upon the bones at the joints, but some tendons to bind the bones together.   The soft flesh, which is full of fluids, is enclosed under the skin in the space between the joints; and as the bones are bigger at the joints than in the space between them, the skin throws off in the progress to manhood that superfluity, and draws nearer to the bones, thinning the whole part together.   But upon the joints it does not lessen, as there is nothing but cartilages and tendons.   For these reasons children are small in the joints, and plump in the space between, as may be observed in their fingers, arms, and narrow shoulders.

* See chap. 87.

Men, on the contrary, are large and full in the joints, in the arms and legs ; and where children have hollows, men are knotty and prominent.

35.—*Of the Joints of the Fingers.*

The joints of the fingers appear larger on all sides when they bend; the more they bend the larger they appear. The contrary is the case when straight. It is the same in the toes, and it will be more perceptible in proportion to their fleshiness.

36.—*Of the Joint of the Wrist.*

The wrist, or joint between the hand and arm, lessens on closing the hand, and grows larger when it opens. The contrary happens in the arm, in the space between the elbow and the hand, on all sides; because in opening the hand the muscles are extended and thinned in the arm, from the elbow to the wrist; but when the hand is shut, the same muscles swell and shorten. The tendons alone start, being stretched by the clenching of the hand.

37.—*Of the Joint of the Foot.*

The increase and diminution in the joint of the foot is produced on that side where the tendons are seen, as D E F, *Plate I.*, which increases when the angle is acute, and diminishes when it becomes obtuse. It must be understood of the joint in the front part of the foot A B C.

38.—*Of the Knee.*

Of all the members which have pliable joints, the knee is the only one that lessens in the bending and becomes larger by extension.

39.—*Of the Joints.*

All the joints of the human body become larger by bending, except that of the leg.

40.—*Of the Naked.*

When a figure is to appear nimble and delicate, its muscles must never be too much marked, nor are any of them to be much swelled; because such figures are expressive of activity and swiftness, and are never loaded with much flesh upon the bones. They are made light by the want of flesh, and where there is but little flesh there cannot be any thickness of muscles.

41.—*Of the Thickness of the Muscles.*

Muscular men have large bones, and are in general thick and short, with very little fat; because the fleshy muscles in their growth contract closer together, and the fat, which in other instances lodges between them, has no room. The muscles in such thin subjects, not being able to extend, grow in thickness, particularly towards their middle, in the parts most removed from the extremities.

42.—*Fat Subjects have small Muscles.*

Though fat people have this in common with muscular men, that they are frequently short and thick, they have thin muscles; but their skin contains a great deal of spongy and soft flesh full of air; for that reason they are lighter upon the water, and swim better than muscular people.

43.—*Which of the Muscles disappear in the Motions of the Body.*

In raising or lowering the arm, the pectoral muscles disappear, or acquire a greater relievo. A similar effect is produced by the hips, when they bend either inwards or outwards. It is to be observed, that there is more variety of appearances in the shoulders, hips, and neck, than in any other joint, because they are susceptible of the greatest variety of motions. But of this subject I shall make a separate treatise.*

* It does not appear that this intention was ever carried into execution; but there are many chapters in this work on the subject

44.—*Of the Muscles.*

The muscles are not to be scrupulously marked all the way, because it would be disagreeable to the sight, and of very difficult execution. But on that side only where the members are in action, they should be pronounced more strongly; for muscles that are at work naturally collect all their parts together, to gain increase of strength, so that some small parts of those muscles will appear, that were not seen before.

45.—*Of the Muscles.*

The muscles of young men are not to be marked strongly, nor too much swelled, because that would indicate full strength and vigour of age, which they have not yet attained. Nevertheless they must be more or less expressed, as they are more or less employed. For those which are in motion are always more swelled and thicker than those which remain at rest. The intrinsic and central line of the members which are bent, never retains its natural length.

46.—*The Extension and Contraction of the Muscles.*

The muscle at the back part of the thigh shows more variety in its extension and contraction than any other in the human body; the second, in that respect, are those which compose the buttocks; the third, those of the back; the fourth, those of the neck; the fifth, those of the shoulders; and the sixth, those of the Abdomen, which, taking their rise under the breast, terminate under the lower belly; as I shall explain when I speak of each.

47.—*Of the Muscle between the Chest and the lower Belly.*

There is a muscle which begins under the breast at the Sternum, and is inserted into, or terminates at the Os

of motion, where all that is necessary for a painter in this branch will be found.

pubis, under the lower belly. It is called the Rectus of
the Abdomen; it is divided, lengthways, into three principal portions, by transverse tendinous intersections or
ligaments, viz., the superior part, and a ligament; the
second part, with its ligaments; and the third part, with
the third ligament; which last unites by tendons to the Os
pubis. These divisions and intersections of the same
muscle are intended by nature to facilitate the motion
when the body is bent or distended. If it were made of
one piece, it would produce too much variety when extended, or contracted, and also would be considerably
weaker. When this muscle has but little variety in the
motion of the body, it is more beautiful.*

48.—Of a Man's complex Strength, but first of the Arm.

The muscles which serve either to straighten or bend
the arm, arise from the different processes of the Scapula;
some of them from the protuberances of the Humerus,
and others about the middle of the Os humeri. The
extensors of the arm arise from behind, and the flexors
from before.

That a man has more power in pulling than in pushing,
has been proved by the ninth proposition De Ponderibus,†
where it is said, that of two equal weights, that will have
the greatest power which is farthest removed from the
pole or centre of its balance. It follows then of course,
that the muscle N B, *Plate II.*, and the muscle N C, being
of equal power, the inner muscle N C will nevertheless be
stronger than the outward one N B, because it is inserted
into the arm at C, a point farther removed from the centre
of the elbow A than B, which is on the other side of such

---

* Anatomists have divided this muscle into four or five sections;
but painters, following the ancient sculptors, show only the three
principal ones; and, in fact, we find that a greater number of them
(as may often be observed in nature) gives a disagreeable meagreness
to the subject. Beautiful nature does not show more than three,
though there may be more hid under the skin.

† A treatise on weights, like many others, intended by this author,
but never published.

Plate 9.

centre, so that that question is determined. But this is a simple power, and I thought it best to explain it before I mentioned the complex power of the muscles, of which I must now take notice. The complex power, or strength, is, for instance, this—when the arm is going to act, a second power is added to it (such as the weight of the body and the strength of the legs, in pulling or pushing), consisting in the extension of the parts, as when two men attempt to throw down a column; the one by pushing, and the other by pulling.*

49.—In which of the two Actions, Pulling or Pushing, a Man has the greatest Power.

(Plate 2.)

A man has the greatest power in pulling, for in that action he has the united exertion of all the muscles of the arm, while some of them must be inactive when he is pushing; because when the arm is extended for that purpose, the muscles which move the elbow cannot act, any more than if he pushed with his shoulders against the column he means to throw down; in which case only the muscles that extend the back, the legs under the thigh, and the calves of the legs, would be active. From which we conclude, that in pulling there is added to the power of extension the strength of the arms, of the legs, of the back, and even of the chest, if the oblique motion of the body require it. But in pushing, though all the parts were employed, yet the strength of the muscles of the arms is wanting; for to push with an extended arm without motion, does not help more than if a piece of wood were placed from the shoulder to the column meant to be pushed down.

50.—Of the bending of Members, and of the Flesh round the bending Joint.

The flesh which covers the bones near and at the joints, swells or diminishes in thickness according to their

* See the next chapter.

C

bending or extension; that is, it increases at the inside of
the angle formed by the bending, and grows narrow and
lengthened on the outward side of the exterior angle.
The middle between the convex and concave angle participates of this increase or diminution, but in a greater or
less degree as the parts are nearer to, or farther from, the
angles of the bending joints.

51.—Of the naked Body.

The members of naked men who work hard in different
attitudes, will show the muscles more strongly on that
side where they act forcibly to bring the part into action;
and the other muscles will be more or less marked, in
proportion as they co-operate in the same motion.

52.—Of a Ligament without Muscles.

Where the arm joins with the hand, there is a ligament,
the largest in the human body, which is without muscles,
and is called the strong ligament of the Carpus; it has a
square shape, and serves to bind and keep close together
the bones of the arm, and the tendous of the fingers, and
prevent their dilating, or starting out.

53.—Of Creases.

In bending the joints the flesh will always form a crease
on the opposite side to that where it is tight.

54.—How near behind the Back one Arm can be brought to the other.

(Plates 3 and 4.)

When the arms are carried behind the back, the elbows
can never be brought nearer than the length from the
elbow to the end of the longest finger; so that the fingers
will not be seen beyond the elbows; and in that situation,
the arms with the shoulders form a perfect square. The
greatest extension of the arm across the chest is, when the

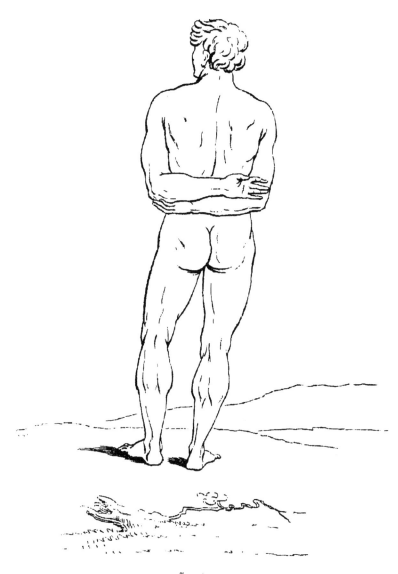

Chap. 51

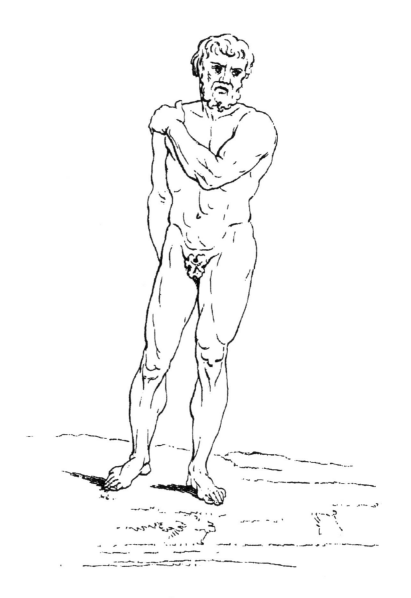

Chap. 53.

elbow comes over the pit of the stomach; the elbow and the shoulder in this position, will form an equilateral triangle.

55.—Of the Muscles.

A naked figure being strongly marked, so as to give a distinct view of all the muscles, will not express any motion; because it cannot move, if some of its muscles do not relax while the others are pulling. Those which relax cease to appear in proportion as the others pull strongly and become apparent.

56.—Of the Muscles.

The muscles of the human body are to be more or less marked according to their degree of action. Those only which act are to be shown, and the more forcibly they act, the stronger they should be pronounced. Those that do not act at all must remain soft and flat.

57.—Of the bending of the Body.

The bodies of men diminish as much on the side which bends, as they increase on the opposite side. That diminution may at last become double in proportion to the extension on the other side. But of this I shall make a separate treatise.*

58.—The same subject.

The body which bends, lengthens as much on one side as it shortens on the other; but the central line between them will never lessen or increase.

59.—The Necessity of Anatomical Knowled

The painter who has obtained a perfect knowledge of the nature of the tendons and muscles, and of those parts

* It is believed that this treatise, like many others promised by the author, was never written.

which contain the most of them, will know to a certainty, in giving a particular motion to any part of the body, which, and how many of the muscles give rise and contribute to it; which of them, by swelling, occasion their shortening, and which of the cartilages they surround.

He will not imitate those who, in all the different attitudes they adopt, or invent, make use of the same muscles, in the arms, back, or chest, or any other parts.

MOTION AND EQUIPOISE OF FIGURES.

60.—*Of the Equipoise of a Figure standing still.*

THE non-existence of motion in any animal resting on its feet, is owing to the equality of weight distributed on each side of the line of gravity.

61.—*Motion produced by the Loss of Equilibrium.*

Motion is created by the loss of due equipoise, that is, by inequality of weight; for nothing can move of itself, without losing its centre of gravity, and the farther that is removed, the quicker and stronger will be the motion.

62.—*Of the Equipoise of Bodies.*
(Plate 5.)

The balance or equipoise of parts in the human body is of two sorts, viz., simple and complex. Simple, when a man stands upon his feet without motion: in that situation, if he extends his arms at different distances from the middle, or stoop, the centre of his weight will always be in a perpendicular line upon the centre of that foot which supports the body; and if he rests equally upon both feet, then the middle of the chest will be perpendicular to the middle of the line which measures the space between the centres of his feet.

Plate 5.

Chap. 62.

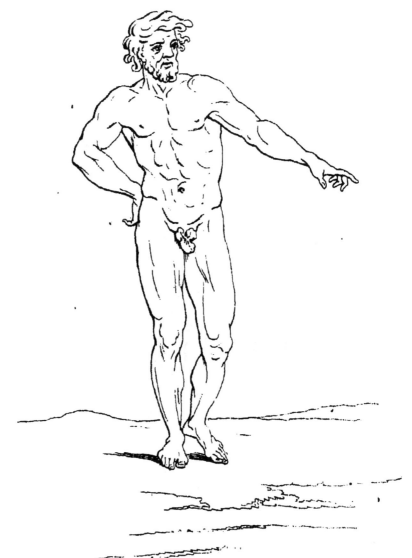

Plate 6.

Chap. 6.

The complex balance is, when a man carries a weight
not his own, which he bears by different motions; as in
the figure of Hercules stifling Anteus, by pressing him
against his breast with his arms, after he has lifted him
from the ground. He must have as much of his own
weight thrown behind the central line of his feet, as the
weight of Anteus adds before.

63.—Of Positions.

The pit of the neck, between the two clavicles, falls
perpendicularly with the foot which bears the weight of
the body. If one of the arms be thrown forwards, this pit
will quit that perpendicular, and if one of the legs goes
back, that pit is brought forwards, and so changes its
situation at every change of posture.

64.—Of balancing the Weight round the Centre of Gravity in Bodies.

A figure standing upon its feet without motion, will
form an equipoise of all its members round the centre of
its support.

If this figure without motion, and resting upon its feet,
happens to move one of its arms forwards, it must
necessarily throw as much of its weight on the opposite
side, as is equal to that of the extended arm of the
accidental weight. And the same I say of every part
which is brought out beyond its usual balance.

65.—Of Figures that have to lift up, or carry, any Weight.

A weight can never be lifted up or carried by any man,
if he do not throw more than an equal weight of his own
on the opposite side.

66.—The Equilibrium of a Man standing upon his Feet.
(Plate 6.)

The weight of a man resting upon one leg will always be

equally divided on each side of the central or perpendicular line of gravity, which supports him.

67.—*Of Walking.*
(Plate 7.)

A man walking will always have the centre of gravity over the centre of the leg which rests upon the ground.

68.—*Of the Centre of Gravity in Men and Animals.*

The legs, or centre of support, in men and animals, will approach nearer to the centre of gravity, in proportion to the slowness of their motion; and, on the contrary, when the motion is quicker, they will be farther removed from that perpendicular line.

69.—*Of the corresponding Thickness of Parts on each Side of the Body.*

The thickness or breadth of the parts in the human body will never be equal on each side, if the corresponding members do not move equally and alike.

70.—*Of the Motions of Animals.*

All bipeds in their motions lower the part immediately over the foot that is raised, more than over that resting on the ground, and the highest parts do just the contrary. This is observable in the hips and shoulders of a man when he walks : and also in birds in the head and rump.

71.—*Of Quadrupeds and their Motions.*

The highest parts of quadrupeds are susceptible of more variation when they walk, than when they are still, in a greater or less degree in proportion to their size. This proceeds from the oblique position of their legs when they touch the ground, which raise the animal when they become straight and perpendicular upon the ground.

Plate 7.   Chap. 6.

Plate 8.   Chap. 74.

72.—*Of the Quickness or Slowness of Motion.*

The motion performed by a man, or any other animal whatever, in walking, will have more or less velocity as the centre of their weight is more or less removed from the centre of that foot upon which they are supported.

73.—*Of the Motion of Animals.*

That figure will appear the swiftest in its course which leans the most forwards.

Any body, moving of itself, will do it with more or less velocity in proportion as the centre of its gravity is more or less removed from the centre of its support. This is mentioned chiefly in regard to the motion of birds, which, without any clapping of their wings, or assistance of wind, move themselves. This happens when the centre of their gravity is out of the centre of their support, viz., out of its usual residence, the middle between the two wings. Because, if the middle of the wings be more backward than the centre of the whole weight, the bird will move forwards and downwards, in a greater or less degree as the centre of its weight is more or less removed from the middle of its wings. From which it follows, that if the centre of gravity be far removed from the other centre, the descent of the bird will be very oblique; but if that centre be near the middle of the wings, the descent will have very little obliquity.

74.—*Of a Figure moving against the Wind.*

(Plate 8.)

A man moving against the wind in any direction, does not keep his centre of gravity duly disposed upon the centre of support.*

* See chap. 64.

75.—*Of the Balance of a Figure resting upon its Feet.*

The man who rests upon his feet, either bears the weight of his body upon them equally, or unequally. If equally, it will be with some accidental weight, or simply with his own ; if it be with an additional weight, the opposite extremities of his members will not be equally distant from the perpendicular of his feet. But if he simply carries his own weight, the opposite extremities will be equally distant from the perpendicular of his feet : and on this subject of gravity I shall write a separate book.*

76.—*A Precept.*

The navel is always in the central or middle line of the body, which passes through the pit of the stomach to that of the neck, and must have as much weight, either accidental or natural, on one side of the human figure as on the other. This is demonstrated by extending the arm, the wrist of which performs the office of a weight at the end of a steelyard ; and will require some weight to be thrown on the other side of the navel, to counterbalance that of the wrist. It is on that account that the heel is often raised.

77.—*Of a Man standing, but resting more upon one Foot than the other.*

After a man, by standing long, has tired the leg upon which he rests, he sends part of his weight upon the other leg. But this kind of posture is to be employed only for old age, infancy, or extreme lassitude, because it expresses weariness, or very little power in the limbs. For that reason, a young man, strong and healthy, will always rest upon one of his legs, and if he removes a little of his weight upon the other, it is only a necessary preparative to motion, without which it is impossible to move ; as we have proved before, that motion proceeds from inequality.†

* See in this work from chap. 60 to 81.
† See chapters 61, 64.

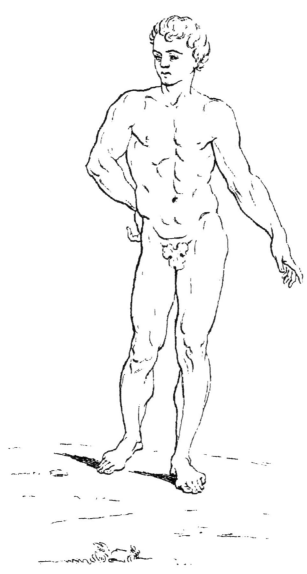

Plate 9.

Chap. 78.

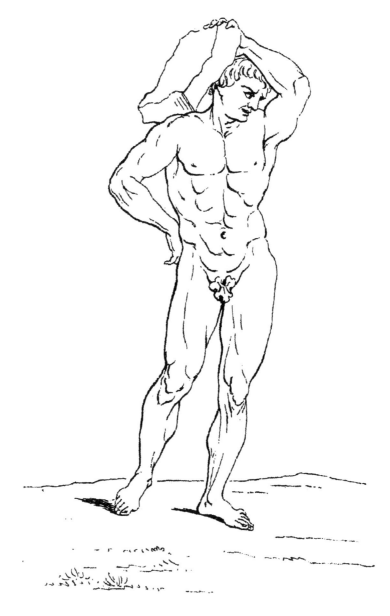

Plate 10.

Chap. 80.

78.—*Of the Balance of Figures.*
(Plate 9.)

If the figure rests upon one foot, the shoulder on that side will always be lower than the other; and the pit of the neck will fall perpendicularly over the middle of that leg which supports the body. The same will happen in whatever other view we see that figure, when it has not the arm much extended, nor any weight on its back, in its hand, or on its shoulder, and when it does not, either behind or before, throw out that leg which does not support the body.

79.—*In what Manner extending one Arm alters the Balance.*

The extending of the arm, which was bent, removes the weight of the figure upon the foot which bears the weight of the whole body : as is observable in rope-dancers, who dance upon the rope with their arms open, without any pole.

80.—*Of a Man bearing a Weight on his Shoulders.*
(Plate 10.)

The shoulder which bears the weight is always higher than the other. This is seen in the figure opposite, in which the centre line passes through the whole, with an equal weight on each side, to the leg on which it rests. If the weight were not equally divided on each side of this central line of gravity, the whole would fall to the ground. But Nature has provided, that as much of the natural weight of the man should be thrown on one side, as of accidental weight on the other, to form a counterpoise. This is effected by the man's bending, and leaning on the side not loaded, so as to form an equilibrium to the accidental weight he carries; and this cannot be done, unless the loaded shoulder be raised, and the other lowered. This is the resource with which Nature has furnished a man on such occasions.

81.—*Of Equilibrium.*

Any figure bearing an additional weight out of the central line, must throw as much natural or accidental weight on the opposite side as is sufficient to form a counterpoise round that line, which passes from the pit of the neck, through the whole mass of weight, to that part of the foot which rests upon the ground. We observe, that when a man lifts a weight with one arm, he naturally throws out the opposite arm; and if that be not enough to form an equipoise, he will add as much of his own weight, by bending his body, as will enable him to resist such accidental load. We see also, that a man ready to fall sideways and backwards at the same time, always throws out the arm on the opposite side.

82.—*Of Motion.*

Whether a man moves with velocity or slowness, the parts above the leg which sustains the weight will always be lower than the others on the opposite side.

83.—*The Level of the Shoulders.*

The shoulders or sides of a man, or any other animal, will preserve less of their level, in proportion to the slowness of their motion; and *vice versâ*, those parts will lose less of their level when the motion is quicker. This is proved by the ninth proposition, treating of local motions, where it is said, any weight will press in the direction of the line of its motion; therefore the whole moving towards any one point, the parts belonging to it will follow the shortest line of the motion of its whole, without giving any of its weight to the collateral parts of the whole.

84.—*Objection to the above answered.*

(Plates 11 and 12.)

It has been objected, in regard to the first part of the above proposition, that it does not follow that a man

B

Chap. 84 .

C

Plate 12

Chap. 84.

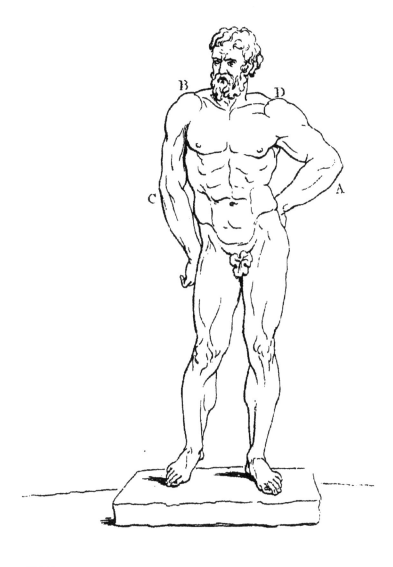

Plate 23.

Chap. 85.

standing still, or moving slowly, has his members always in perfect balance upon the centre of gravity; because we do not find that Nature always follows that rule, but, on the contrary, the figure will sometimes bend sideways, standing upon one foot; sometimes it will rest part of its weight upon that leg which is bent at the knee, as is seen in the figures B. C. But I shall reply thus, that what is not performed by the shoulders in the figure C, is done by the hip, as is demonstrated in another place.

85.—*Of the Position of Figures.*
(Plate 13.)

In the same proportion as that part of the naked figure marked D A lessens in height from the shoulder to the hip, on account of its position the opposite side increases. And this is the reason: the figure resting upon one (suppose the left) foot, that foot becomes the centre of all the weight above; and the pit of the neck, formed by the junction of the two clavicles, quits also its natural situation at the upper extremity of the perpendicular line (which passes through the middle surface of the body), to bend over the same foot; and as this line bends with it, it forces the transverse lines, which are always at right angles, to lower their extremities on that side where the foot rests, as appears in A B C. The navel and middle parts always preserve their natural height.

86.—*Of the Joints.*

In the bending of the joints it is particularly useful to observe the difference and variety of shape they assume; how the muscles swell on one side, while they flatten on the other; and this is more apparent in the neck, because the motion of it is of three sorts, two of which are simple motions, and the other complex, participating also of the other two.

The simple motions are, first, when the neck bends towards the shoulder, either to the right or left, and when it raises or lowers the head. The second is, when it twists to the right or left, without rising or bending, but straight, with the head turned towards one of the shoulders. The third motion, which is called complex, is, when to the bending of it is added the twisting, as when the ear leans towards one of the shoulders, the head turning the same way, and the face turned upwards.

87.—*Of the Shoulders.*

Of those which the shoulders can perform, simple motions are the principal, such as moving the arm upwards and downwards, backwards and forwards. Though one might almost call those motions infinite, for if the arm can trace a circle upon a wall, it will have performed all the motions belonging to the shoulders. Every continued quantity being divisible *ad infinitum*, and this circle being a continued quantity, produced by the motion of the arm going through every part of the circumference, it follows, that the motions of the shoulders may also be said to be infinite.

88.—*Of the Motions of a Man.*

When you mean to represent a man removing a weight, consider that the motions are various, viz., either a simple motion, by bending himself to raise the weight from the ground upwards, or when he drags the weight after him, or pushes it before him, or pulls it down with a rope passing through a pulley. It is to be observed, that the weight of the man's body pulls the more in proportion as the centre of his gravity is removed from the centre of his support. To this must be added the strength of the effort that the legs and back make when they are bent, to return to their natural straight situation.

A man never ascends or descends, nor walks at all in any direction, without raising the heel of the back foot.

89.—*Of the Dispositions of Members preparing to act with great Force.*
(Plate 14.)

When a man prepares himself to strike a violent blow, he bends and twists his body as far as he can to the side

Plate 14.

Chap. 89.

Plate 15.

Chap. 90.

E

B

A

Plate 16.

Chap. 91.

contrary to that which he means to strike, and collecting all his strength, he by a complex motion, returns and falls upon the point he has in view.*

90.—*Of throwing Anything with Violence.*
(Plate 15.)

A man throwing a dart, a stone, or anything else with violence, may be represented, chiefly, two different ways; that is, he may be preparing to do it, or the act may be already performed. If you mean to place him in the act of preparation, the inside of the foot upon which he rests will be under the perpendicular line of the pit of the neck; and if it be the right foot, the left shoulder will be perpendicular over the toes of the same foot.

91.—*On the Motion of driving Anything into, or drawing it out of, the Ground.*

He who wishes to pitch a pole into the ground, or draw one out of it, will raise the leg and bend the knee opposite to the arm which acts, in order to balance himself upon the foot that rests, without which he could neither drive in, nor pull out anything.

92.—*Of forcible Motions.*
(Plate 16.)

Of the two arms, that will be most powerful in its effort, which, having been farthest removed from its natural situation, is assisted more strongly by the other parts to bring it to the place where it means to go. As the man A, who moves the arm with a club E, and brings it to the opposite side B, assisted by the motion of the whole body.

93.—*The Action of Jumping.*

Nature will of itself, and without any reasoning in the mind of a man going to jump, prompt him to raise his

* See chapters 104, 154.

arms and shoulders by a sudden motion, together with a great part of his body, and to lift them up high, till the power of the effort subsides. This impetuous motion is accompanied by an instantaneous extension of the body which had bent itself, like a spring or bow, along the back, the joints of the thighs, knees, and feet, and is let off obliquely, that is upwards and forwards; so that the disposition of the body tending forwards and upwards, makes it describe a great arch when it springs up, which increases the leap.

94.—Of the three Motions in jumping upwards.

When a man jumps upwards, the motion of the head is three times quicker than that of the heel, before the extremity of the foot quits the ground, and twice as quick as that of the hips; because three angles are opened and extended at the same time: the superior one is that formed by the body at its joint with the thigh before, the second is at the joint of the thighs and legs behind, and the third is at the instep before.*

95.—Of the easy Motions of Members.

In regard to the freedom and ease of motions, it is very necessary to observe, that when you mean to represent a figure which has to turn itself a little round, the feet and all the other members are not to move in the same direction

* The author here means to compare the different quickness of the motion of the head and the heel, when employed in the same action of jumping; and he states the proportion of the former to be three times that of the latter. The reason he gives for this is in substance, that as the head has but one motion to make, while in fact the lower part of the figure has three successive operations to perform at the places he mentions, three times the velocity, or, in other words, three times the degree of effort, is necessary in the head, the prime mover, to give the power of influencing the other parts; and the rule deducible from this axiom is, that where two different parts of the body concur in the same action, and one of them has to perform one motion only, while the other is to have several, the proportion of velocity or effort in the former must be regulated by the number of operations necessary in the latter.

Plate 17.

Chap. 96.

as the head. But you will divide that motion among four joints, viz. the feet, the knees, the hips, and the neck. If it rests upon the right leg, the left knee should be a little bent inward, with its foot somewhat raised outward. The left shoulder should be lower than the other, and the nape of the neck turned on the same side as the outward ankle of the left foot, and the left shoulder perpendicular over the great toe of the right foot. And take it as a general maxim, that figures do not turn their heads straight with the chest, Nature having for our convenience formed the neck so as to turn with ease on every side when the eyes want to look round; and to this the other joints are in some measure subservient. If the figure be sitting, and the arms have some employment across the body, the breast will turn over the joint of the hip.

96.—*The greatest Twist which a Man can make, in turning to look at himself behind.*

(Plate 17.)

The greatest twist that the body can perform is when the back of the heels and the front of the face are seen at the same time. It is not done without difficulty, and is effected by bending the leg and lowering the shoulder on that side towards which the head turns. The cause of this motion, and also which of the muscles move first and which last, I shall explain in my treatise on anatomy.*

97.—*Of turning the Leg without the Thigh.*

It is impossible to turn the leg inwards or outwards without turning the thigh by the same motion, because the setting in of the bones at the knee is such, that they have no motion but backwards and forwards, and no more than is necessary for walking or kneeling; never sideways, because the form of the bones at the joint of the knee does not allow it. If this joint had been made pliable on all

* It is explained in this work, or at least there is something respecting it in the preceding chapter, and in chap. 151.

sides, as that of the shoulder, or that of the thigh bone
with the hip, a man would have had his legs bent on each
side as often as backwards and forwards, and seldom or
never straight with the thigh. Besides, this joint can
bend only one way, so that in walking it can never go
beyond the straight line of the leg; it bends only forwards,
for if it could bend backwards, a man could never get up
again upon his feet, if once he were kneeling; as when he
means to get up from the kneeling posture (on both knees),
he gives the whole weight of his body to one of the knees
to support, unloading the other, which at that time feels
no other weight than its own, and therefore is lifted up
with ease, and rests his foot flat upon the ground;
then returning the whole weight upon that foot, and
leaning his hand upon his knee, he at once extends the
other arm, raises his head, and straightening the thigh
with the body, he springs up, and rests upon the same foot,
while he brings up the other.

98.—*Postures of Figures.*

Figures that are set in a fixed attitude, are nevertheless
to have some contrast of parts. If one arm come before,
the other remains still or goes behind. If the figure rests
upon one leg, the shoulder on that side will be lower than
the other. This is observed by artists of judgment, who
always take care to balance the figure well upon its feet,
for fear it should appear to fall. Because by resting upon
one foot, the other leg being a little bent, does not support
the body any more than if it were dead; therefore it is
necessary that the parts above that leg should transfer the
centre of their weight upon the leg which supports the
body.

99.—*Of the Gracefulness of the Members.*

The members are to be suited to the body in graceful
motions, expressive of the meaning which the figure is
intended to convey. If it had to give the idea of genteel
and agreeable carriage, the members must be slender and

well turned, but not lean; the muscles very slightly marked, indicating in a soft manner such as must necessarily appear; the arms, particularly, pliant, and no member in a straight line with any other adjoining member. If it happen, on account of the motion of the figure, that the right hip be higher than the left, make the joint of the shoulder fall perpendicularly on the highest part of that hip; and let that right shoulder be lower than the left. The pit of the neck will always be perpendicular over the middle of the instep of the foot that supports the body. The leg that does not bear will have its knee a little lower than the other, and near the other leg.

In regard to the positions of the head and arms, they are infinite, and for that reason I shall not enter into any detailed rule concerning them; suffice it to say, that they are to be easy and free, graceful, and varied in their bendings, so that they may not appear stiff like pieces of ·wood.

100.—*That it is impossible for any Memory to retain the Aspects and Changes of the Members.*

It is impossible that any memory can be able to retain all the aspects or motions of any member of any animal

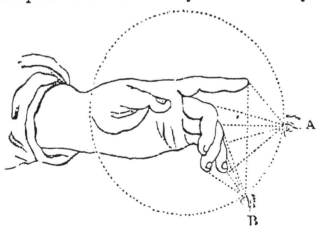

whatever. This case we shall exemplify by the appearance of the hand. And because any continued quantity is

divisible *ad infinitum*, the motion of the eye which looks
at the hand, and moves from A to B, moves by a space
A B, which is also a continued quantity and consequently
divisible *ad infinitum*, and in every part of the motion
varies to its view the aspect and figure of the hand; and
so it will do if it move round the whole circle. The same
will the hand do which is raised in its motion; that is, it
will pass over a space, which is a continued quantity.*

101.—*The Motions of Figures.*

Never put the head straight upon the shoulders, but a
little turned sideways to the right or left, even though the
figures should be looking up or down or straight, because
it is necessary to give them some motion of life and spirit.
Nor ever compose a figure in such a manner, either in a
front or back view, as that every part falls straight upon
another from the top to the bottom. But if you wish to
introduce such a figure, use it for old age. Never repeat
the same motions of arms or of legs, not only not in the
same figure, but in those which are standing by or near, if
the necessity of the case, or the expression of the subject
you represent, do not oblige you to it.†

102.—*Of common Motions.*

The variety of motions in man are equal to the variety
of accidents or thoughts affecting the mind, and each of
these thoughts, or accidents, will operate more or less,
according to the temper and age of the subject; for the
same cause will in the actions of youth, or of old age,
produce very different effects.

---

* The eyeball moving up and down to look at the hand, describes
a part of a circle, from every point of which it sees it in an infinite
variety of aspects. The hand also is movable *ad infinitum* (for it
can go round the whole circle—see chap. 87), and consequently show
itself in an infinite variety of aspects, which it is impossible for any
memory to retain.
† See chapters 20, 155.

103.—*Of simple Motion.*

Simple motion is that which a man performs in merely bending backwards or forwards.

104.—*Complex Motion.*

Complex motion is that which, to produce some particular action, requires the body to bend downwards and sideways at the same time. The painter must be careful in his compositions to apply these complex motions according to the nature of the subject, and not to weaken or destroy the effect of it by introducing figures with simple motions, without any connection with the subject.

105.—*Motions appropriated to the Subject.*

The motions of your figures are to be expressive of the quantity of strength requisite to the force of the action. Let not the same effort be used to take up a stick as would easily raise a piece of timber. Therefore show great variety in the expression of strength, according to the quality of the load to be managed.

106.—*Appropriate Motions.*

There are some emotions of the mind which are not expressed by any particular motion of the body, while in others, the expression cannot be shown without it. In the first, the arms fall down, the hands and all the other parts which in general are the most active, remain at rest. But such emotions of the soul as produce bodily action, must put the members into such motions as are appropriated to the intention of the mind. This, however, is an ample subject, and we have a great deal to say upon it. There is a third kind of motion, which participates of the two already described; and a fourth, which depends neither on the one nor the other. This last belongs to insensibility or fury, and should be ranked with madness or stupidity and so adapted only to grotesque or Moresco work.

107.—*Of the Postures of Women and young People.*

It is not becoming in women and young people to have their legs too much asunder, because it denotes boldness; while the legs close together show modesty.

108.—*Of the Postures of Children.*

Children and old people are not to express quick motions, in what concerns their legs.

109.—*Of the Motion of the Members.*

Let every member be employed in performing its proper functions. For instance, in a dead body, or one asleep, no member should appear alive or awake. A foot bearing the weight of the whole body, should not be playing its toes up and down, but flat upon the ground; except when it rests entirely upon the heel.

110.—*Of mental Motions.*

A mere thought, or operation of the mind, excites only simple and easy motions of the body; not this way, and that way, because its object is in the mind, which does not affect the senses when it is collected within itself.

111.—*Effect of the Mind upon the Motions of the Body, occasioned by some outward Object.*

When the motion is produced by the presence of some object, either the cause is immediate or not. If it be immediate, the figure will first turn towards it the organs most necessary, the eyes; leaving its feet in the same place; and will only move the thighs, hips, and knees a little towards the same side to which the eyes are directed.

LINEAR PERSPECTIVE.

112.—*Of those who apply themselves to the Practice, without having learnt the Theory of the Art.*

THOSE who become enamoured of the practice of the art, without having previously applied to the diligent study of the scientific part of it, may be compared to mariners, who put to sea in a ship without rudder or compass, and therefore cannot be certain of arriving at the wished-for port.

Practice must always be founded on good theory; to this, Perspective is the guide and entrance, without which nothing can be well done.

113.—*Precepts in Painting.*

PERSPECTIVE is to Painting what the bridle is to a horse, and the rudder to a ship.

The size of a figure should denote the distance at which it is situated.

If a figure be seen of the natural size, remember that it denotes its being near to the eye.

114.—*Of the Boundaries of Objects, called Outlines or Contours.*

The outlines or contours of bodies are so little perceivable, that at any small distance between that and the object, the eye will not be able to recognize the features of a friend or relation, if it were not for their clothes and general appearance. So that by the knowledge of the whole it comes to know the parts.

115.—*Of linear Perspectiv*

LINEAR Perspective consists in giving, by established rules, the true dimensions of objects, according to their respective distances; so that the second object be less than

the first, the third than the second, and by degrees at last
they become invisible. I find by experience, that, if the
second object be at the same distance from the first, as the
first is from the eye, though they be of the same size,
the second will appear half the size of the first; and, if
the third be at the same distance behind the second, it
will diminish two-thirds; and so on, by degrees, they will
at equal distances, diminish in proportion; provided that
the interval be not more than twenty cubits;* at which
distance it will lose two-fourths of its size; at forty it will
diminish three-fourths; and at sixty it will lose five-sixths,
and so on progressively. But you must be distant from
your picture twice the size of it; for, if you be only once
the size, it will make a great difference in the measure
from the first to the second.

116.—*What Parts of Objects disappear first by Distance.*

Those parts which are of less magnitude will first vanish
from the sight.† This happens, because the shape of
small objects, at an equal distance, comes to the eye under
a more acute angle than the large ones, and the perception
is less, in proportion as they are less in magnitude. It
follows then, that if the large objects, by being removed
to a great distance, and consequently coming to the eye
by a small angle, are almost lost to the sight, the small
objects will entirely disappear.

117.—*Of remote Objects.*

The outlines of objects will be less seen, in proportion
as they are more distant from the eye.

118.—*Of the Point of Sight.*

The point of sight must be on a level with the eyes of
a common-sized man, and placed upon the horizon, which

---

* About thirteen yards of our measure; the Florentine braccia,
or cubit, by which the author measures, being 1 foot 10 inches
7-8ths English measure.　　　　† See chapters 121 and 305.

is the line formed by a flat country terminating with the sky. An exception must be made as to mountains, which are above that line.

119.—*A Picture is to be viewed from one Point only.*

This will be proved by one single example. If you mean to represent a round ball very high up, on a flat and perpendicular wall, it will be necessary to make it oblong, like the shape of an egg, and to place yourself (that is, the eye, or point of view) so far back, as that its outline or circumference may appear round.

120.—*Of the Dimensions of the first Figure in an historical Painting.*

The first figure in your picture will be less than Nature, in proportion as it recedes from the front of the picture, or the bottom line; and by the same rule the others behind it will go on lessening in an equal degree.*

121.—*Of Objects that are lost to the Sight in Proportion to their Distance.*

The first things that disappear, by being removed to some distance, are the outlines or boundaries of objects. The second, as they remove farther, are the shadows which divide contiguous bodies. The third are the thickness of legs and feet; and so in succession the small parts are lost to the sight, till nothing remains but a confused mass, without any distinct parts.

---

* It is supposed that the figures are to appear of the natural size, and not bigger. In that case, the measure of the first, to be of the exact dimension, should have its feet resting upon the bottom line; but as you remove it from that, it should diminish.

No allusion is here intended to the distance at which a picture is to be placed from the eye.

122.—*Errors not so easily seen in small Objects as in large ones.*

Supposing this small object to represent a man, or any other animal, although the parts, by being so much diminished or reduced, cannot be executed with the same exactness of proportion, nor finished with the same accuracy, as if on a larger scale, yet on that very account the faults will be less conspicuous. For example, if you look at a man at the distance of two hundred yards, and with all due attention mean to form a judgment, whether he be handsome or ugly, deformed or well made, you will find that, with all your endeavours, you can hardly venture to decide. The reason is, that the man diminishes so much by the distance, that it is impossible to distinguish the parts minutely. If you wish to know by demonstration the diminution of the above figure, hold your finger up before your eye at about nine inches distance, so that the top of your finger corresponds with the top of the head of the distant figure : you will perceive that your finger covers, not only its head, but part of its body ; which is an evident proof of the apparent diminution of that object. Hence it often happens that we are doubtful, and can scarcely, at some distance, distinguish the form of even a friend.

123.—*Historical Subjects one above another on the same Wall to be avoided.*

This custom, which has been generally adopted by painters on the front and sides of chapels, is much to be condemned. They begin with an historical picture, its landscape and buildings, in one compartment. After which, they raise another compartment, and execute another history with other buildings upon another level; and from thence they proceed to a third and fourth, varying the point of sight, as if the beholder was going up steps, while, in fact, he must look at them all from below, which is very ill-judged in those matters.

We know that the point of sight is the eye of the spectator; and if you ask, How is a series of subjects, such as the life of a saint, to be represented, in different compartments on the same wall? I answer, that you are to place the principal event in the largest compartment, and make the point of sight as high as the eye of the spectator. Begin that subject with large figures; and as you go up, lessen the objects, as well the figures as buildings, varying the plans according to the effect of perspective; but never varying the point of sight: and so complete the series of subjects, till you come to a certain height, where terrestrial objects can be seen no more, except the tops of trees, or clouds and birds; or if you introduce figures, they must be aerial, such as angels, or saints in glory, or the like, if they suit the purpose of your history. If not, do not undertake this kind of painting, for your work will be faulty, and justly reprehensible.*

124.—Why Objects in Painting can never detach, as natural Objects do.

Painters often despair of being able to imitate Nature, from observing, that their pictures have not the same relief, nor the same life, as natural objects have in a looking-glass, though they both appear upon a plain surface. They say, they have colours which surpass in brightness the quality of the lights, and in darkness the quality of the shades of the objects seen in the looking-glass; but attribute this circumstance to their own ignorance, and not to the true cause, because they do not know it. It is impossible that

---

* The author does not mean here to say, that one historical picture cannot be hung over another. It certainly may, because in viewing each, the spectator is at liberty (especially if they are subjects independent of each other) to shift his place so as to stand at the true point of sight for viewing every one of them ; but in covering a wall with a succession of subjects from the same history, the author considers the whole as in fact but one picture, divided into compartments, and to be seen at one view, and which cannot therefore admit more than one point of sight. In the former case the pictures are, in fact, so many distinct subjects unconnected with each other.

objects in painting should appear with the same relief as those in the looking-glass, unless we look at them with only one eye.

The reason is this.   The two eyes A B looking at objects one behind another, as M and N, see them both: because M cannot entirely occupy the space of N, by reason that the base of the visual rays is so broad that the second object is seen behind the first.   But if one eye be shut, and you look with the other S, the body F will entirely cover the body R, because the visual rays beginning at one point, form a triangle, of which the body F is the base, and being prolonged, they form two diverging tangents at the two extremities of F, which cannot touch the body R behind it, therefore can never see it.*

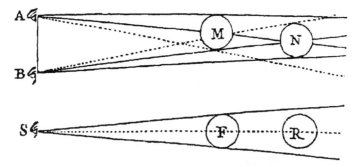

* See chap. 348.

This chapter is obscure, and may probably be made clear by merely stating it in other words.   Leonardo objects to the use of both eyes, because, in viewing in that manner the objects here mentioned, two balls, one behind the other, the second is seen, which would not be the case, if the angle of the visual rays were not too big for the first object.   Whoever is at all acquainted with optics, need not be told, that the visual rays commence in a single point in the centre, or nearly the centre of each eye, and continue diverging. But, in using both eyes, the visual rays proceed not from one and the same centre, but from a different centre in each eye, and intersecting each other, as they do a little before passing the first object, they become together broader than the extent of the first object, and consequently give a view of part of the second.   On the contrary, in using but one eye, the visual rays proceed but from one centre; and as, therefore, there cannot be any intersection, the visual rays, when they reach the first object are not broader than the first object, and the second is completely hidden.   Properly speaking, therefore,

125.—*How to give the proper Dimension to Objects in Painting.*

In order to give the appearance of the natural size, if the piece be small (as miniatures), the figures on the foreground are to be finished with as much precision as those of any large painting, because being small they are to be brought up close to the eye. But large paintings are seen at some distance; whence it happens, that though the figures in each are so different in size, in appearance they will be the same. This proceeds from the eye receiving those objects under the same angle; and it is proved thus: Let the large painting be B C, the eye A, and D E a pane of glass, through which are seen the figures situated at

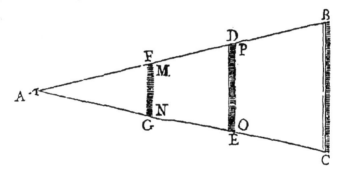

in using both eyes we introduce more than one point of sight, which renders the perspective false in the painting; but in using one eye only, there can be, as there ought, but one point of sight. There is, however, this difference between viewing real objects and those represented in painting, that in looking at the former, whether we use one or both eyes, the objects, by being actually detached from the back ground, admit the visual rays to strike on them, so as to form a correct perspective, from whatever point they are viewed, and the eye accordingly forms a perspective of its own; but in viewing the latter, there is no possibility of varying the perspective; and, unless the picture is seen precisely under the same angle as it was painted under, the perspective in all other views must be false. This is observable in the perspective views painted for scenes at the playhouse. If the beholder is seated in the central line of the house, whether in the boxes or pit, the perspective is correct; but, in proportion as he is placed at a greater or less distance to the right or left of that line, the perspective appears to him more or less faulty. And hence arises the necessity of using but one eye in viewing a painting, in order thereby to reduce it to one point of sight.

B C. I say that the eye being fixed, the figures in the copy of the painting B C are to be smaller, in proportion as the glass D E is nearer the eye A, and are to be as precise and finished. But if you will execute the picture B C upon the glass D E, this ought to be less finished than the picture B C, and more so than the figure M N transferred upon the glass F G; because, supposing the figure O P to be as much finished as the natural one in B C, the perspective of O P would be false, since, though in regard to the diminution of the figure it would be right, B C being diminished in O P, the finishing would not agree with the distance, because in giving it the perfection of the natural B C, B C would appear as near as O P; but, if you search for the diminution of O P, O P will be found at the distance B C, and the diminution of the finishing as at F G.

126.—*How to draw accurately any particular Spot.*

Take a glass as large as your paper, fasten it well between your eye and the object you mean to draw, and fixing your head in a frame (in such a manner as not to be able to move it) at the distance of two feet from the glass; shut one eye, and draw with a pencil accurately upon the glass all that you see through it. After that, trace upon paper what you have drawn on the glass, which tracing you may paint at pleasure, observing the aerial perspective.

127.—*Disproportion to be avoided, even in the accessory Parts.*

A great fault is committed by many painters, which is highly to be blamed, that is, to represent the habitations of men, and other parts of their compositions, so low, that the doors do not reach as high as the knees of their inhabitants, though, according to their situation, they are nearer to the eye of the spectator, than the men who seem willing to enter them. I have seen some pictures with porticos, supported by columns loaded with figures; one grasping a column against which it leans, as if it were a walking stick, and other similar errors, which are to be avoided with the greatest care.

INVENTION, OR COMPOSITION.

128.—*Precept for avoiding a bad Choice in the Style or Proportion of Figures.*

THE painter ought to form his style upon the most proportionate model in Nature; and after having measured that, he ought to measure himself also, and be perfectly acquainted with his own defects or deficiencies; and having acquired this knowledge, his constant care should be to avoid conveying into his work those defects which he has found in his own person; for these defects, becoming habitual to his observation, mislead his judgment, and he perceives them no longer. We ought, therefore, to struggle against such a prejudice, which grows up with us; for the mind, being fond of its own habitation, is apt to represent it to our imagination as beautiful. From the same motive it may be, that there is not a woman, however plain in her person, who may not find her admirer, if she be not a monster. Against this bent of the mind you ought very cautiously to be on your guard.

129.—*Variety in Figures.*

A painter ought to aim at universal excellence; for he will be greatly wanting in dignity, if he do one thing well and another badly, as many do, who study only the naked figure, measured and proportioned by a pair of compasses in their hands, and do not seek for variety. A man may be well proportioned, and yet be tall or short, large or lean, or of a middle size; and whoever does not make great use of these varieties, which are all existing in Nature in its most perfect state, will produce figures as if cast in one and the same mould, which is highly reprehensible.

130.—*How a Painter ought to proceed in his Studies.*

The painter ought always to form in his mind a kind of system of reasoning or discussion within himself on any remarkable object before him. He should stop, take notes, and form some rule upon it; considering the place, the circumstances, the lights and shadows.

131.—*Of sketching Histories and Figures.*

Sketches of historical subjects must be slight, attending only to the situation of the figures, without regard to the finishing of particular members, which may be done afterwards at leisure, when the mind is so disposed.

132.—*How to study Composition.*

The young student should begin by sketching slightly some single figure, and turn that on all sides, knowing already how to contract, and how to extend the members; after which, he may put two together in various attitudes, we will suppose in the act of fighting boldly. This composition also he must try on all sides, and in a variety of ways, tending to the same expression. Then he may imagine one of them very courageous, while the other is a coward. Let these attitudes, and many other accidental affections of the mind, be with great care studied, examined, and dwelt upon.

133.—*Of the Attitudes of Men.*

The attitudes and all the members are to be disposed in such a manner, that by them the intentions of the mind may be easily discovered.

134.—*Variety of Positions.*

The positions of the human figure are to be adapted to the age and rank; and to be varied according to the difference of the sexes, men or women.

135.—*Of Studies from Nature for History.*

It is necessary to consider well the situation for which the history is to be painted, particularly the height; and let the painter place accordingly the model from which he means to make his studies for that historical picture; and set himself as much below the object, as the picture is to be above the eye of the spectator, otherwise the work will be faulty.

136.—*Of the Variety of Figures in History Painting.*

History painting must exhibit variety in its fullest extent. In temper, size, complexion, actions, plumpness, leanness, thick, thin, large, small, rough, smooth, old age and youth, strong and muscular, weak, with little appearance of muscles, cheerfulness, and melancholy. Some should be with curled hair, and some with straight; some short, some long, some quick in their motions, and some slow, with a variety of dresses and colours, according as the subject may require.

137.—*Of Variety in History.*

A painter should delight in introducing great variety into his compositions, avoiding repetition, that by this fertility of invention he may attract and charm the eye of the beholder. If it be requisite, according to the subject meant to be represented, that there should be a mixture of men differing in their faces, ages, and dress, grouped with women, children, dogs, and horses, buildings, hills, and flat country; observe dignity and decorum in the principal figure; such as a king, magistrate, or philosopher, separating them from the low classes of the people. Mix not afflicted

or weeping figures with joyful and laughing ones; for
Nature dictates that the cheerful be attended by others of
the same disposition of mind. Laughter is productive of
laughter, and *vice versâ*.

138.—*Of the Age of Figures.*

Do not bring together a number of boys with as many
old men, nor young men with infants, nor women with
men; if the subject you mean to represent does not oblige
you to it.

139.—*Of Variety of Faces.*

The Italian painters have been accused of a common
fault, that is, of introducing into their compositions the
faces, and even the whole figures, of Roman emperors, which
they take from the antique. To avoid such an error, let
no repetition take place, either in parts, or the whole of a
figure; nor let there be even the same face in another
composition; and the more the figures are contrasted, viz.
the deformed opposed to the beautiful, the old to the young,
the strong to the feeble, the more the picture will please
and be admired. These different characters, contrasted
with each other, will increase the beauty of the whole.

It frequently happens that a painter, while he is composing, will use any little sketch or scrap of drawing he
has by him, and endeavour to make it serve his purpose;
but this is extremely injudicious, because he may very
often find that the members he has drawn have not the
motion suited to what he means to express; and after he
has adopted, accurately drawn, and even well finished them,
he will be loth to rub out and change them for others.

140.—*A Fault in Painters.*

It is a very great fault in a painter to repeat the same
motions in figures, and the same folds in draperies in the
same composition, as also to make all the faces alike.

141. —*How you may learn to compose Groups for History Painting.*

When you are well instructed in perspective, and know perfectly how to draw the anatomy and forms of different bodies or objects, it should be your delight to observe and consider in your walks the different actions of men, when they are talking, or quarrelling; when they laugh, and when they fight. Attend to their positions, and to those of the spectators; whether they are attempting to separate those who fight, or merely lookers-on. Be quick in sketching these with slight strokes in your pocket-book, which should always be about you, and made of stained paper, as you ought not to rub out. When it is full, take another, for these are not things to be rubbed out, but kept with the greatest care; because forms and motions of bodies are so infinitely various, that the memory is not able to retain them; therefore preserve these sketches as your assistants and masters.

142.—*How to study the Motions of the human Body.*

The first requisite towards a perfect acquaintance with the various motions of the human body, is the knowledge of all the parts, particularly the joints, in all the attitudes in which it may be placed. Then make slight sketches in your pocket-book as opportunities occur, of the actions of men, as they happen to meet your eye, without being perceived by them; because, if they were to observe you, they would be disturbed from that freedom of action, which is prompted by inward feeling; as when two men are quarrelling and angry, each of them seeming to be in the right, and with great vehemence move their eyebrows, arms, and all the other members, using motions appropriated to their words and feelings. This they could not do, if you wanted them to imitate anger, or any other accidental emotion, such as laughter, weeping, pain, admiration, fear and the like. For that reason take care never to be without a little book, for the purpose of sketching those various motions, and also groups of people standing by.

E

This will teach you how to compose history. Two things demand the principal attention of a good painter. One is the exact outline and shape of the figure; the other, the true expression of what passes in the mind of that figure, which he must feel, and that is very important.

143.—Of Dresses, and of Draperies and Folds.

The draperies with which you dress figures ought to have their folds so accommodated as to surround the parts they are intended to cover; that in the mass of light there be not any dark fold, and in the mass of shadows none receiving too great a light. They must go gently over, describing the parts; but not with lines across, cutting the members with hard notches, deeper than the part can possibly be; at the same time, it must fit the body, and not appear like an empty bundle of cloth: a fault of many painters, who, enamoured of the quantity and variety of folds, have encumbered their figures, forgetting the intention of clothes, which is to dress and surround the parts gracefully wherever they touch; and not to be filled with wind, like bladders puffed up where the parts project. I do not deny that we ought not to neglect introducing some handsome folds among these draperies, but it must be done with great judgment, and suited to the parts, where, by the actions of the limbs and position of the whole body, they gather together. Above all, be careful to vary the quality and quantity of your folds in compositions of many figures; so that, if some have large folds, produced by thick woollen cloth, others, being dressed in thinner stuff, may have them narrower; some sharp and straight, others soft and undulating.

144.—Of the Nature of Folds in Draperies.

Many painters prefer making the folds of their draperies with acute angles, deep and precise; others with angles hardly perceptible; and some with none at all: but instead of them, certain curved lines.

Chap. 145.

145.— *How the Folds of Draperies ought to be represented.*
(Plate 18.)

That part of the drapery which is the farthest from the place where it is gathered will appear more approaching its natural state Everything naturally inclines to preserve its primitive form.   Therefore a stuff or cloth, which is of equal thickness on both sides, will always incline to remain flat.   For that reason, when it is constrained by some fold to relinquish its flat situation, it is observed that, at the part of its greatest restraint, it is continually making efforts to return to its natural shape ; and the parts most distant from it re-assume more of their primitive state by ample and distended folds.   For example, let A B C be the drapery mentioned above ; A B the place where it is folded or restrained.   I have said that the part, which is farthest from the place of its restraint, would return more toward its primitive shape. Therefore C being the farthest, will be broader and more extended than any other part.

146.—*How the Folds in Draperies ought to be made.*

Draperies are not to be encumbered with many folds : on the contrary, there ought to be some only where they are held up with the hands or arms of the figures, and the rest left to fall with natural simplicity.   They ought to be studied from nature ; that is to say, if a woollen cloth be intended, the folds ought to be drawn after such cloth ; if it be of silk, or thin stuff, or else very thick for labourers, let it be distinguished by the nature of the folds. But never copy them, as some do, after models dressed in paper, or thin leather, for it greatly misleads.

147.—*Fore-shortening of Folds.*
(Plate 19.)

Where the figure is fore-shortened, there ought to appear a greater number of folds than on the other parts, all surrounding it in a circular manner.   Let E be the situation of the eye. M N will have the middle of every circular fold successively removed farther from its outline, in proportion as it is more distant from the eye. In M O of the other figure the outlines of these circular folds will appear almost straight, because it is situated opposite the eye; but in P and Q quite the contrary, as in N and M.

148.—*Of Folds.*

The folds of draperies, whatever be the motion of the figure, ought always to show, by the form of their outlines, the attitude of such figure; so as to leave, in the mind of the beholder, no doubt or confusion in regard to the true position of the body; and let there be no fold, which, by its shadow, breaks through any of the members; that is to say, appearing to go in deeper than the surface of the part it covers. And if you represent the figure clothed with several garments, one over the other, let it not appear as if the upper one covered only a mere skeleton; but let it express that it is also well furnished with flesh, and a thickness of folds, suitable to the number of its under garments.

The folds surrounding the members ought to diminish in thickness near the extremities of the part they surround.

The length of the folds, which are close to the members, ought to produce other folds on that side where the member is diminished by fore-shortening, and be more extended on the opposite side.

149.—*Of Decorum.*

Observe decorum in everything you represent; that is, fitness of action, dress, and situation, according to the dignity or meanness of the subject to be represented. Be careful that a king, for instance, be grave and majestic in his countenance and dress; that the place be well decorated; and that his attendants, or the bystanders, express reverence and admiration, and appear as noble, in dresses suitable to a royal court.

On the contrary, in the representation of a mean subject, let the figures appear low and despicable; those about them with similar countenances and actions, denoting base and presumptuous minds, and meanly clad. In short, in both cases, the parts must correspond with the genera. sentiment of the composition.

The motions of old age should not be similar to those of youth; those of a woman to those of a man; nor should the latter be the same as those of a boy.

150.—*The Character of Figures in Composition.*

In general, the painter ought to introduce very few old men in the ordinary course of historical subjects, and those few separated from young people; because old people are few, and their habits do not agree with those of youth. Where there is no conformity of custom, there can be no intimacy, and, without it, a company is soon separated. But if the subject require an appearance of gravity, a meeting on important business, as a council, for instance, let there be few young men introduced, for youth willingly avoids such meetings.

151.—*The Motion of the Muscles, when the Figures are in natural Positions.*

A figure which does not express by its position the sentiments and passions by which we suppose it animated, will appear to indicate that its muscles are not obedient to its will, and the painter very deficient in judgment. For that reason, a figure is to show great eagerness and meaning; and its position is to be so well appropriated to that meaning, that it cannot be mistaken, nor made use of for any other.

152.—*A Precept in Painting.*

The painter ought to notice those quick motions, which men are apt to make without thinking, when impelled by strong and powerful affections of the mind. He ought to take memorandums of them, and sketch them in his pocket-book, in order to make use of them when they may answer his purpose; and then to put a living model in the same position, to see the quality and aspect of the muscles which are in action.

153.—*Of the Motion of Man.*
(Plates 20 and 21.)

The first and principal part of the art is composition of any sort, or putting things together. The second relates to the expression and motion of the figures, and requires that they be well appropriated, and seeming attentive to what they are about; appearing to move with alacrity and spirit, according to the degree of expression suitable to the occasion; expressing slow and tardy motions, as well as those of eagerness in pursuit: and that quickness and ferocity be expressed with such force as to give an idea of the sensations of the actors. When a figure is to throw a dart, stones, or the like, let it be seen evidently by the attitude and disposition of all the members, that such is its intention; of which there are two examples in the opposite plates, varied both in action and power. The first in point of vigour is A. The second is B. But A will throw his weapon farther than B, because, though they seem desirous of throwing it to the same point, A having turned his feet towards the object, while his body is twisted and bent back the contrary way, to increase his power, returns with more velocity and force to the point to which he means to throw. But the figure B having turned his feet the same way as his body, it returns to its place with great inconvenience, and consequently with weakened powers. For in the expression of great efforts, the preparatory motions of the body must be strong and violent, twisting and bending, so that it may return with convenient ease, and by that means have a great effect. In the same manner, if a cross-bow be not strung with force, the motion of whatever it shoots will be short and without effect; because, where there is no impulse, there can be no motion; and, if the impulse be

Plate 20.   Chap. 13.

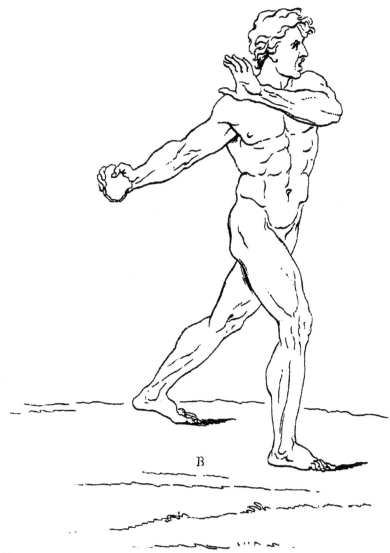

B

Plate 21.

Chap.153.

not violent, the motion is but tardy and feeble. So a bow which is not strung has no motion; and if it be strung, it will remain in that state till the impulse be given by another power which puts it in motion, and it will shoot with a violence equal to that which was employed in bending it. In the same manner, the man who does not twist and bend his body will have acquired no power. Therefore, after A has thrown his dart, he will find himself twisted the contrary way, viz., on the side where he has thrown; and he will have acquired only power sufficient to serve him to return to where he was at first.

154.—*Of Attitudes and the Motions of the Members.*

The same attitude is not to be repeated in the same picture, nor the same motion of members in the same figure, nay, not even in the hands or fingers.

And if the history requires a great number of figures, such as a battle, or a massacre of soldiers, in which there are but three ways of striking, viz., thrusting, cutting, or back-handed; in that case you must take care, that all those who are cutting be expressed in different views; some turning their backs, some their sides, and others be seen in front; varying in the same manner the three different ways of fighting, so that all the actions may have a relation to those three principles. In battles, complex motions display great art, giving spirit and animation to the whole. By complex motion is meant, for instance, that of a single figure showing the front of the legs, and the same time the profile of the shoulder. But of this I I shall treat in another place.*

155.—*Of a single Figure separate from an historical Group.*

The same motion of members should not be repeated in a figure which you mean to be alone; for instance, if the figure be represented running it must not throw both hands forward, but one forward and the other backward,

* Chapters 96 and 104.

or else it cannot run. If the right foot come forward, the right arm must go backward and the left forward, because, without such disposition and contrast of parts, it is impossible to run well. If another figure be supposed to follow this, one of its legs should be brought somewhat forward, and the other be perpendicular under the head; the arm on the same side should pass forward. But of this we shall treat more fully in the book on motion.*

156.—*On the Attitudes of the human Figure.*

A painter is to be attentive to the motions and actions of men, occasioned by some sudden accident. He must observe them on the spot, take sketches, and not wait till he wants such expression, and then have it counterfeited for him; for instance, setting a model to weep when there is no cause; such an expression without a cause will be neither quick nor natural. But it will be of great use to have observed every action from nature as it occurs, and then to have a model set in the same attitude to help the recollection, and find out something to the purpose, according to the subject in hand.

157.—*How to represent a Storm.*

To form a just idea of a storm, you must consider it attentively in its effects. When the wind blows violently over the sea or land, it removes and carries off with it everything that is not firmly fixed to the general mass. The clouds must appear straggling and broken, carried according to the direction and the force of the wind, and blended with clouds of dust raised from the sandy shore. Branches and leaves of trees must be represented as carried along by the violence of the storm, and together with numberless other light substances, scattered in the air. Trees and grass must be bent to the ground, as if yielding to the course of the wind. Boughs must be twisted out of their natural form, with their leaves reversed and

* See the Life of the Author; also chapters 20 and 101 of the present w· ·

entangled. Of the figures dispersed in the picture, some should appear thrown on the ground, so wrapped up in their cloaks and covered with dust, as to be scarcely distinguishable. Of those who remain on their feet, some should be sheltered by, and holding fast behind, some great trees, to avoid the same fate: others bending to the ground, their hands over their faces to ward off the dust; their hair and their clothes flying straight up at the mercy of the wind.

The high tremendous waves of the stormy sea will be covered with foaming froth; the most subtle parts of which, being raised by the wind, like a thick mist, mix with the air. What vessels are seen should appear with broken cordage, and torn sails, fluttering in the wind; some with broken masts fallen across the hulk, already on its side amidst the tempestuous waves. Some of the crew should be represented as if crying aloud for help, and clinging to the remains of the shattered vessel. Let the clouds appear as driven by tempestuous winds against the summits of lofty mountains, enveloping those mountains, and breaking and recoiling with redoubled force, like waves against a rocky shore. The air should be rendered awfully dark, by the mist, dust, and thick clouds.

158.—How to compose a Battle.

First, let the air exhibit a confused mixture of smoke, arising from the discharge of artillery and musketry, and the dust raised by the horses of the combatants; and observe that dust, being of an earthy nature, is heavy; but yet, by reason of its minute particles, it is easily impelled upwards, and mixes with the air; nevertheless, it naturally fall downwards again, the most subtle parts of it alone gaining any considerable degree of elevation, and at its utmost height it is so thin and transparent, as to appear nearly of the colour of the air. The smoke, thus mixing with the dusty air, forms a kind of dark cloud, at the top of which it is distinguished from the dust by a bluish cast, the dust retaining more of its natural colour. On that part from which the light proceeds, this mixture of

air, smoke, and dust, will appear much brighter than on
the opposite side. The more the combatants are involved
in this turbulent mist, the less distinctly they will be seen,
and the more confused will they be in their lights and
shades. Let the faces of the musketeers, their bodies, and
every object near them, be tinged with a reddish hue, even
the air or cloud of dust; in short, all that surrounds them.
This red tinge you will diminish, in proportion to their
distance from the primary cause. The group of figures,
which appear at a distance between the spectator and the
light, will form a dark mass upon a light ground; and
their legs will be more undetermined and lost as they
approach nearer to the ground; because there the dust is
heavier and thicker.

If you mean to represent some straggling horses running
out of the main body, introduce also some small clouds of
dust, as far distant from each other as the leap of the
horse, and these little clouds will become fainter, more
scanty, and diffused, in proportion to their distance from
the horse. That nearest to his feet will consequently be
the most determined, smallest, and the thickest of all.

Let the air be full of arrows, in all directions; some
ascending, some falling down, and some darting straight
forwards. The bullets of the musketry, though not seen,
will be marked in their course by a train of smoke, which
breaks through the general confusion. The figures in the
foreground should have their hair covered with dust, as
also their eyebrows, and all parts liable to receive it.

The victorious party will be running forwards, their
hair and other light parts flying in the wind, their eyebrows lowered, and the motion of every member properly
contrasted; for instance, in moving the right foot forwards,
the left arm must be brought forward also. If you make
any of them fallen down, mark the trace of his fall on the
slippery, gore-stained dust; and where the ground is less
impregnated with blood, let the print of men's feet and of
horses, that have passed that way, be marked. Let there
be some horses dragging the bodies of their riders, and
leaving behind them a furrow, made by the body thus
trailed along.

The countenances of the vanquished will appear pale and dejected. Their eyebrows raised, and much wrinkled about the forehead and cheeks. The tip of their noses somewhat divided from the nostrils by arched wrinkles terminating at the corner of the eyes, those wrinkles being occasioned by the opening and raising of the nostrils. The upper lips turned up, discovering the teeth. Their mouths wide open, and expressive of violent lamentation. One may be seen fallen wounded on the ground, endeavouring with one hand to support his body, and covering his eyes with the other, the palm of which is turned towards the enemy. Others running away, and with open mouths seeming to cry aloud. Between the legs of the combatants let the ground be strewed with all sorts of arms; as broken shields, spears, swords, and the like. Many dead bodies should be introduced, some entirely covered with dust, others in part only; let the blood, which seems to issue immediately from the wound, appear of its natural colour, and running in a winding course, till, mixing with the dust, it forms a reddish kind of mud. Some should be in the agonies of death; their teeth shut, their eyes wildly staring, their fists clenched, and their legs in a distorted position. Some may appear disarmed, and beaten down by the enemy, still fighting with their fists and teeth, and endeavouring to take a passionate, though unavailing revenge. There may be also a straggling horse without a rider, running in wild disorder; his mane flying in the wind, beating down with his feet all before him and doing a deal of damage. A wounded soldier may also be seen falling to the ground, and attempting to cover himself with his shield, while an enemy bending over him endeavours to give him the finishing stroke. Several dead bodies should be heaped together under a dead horse. Some of the conquerors, as having ceased fighting, may be wiping their faces from the dirt, collected on them by the mixture of dust with the water from their eyes.

The *corps de reserve* will be seen advancing gaily, but cautiously, their eyebrows directed forwards, shading their eyes with their hands to observe the motions of the enemy, amidst clouds of dust and smoke, and seeming attentive to the orders of their chief. You may also make their commander holding up his staff, pushing forwards, and pointing towards the place where they are wanted. A river may likewise be introduced, with horses fording it, dashing the water about between their legs, and in the air, covering all the adjacent ground with water and foam. Not a spot is to be left without some marks of blood and carnage.

159.—*The Representation of an Orator and his Audience.*

If you have to represent a man who is speaking to a large assembly of people, you are to consider the subject matter of his discourse, and to adapt his attitude to such subject. If he means to persuade, let it be known by his gesture. If he is giving an explanation, deduced from several reasons, let him put two fingers of the right hand within one of the left, having the other two bent close, his face turned towards the audience, with the mouth half open, seeming to speak. If he is sitting, let him appear as going to raise himself up a little, and his head be forward. But if he is represented standing, let him bend his chest and his head forward towards the people.

The auditory are to appear silent and attentive, with their eyes, upon the speaker, in the act of admiration. There should be some old men, with their mouths close shut, in token of approbation, and their lips pressed together, so as to form wrinkles at the corners of the mouth and about the cheeks, and forming others about the forehead, by raising the eyebrows, as if struck with astonishment. Some others of those sitting by should be seated with their hands within each other, round one of their knees; some with one knee upon the other, and upon that, one hand receiving the elbow, the other supporting the chin, covered with a venerable beard.

160.—*Of demonstrative Gestures.*

The action by which a figure points at anything near, either in regard to time or situation, is to be expressed by the hand very little removed from the body. But if the same thing is far distant, the hand must also be far removed from the body, and the face of the figure pointing must be turned towards those to whom he is pointing it out.

161.—*Of the Attitudes of the Bystanders at some remarkable Event.*

All those who are present at some event deserving notice express their admiration, but in various manners: as when the hand of justice punishes some malefactor. If the subject be an act of devotion, the eyes of all present should be directed towards the object of their adoration, aided by a variety of pious actions with the other members: as at the elevation of the host at mass, and other similar ceremonies. If it be a laughable subject, or one exciting compassion and moving to tears, in those cases it will not be necessary for all to have their eyes turned towards the object, but they will express their feelings by different actions; and let there be several assembled in groups, to rejoice or lament together. If the event be terrific, let the faces of those who run away from the sight, be strongly expressive of fright, with various motions; as shall be described in the tract on motion.

162.—*How to represent Night.*

Those objects which are entirely deprived of light, are lost to the sight, as in the night; therefore if you mean to paint a history under those circumstances, you must suppose a large fire, and those objects that are near it to be tinged with its colour, and the nearer they are the more they will partake of it. The fire being red, all those objects which receive light from it will appear of a reddish colour, and those that are most distant from it will partake of the darkness that surrounds them. The figures which are represented before the fire will appear dark in proportion to the brightness of the fire, because those parts of them which we see, are tinged by that darkness of the night, and not by the light of the fire, which they intercept.

Those that are on either side of the fire, will be half in the shade of night, and half in the red light. Those seen beyond the extent of the flames, will be all of a reddish light upon a black ground. In regard to their attitudes, let those who are nearest the fire, make screens of their hands and cloaks, against the scorching heat, with their faces turned on the contrary side, as if ready to run away from it. The most remote will only be shading their eyes with their hands, as if hurt by the too great glare.

163.—*The Method of awakening the Mind to a Variety of Inventions.*

I will not omit to introduce among these precepts a new kind of speculative invention, which though apparently trifling, and almost laughable, is nevertheless of great utility in assisting the genius to find variety for composition.

By looking attentively at old and smeared walls, or stones and veined marble of various colours, you may fancy that you see in them several compositions, landscapes, battles, figures in quick motion, strange countenances, and dresses, with an infinity of other objects. By these confused lines the inventive genius is excited to new exertions.

164.—*Of Composition in History.*

When the painter has only a single figure to represent, he must avoid any shortening whatever, as well of any particular member, as of the whole figure, because he would have to contend with the prejudices of those who have no knowledge in that branch of the art. But in subjects of history, composed of many figures, shortenings may be introduced with great propriety; nay, they are indispensable, and ought to be used without reserve, as the subject may require; particularly in battles, where, of course, many shortenings and contortions of figures happen, amongst such an enraged multitude of actors, possessed, as it were, of a brutal madness.

EXPRESSION AND CHARACTER.

165.—*Of expressive Motions.*

LET your figures have actions appropriated to what they are intended to think or say, and these will be well learnt by imitating the deaf, who by the motion of their hands, eyes, eyebrows, and the whole body, endeavour to express the sentiments of their mind. Do not ridicule the thought of a master without a tongue teaching you an art he does not understand; he will do it better by his expressive motions, than all the rest by their words and examples. Let then the painter, of whatever school, attend well to this maxim, and apply it to the different qualities of the figures he represents, and to the nature of the subject in which thay are actors.

166.—*How to paint Children.*

Children are to be represented with quick and contorted motions, when they are sitting; but when standing, with fearful and timid motions.

167.—*How to represent old Men.*

Old men must have slow and heavy motions; their legs and knees must be bent when they are standing, and their feet placed parallel and wide asunder. Let them be bowed downwards, the head leaning much forward, and their arms very little extended.

168.—*How to paint old Women.*

Old women, on the contrary, are to be represented bold and quick, with passionate motions, like furies.* But the

* The author here speaks of unpolished nature; and indeed it is from such subjects only, that the genuine and characteristic operations of nature are to be learnt. It is the effect of education to correct the natural peculiarities and defects, and, by so doing, to assimilate one person to the rest of the world.

motions are to appear a great deal quicker in their arms than in their legs.

169.—How to paint Women.

Women are to be represented in modest and reserved attitudes, with their knees rather close, their arms drawing near each other, or folded about the body; their heads looking downwards, and leaning a little on one side.

170.—Of the Variety of Faces.

The countenances of your figures should be expressive of their different situations : men at work, at rest, weeping, laughing, crying out, in fear, or joy, and the like. The attitudes also, and all the members, ought to correspond with the sentiment expressed in the faces.

171.—The Parts of the Face and their Motions.

The motions of the different parts of the face, occasioned by sudden agitations of the mind, are many. The principal of these are Laughter, Weeping, Calling out, Singing, either in a high or low pitch, Admiration, Anger, Joy, Sadness, Fear, Pain, and others, of which I propose to treat. First, of Laughing and Weeping, which are very similar in the motion of the mouth, the cheeks, the shutting of the eyebrows, and the space between them ; as we shall explain in its place, in treating of the changes which happen in the face, hands, fingers, and all the other parts of the body, as they are affected by the different emotions of the soul ; the knowledge of which is absolutely necessary to a painter, or else his figures may be said to be twice dead. But it is very necessary also that he be careful not to fall into the contrary extreme ; giving extraordinary motions to his figures, so that in a quiet and peaceable subject, he does not seem to represent a battle, or the revellings of drunken men. But, above all, the actors in any point of history must be attentive to what they are about, or to what is going forward; with actions that denote admiration, respect, pain, suspicion, fear, and joy, according as the occasion for which they are brought together, may require. Endeavour that different points of history be not placed one above the other on the same canvas, nor walls with different horizons,* as if it were a jeweller's shop, showing the goods in different square caskets.

172.—*Laughing and Weeping.*

Between the expression of laughter and that of weeping there is no difference in the motion of the features, either in the eyes, mouth, or cheeks; only in the ruffling of the brows, which is added when weeping, but more elevated and extended in laughing. One may represent the figure weeping, as tearing his clothes, or some other expression, as various as the cause of his feeling may be; because some weep for anger, some through fear, others for tenderness and joy, or for suspicion; some for real pain and torment; whilst others weep through compassion, or regret at the loss of some friend and near relation. These different feelings will be expressed by some with marks of despair, by others with moderation; some only shed tears, others cry, aloud, while another has his face turned towards heaven, with his hand depressed, and his fingers twisted. Some again will be full of apprehension, with their shoulders raised up to their ears; and so on, according to the above causes.

Those who weep, raise the brows, and bring them close together above the nose, forming many wrinkles on the forehead, and the corners of the mouth are turned downwards. Those who laugh have them turned upwards, and the brows open and extended.

173.—*Of Anger.*

If you represent a man in a violent fit of anger, make him seize another by the hair, holding his head writhed

* See chap. 123.

F

down against the ground, with his knee fixed upon the ribs of his antagonist; his right arm up, and his fist ready to strike; his hair standing on end, his eyebrows low and straight; his teeth close, and seen at the corner of the mouth; his neck swelled, and his body covered in the abdomen with creases, occasioned by his bending over his enemy, and the excess of his passion.

174.—*Despair.*

The last act of despondency is, when a man is in the act of putting a period to his own existence. He should be represented with a knife in one hand, with which he has already inflicted the wound, and tearing it open with the other. His garments and hair should be already torn. He will be standing with his feet asunder, his knees a little bent, and his body leaning forward, as if ready to fall to the ground.

LIGHT AND SHADOW.

175.—*The Course of Study to be pursued.*

THE student who is desirous of making great proficiency in the art of imitating the works of Nature, should not only learn the shape of figures or other objects, and be able to delineate them with truth and precision, but he must also accompany them with their proper lights and shadows, according to the situation in which those objects appear.

176.—*Which of the two is the most useful Knowledge, the Outlines of Figures, or that of Light and Shadow.*

The knowledge of the outline is of most consequence, and yet may be acquired to great certainty by dint of study; as the outlines of the human figure, particularly those which do not bend, are invariably the same. But the knowledge of the situation, quality, and quantity of shadows, being infinite, requires the most extensive study.

177.—*Which is the most important, the Shadows or Outlines in Painting.*

It requires much more observation and study to arrive at perfection in the shadowing of a picture, than in merely drawing the lines of it. The proof of this is, that the lines may be traced upon a veil or a flat glass placed

between the eye and the object to be imitated. But that
cannot be of any use in shadowing, on account of the
infinite gradation of shades, and the blending of them,
which does not allow of any precise termination; and most
frequently they are confused, as will be demonstrated in
another place.*

178.—*What is a Painter's first Aim and Object.*

The first object of a painter is to make a simple flat
surface appear like a relievo, and some of its parts detached
from the ground; he who excels all others in that part of
the art, deserves the greatest praise. This perfection of
the art depends on the correct distribution of lights and
shades, called *Chiaro-scuro*. If the painter, then, avoids
shadows, he may be said to avoid the glory of the art, and
to render his work despicable to real connoisseurs, for the
sake of acquiring the esteem of vulgar and ignorant
admirers of fine colours, who never have any knowledge of
relievo.

179.—*The Difference of Superficies, in regard to Painting.*

Solid bodies are of two sorts: the one has the surface
curvilinear, oval, or spherical; the other has several
surfaces, or sides producing angles, either regular or
irregular. Spherical, or oval bodies, will always appear
detached from their ground, though they are exactly of
the same colour. Bodies also of different sides and angles
will always detach, because they are always disposed so as
to produce shades on some of their sides, which cannot
happen to a plain superficies.†

180.—*How a Painter may become universal.*

The painter who wishes to be universal, and please a
variety of judges, must unite in the same composition.
objects susceptible of great force in the shadows, and great

* See chap. 264.   † See chap. 267.

sweetness in the management of them; accounting, how-ever, in every instance, for such boldness and softenings.

181.—*Accuracy ought to be learnt before Despatch in the Execution.*

If you wish to make good and useful studies, use great deliberation in your drawings, observe well among the lights, which, and how many, hold the first rank in point of brightness; and so among the shadows, which are darker than others, and in what manner they blend together; compare the quality and quantity of one with the other. and observe to what part they are directed. Be careful also in your outlines, or divisions of the members. Remark well what quantity of parts are to be on one side, and what on the other; and where they are more or less apparent, or broad, or slender. Lastly, take care that the shadows and lights be united, or lost in each other; without any hard strokes or lines; as smoke loses itself in the air, so are your lights and shadows to pass from the one to the other, without any apparent separation.

When you have acquired the habit, and formed your hand to accuracy, quickness of execution will come of itself.*

182.—*How the Painter is to place himself in regard to the Light and his Model.*

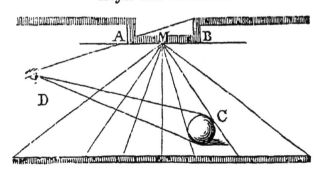

Let A B be the window, M the centre of it, C the model.

* Sir Joshua Reynolds frequently inculcated these precepts in his lectures, and indeed they cannot be too often enforced.

The best situation for the painter will be a little sideways, between the window and his model, as D, so that he may see his object partly in the light and partly in the shadow.

183.—*Of the best Light.*

The light from on high, and not too powerful, will be found the best calculated to show the parts to advantage.

184.—*Of Drawing by Candle-light.*

To this artificial light apply a paper blind, and you will see the shadows undetermined and soft.

185.—*Of those Painters who draw at Home from one Light, and afterwards adapt their studies to another Situation in the Country, and a different Light.*

It is a great error in some painters who draw a figure from nature at home, by any particular light, and afterwards make use of that drawing in a picture representing an open country, which receives the general light of the sky, where the surrounding air gives light on all sides. This painter would put dark shadows, where Nature would either produce none, or, if any, so very faint as to be almost imperceptible; and he would throw reflected lights where it is impossible there should be any.

186.—*How high the Light should be in drawing from Nature.*

To paint well from Nature, your window should be to the North, that the lights may not vary. If it be to the South, you must have paper blinds, that the sun, in going round, may not alter the shadows. The situation of the light should be such as to produce upon the ground a shadow from your model as long as that is high.

187.—*What Light the Painter must make Use of to give most Relief to his Figures.*

The figures which receive a particular light show more relief than those which receive an universal one; because the particular light occasions some reflexes, which proceed from the light of one object upon the shadows of another, and help to detach it from the dark ground. But a figure placed in front of a dark and large space, and receiving a particular light, can receive no reflection from any other objects, and nothing is seen of the figure but what the light strikes on, the rest being blended and lost in the darkness of the back ground. This is to be applied only to the imitation of night subjects with very little light

188.—*Advice to Painters.*

Be very careful, in painting, to observe, that between the shadows there are other shadows, almost imperceptible, both for darkness and shape; and this is proved by the third proposition,* which says, that the surfaces of globular or convex bodies have as great a variety of lights and shadows as the bodies that surround them have.

189.—*Of Shadows.*

Those shadows which in Nature are undetermined, and the extremities of which can hardly be perceived, are to be copied in your painting in the same manner, never to be precisely finished, but left confused and blended. This apparent neglect will show great judgment, and be the ingenious result of your observation of Nature.

190.—*Of the Kind of Light proper for drawing from Relievos, or from Nature.*

Lights separated from the shadows with too much precision, have a very bad effect. In order, therefore, to avoid

---

* Probably this would have formed a part of his intended treatise on light and shadow, but no such proposition occurs in the present work.

this inconvenience, if the object be in the open country, you need not let your figures be illumined by the sun ; but may suppose some transparent clouds interposed, so that the sun not being visible, the termination of the shadows will be also imperceptible and soft.

191.—*Whether the Light should be admitted in Front or Side-ways ; and which is most pleasing and graceful.*

The light admitted in front of heads situated opposite to side walls that are dark, will cause them to have great relievo, particularly if the light be placed high ; and the reason is, that the most prominent parts of those faces are illumined by the general light striking them in front, which light produces very faint shadows on the part where it strikes ; but as it turns towards the sides, it begins to participate of the dark shadows of the room, which grow darker in proportion as it sinks into them. Besides, when the light comes from on high, it does not strike on every part of the face alike, but one part produces great shadows upon another ; as the eyebrows, which deprive the whole sockets of the eyes of light. The nose keeps it off from great part of the mouth, and the chin from the neck, and such other parts. This, by concentrating the light upon the most projecting parts, produces a very great relief.

192.—*Of the Difference of Lights according to the Situation.*

A small light will cast large and determined shadows upon the surrounding bodies. A large light, on the contrary, will cast small shadows on them, and they will be much confused in their termination. When a small but strong light is surrounded by a broad but weaker light, the latter will appear like a demi-tint to the other, as the sky round the sun. And the bodies which receive the light from the one, will serve as demi-tints to those which receive the light from the other.

193.—*How to distribute the Light on Figures.*

The lights are to be distributed according to the natural situation you mean your figures should occupy. If you suppose them in sunshine, the shades must be dark, the lights broad and extended, and the shadows of all the surrounding objects distinctly marked upon the ground. If seen in a gloomy day, there will be very little difference between the lights and shades, and no shadows at the feet. If the figures be represented within doors, the lights and shadows will again be distinctly divided, and produce shadows on the ground. But if you suppose a paper blind at the window, and the walls painted white, the effect will be the same as in a gloomy day, when the lights and shadows have little difference. If the figures are enlightened by the fire, the lights must be red and powerful, the shadows dark, and the shadows upon the ground and upon the walls must be precise; observing that they spread wider as they go off from the body. If the figures be enlightened, partly by the sky and partly by the fire, that side which receives the light from the sky will be the brightest, and on the other side it will be reddish, somewhat of the colour of the fire. Above all, contrive that your figures receive a broad light, and that from above; particularly in portraits, because the people we see in the street receive all the light from above; and it is curious to observe, that there is not a face ever so well known amongst your acquaintance, but would be recognised with difficulty, if it were enlightened from beneath.

194.—*Of the Beauty of Faces.*

You must not mark any muscles with hardness of line, but let the soft light glide upon them, and terminate imperceptibly in delightful shadows; from this will arise grace and beauty to the face.

195.—*How, in drawing a Face, to give it Grace, by the Management of Light and Shade.*

A face placed in the dark part of a room, acquires great

additional grace by means of light and shadow. The
shadowed part of the face blends with the darkness of the
ground, and the light part receives an increase of brightness from the open air, the shadows on this side becoming
almost insensible; and from this augmentation of light and
shadow, the face has much relief, and acquires great
beauty.

196.—*How to give Grace and Relief to Faces.*

In streets running towards the west, when the sun is in
the meridian, and the walls on each side so high that they
cast no reflections on that side of the bodies which is in
shade, and the sky is not too bright, we find the most
advantageous situation for giving relief and grace to
figures, particularly to faces; because both sides of the
face will participate of the shadows of the walls. The
sides of the nose and the face towards the west, will be
light, and the man whom we supposed placed at the
entrance, and in the middle of the street, will see all the
parts of that face, which are before him, perfectly
illumined, while both sides of it, towards the walls, will
be in shadow. What gives additional grace is, that these
shades do not appear cutting, hard, or dry, but softly
blended and lost in each other. The reason of it is, that
the light which is spread all over in the air, strikes also
the pavement of the street, and reflecting upon the shady
part of the face, it tinges that slightly with the same hue:
while the great light which comes from above being confined
by the tops of houses, strikes on the face with different
points, almost to the very beginning of the shadows under
the projecting parts of the face. It diminishes by degrees
the strength of them, increasing the light till it comes
upon the chin, where it terminates, and loses itself, blending softly into the shades on all sides. For instance, if
such light were A E, the line F E would give light even to
the bottom of the nose. The line C F will give light only
to the under lip; but the line A H would extend the
shadow to all the under parts of the face, and under the
chin.

In this situation the nose receives a very strong light from all the points A B C D E.

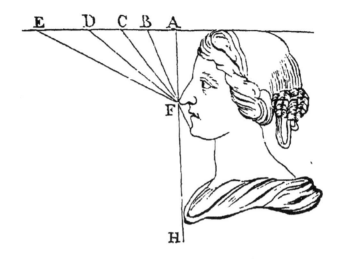

197.—*Of the Termination of Bodies upon each other.*

When a body, of a cylindrical or convex surface, terminates upon another body of the same colour, it will appear darker on the edge than the body upon which it terminates. And any flat body, adjacent to a white surface, will appear very dark; but upon a dark ground it will appear lighter than any other part, though the lights be equal.

198.—*Of the Backgrounds of painted Objects.*

The ground which surrounds the figures in any painting, ought to be darker than the light part of those figures, and lighter than the shadowed part.

199.—*How to detach and bring forward Figures out of their Background.*

If your figure be dark, place it on a light ground; if it be light, upon a dark ground; and if it be partly light and partly dark, as is generally the case, contrive that the dark part of the figure be upon the light part of the ground, and the light side of it against the dark.*

200.—*Of proper Backgrounds.*

It is of the greatest importance to consider well the nature of backgrounds, upon which any opaque body is to be placed. In order to detach it properly, you should place the light part of such opaque body against the dark part of the background, and the dark parts on a light ground; † as in the cut.‡

* See chapters 200 and 219.
† See chapter 209.
‡ This cannot be taken as an absolute rule; it must be left in a great measure to the judgment of the painter. For much graceful softness and grandeur is acquired, sometimes, by blending the lights of the figures with the light part of the ground; and so of the shadows; as Leonardo himself has observed in chapters 194, 195, and Sir Joshua Reynolds has often put in practice with success.

201.—*Of the general Light diffused over Figures.*

In compositions of many figures and animals, observe, that the parts of these different objects ought to be darker in proportion as they are lower, and as they are nearer the middle of the groups, though they are all of an uniform colour. This is necessary, because a smaller proportion of the sky (from which all bodies are illuminated) can give light to the lower spaces between these different figures, than to the upper parts of the spaces. It is proved thus:

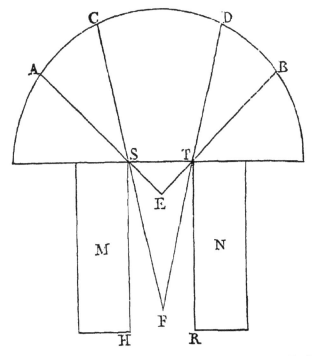

A B C D is that portion of the sky which gives light to all the objects beneath; M and N are the bodies which occupy the space S T R H, in which it is evidently perceived, that the point F, receiving the light only from the portion of the sky C D, has a smaller quantity of it than the point E which receives it from the whole space A B (a larger portion than C D); therefore it will be lighter in E than in F.

202.—*Of those Parts in Shadows which appear the darkest at a Distance.*

The neck, or any other part which is raised straight upwards, and has a projection over it, will be darker than the perpendicular front of that projection; and this projecting part will be lighter, in proportion as it presents a larger surface to the light.

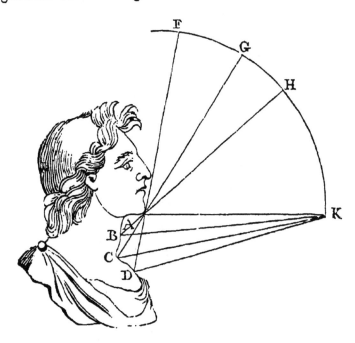

For instance, the recess A receives no light from any part of the sky G K, but B begins to receive the light from the part of the sky H K, and C from G K; and the point D receives the whole of F K. Therefore the chest will be as light as the forehead, nose, and chin. But what I have particularly to recommend, in regard to faces, is, that you observe well those different qualities of shades which are lost at different distances (while there remain only the first and principal spots or strokes of shades, such as those of the sockets of the eyes, and other similar recesses, which are always dark), and at last the whole face become-obscured; because the greatest lights (being small in proportion to the demi-tints) are lost. The quality, therefore, and quantity of the principal lights and shades are by means of great distance blended together into a general half-tint; and this is the reason why trees and other objects are found to be in appearance darker at some distance than they are in reality, when nearer to the eye. But then the air, which interposes between the objects and the eye, will render them light again by tinging them with azure, rather in the shades than in the lights; for the lights will preserve the truth of the different colours much longer.

203.—*Of the Eye viewing the Folds of Draperies surrounding a Figure.*

The shadows between the folds of a drapery surrounding the parts of the human body will be darker as the deep hollows where the shadows are generated are more directly opposite the eye. This is to be observed only when the eye is placed between the light and the shady part of the figure.

204.—*Of the Relief of Figures remote from the Eye.*

Any opaque body appears less relieved in proportion as it is farther distant from the eye; because the air, interposed between the eye and such body, being lighter than the shadow of it, it tarnishes and weakens that shadow, lessens its power, and consequently lessens also its relief.

205.—*Of Outlines of Objects on the Side towards the Light.*

The extremities of any object on the side which receives the light, will appear darker if upon a lighter ground, and lighter if seen upon a darker ground. But if such body be flat, and seen upon a ground equal in point of light with itself and of the same colour, such boundaries, or outlines, will be entirely lost to the sight.*

* See chap. 265.

206.—*How to make Objects detach from their Ground, that is to say, from the Surface on which they are painted.*

Objects contrasted with a light ground will appear much more detached than those which are placed against a dark one. The reason is, that if you wish to give relief to your figures, you will make those parts which are the farthest from the light, participate the least of it; therefore they will remain the darkest, and every distinction of outline would be lost in the general mass of shadows. But to give it grace, roundness, and effect, those dark shades are always attended by reflexes, or else they would either cut too hard upon the ground, or stick to it, by the similarity of shade, and relieve the less as the ground is darker; for at some distance nothing would be seen but the light parts, therefore your figures would appear mutilated of all that remains lost in the background.

CONTRAST AND EFFECT.

207.—*A Precept.*

FIGURES will have more grace, placed in the open and general light, than in any particular or small one; because the powerful and extended light will surround and embrace the objects: and works done in that kind of light appear pleasant and graceful when placed at a distance,* while those which are drawn in a narrow light will receive great force of shadow, but will never appear at a great distance, but as painted objects.

208.—*Of the Interposition of transparent Bodies between the Eye and the Object.*

The greater the transparent interposition is between the eye and the object, the more the colour of that object

* See chap. 196.

will participate of, or be changed into, that of the transparent medium.*

When an opaque body is situated between the eye and the luminary, so that the central line of the one passes also through the centre of the other, that object will be entirely deprived of light.

209.—Of proper Backgrounds for Figures.

As we find by experience that all bodies are surrounded by lights and shadows, I would have the painter to accommodate that part which is enlightened, so as to terminate upon something dark; and to manage the dark parts so that they may terminate on a light ground. This will be of great assistance in detaching and bringing out his figures.†

210.—Of Backgrounds.

To give a great effect to figures, you must oppose to a light one a dark ground, and to a dark figure a light ground, contrasting white with black, and black with white. In general, all contraries give a particular force and brilliancy of effect by their opposition.‡

REFLEXES.

211.—Of Objects placed on a light Ground, and why such a Practice is useful in Painting.

WHEN a darkish body terminates upon a light ground, it will appear detached from that ground; because all opaque

* He means here to say, that in proportion as the body interposed between the eye and the object is more or less transparent, the greater or less quantity of the colour of the body interposed will be communicated to the object.

† See the note to chap. 100.

‡ See the preceding chapter, and chap. 200.

bodies of a curved surface are not only dark on that side which receives no light, and consequently very different from the ground, but even that side of the curved surface which is enlightened will not carry its principal light to the extremities, but have between the ground and the principal light a certain demi-tint, darker than either the ground or that light.

212.—*Of the different Effects of White, according to the Difference of Backgrounds.*

Anything white will appear whiter by being opposed to a dark ground; and, on the contrary, darker upon a light ground. This we learn from observing snow as it falls; while it is descending it appears darker against the sky than when we see it against an open window, which (owing to the darkness of the inside of the house) makes it appear very white. Observe also, that snow appears to fall very quick and in a great quantity when near the eye; but when at some distance, it seems to come down slowly, and in a smaller quantity.*

213.—*Of Reverberation.*

Reverberations are produced by all bodies of a bright nature, that have a smooth and tolerably hard surface, which, repelling the light it receives, makes it rebound like a foot-ball against the first object opposed to it.

214.—*Where there cannot be any Reverberation of Light.*

The surfaces of hard bodies are surrounded by various qualities of light and shadow. The lights are of two sorts; one is called original, the other derivative. The original light is that which comes from the sun, or the brightness of fire, or else from the air. The derivative is a reflected light. But to return to our definition, I say,

---

* The appearance of motion is lessened according to the distance, in the same proportion as objects diminish in size.

there can be no reflection on that side which is turned towards any dark body—such as roofs either high or low, shrubs, grass, wood, either dry or green—because, though, every individual part of those objects be turned towards the original light, and struck by it, yet the quantity of shadow which every one of these parts produces upon the others is so great that, upon the whole, the light, not forming a compact mass, loses its effect, so that those objects cannot reflect any light upon the opposite bodies.

215.—*In what Part the Reflexes have more or less Brightness.*

The reflected lights will be more or less apparent or bright, in proportion as they are seen against a darker or fainter ground; because if the ground be darker than the reflex, then this reflex will appear stronger on account of the great difference of colour. But, on the contrary, if this reflection has behind it a ground lighter than itself, it will appear dark, in comparison to the brightness which is close to it, and therefore it will be hardly perceptible.*

216.—*Of the reflected Lights which surround the Shadows.*

The reflected lights which strike upon the midst of shadows, will brighten up or lessen their obscurity in proportion to the strength of those lights, and their proximity to those shadows. Many painters neglect this observation, while others attend to and deduce their practice from it. This difference of opinion and practice divides the sentiments of artists, so that they blame each other for not thinking and acting as they themselves do. The best way is to steer a middle course, and not to admit of any reflected light, but when the cause of it is evident to every eye; and *vice versâ*, if you introduce none at all, let it appear evident that there was no reasonable cause for it. In doing so, you will neither be totally blamed nor praised by the variety of opinion, which, if not proceeding from entire ignorance, will insure to you the approbation of both parties.

* See chapters 217 and 219.

217.—*Where Reflexes are to be most apparent.*

Of all reflected lights, that is to be the most apparent,
bold, and precise, which detaches from the darkest ground;
and, on the contrary, that which is upon a lighter ground
will be less apparent. And this proceeds from the contrast of shades, by which the faintest makes the dark ones
appear still darker; so in contrasted lights, the brightest
cause the others to appear less bright than they really
are.*

218.—*What Part of a Reflex is to be the lightest.*

That part will be the brightest which receives the reflected light between angles the most nearly equal. For

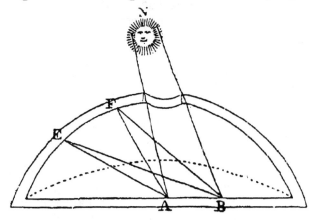

example, let N be the luminary, and A B the illuminated
part of the object, reflecting the light over all the shady
part of the concavity opposite to it. The light which
reflects upon F will be placed between equal angles. But
E at the base will not be reflected by equal angles, as it is
evident that the angle E A B is more obtuse than the angle
E B A. The angle A F B, however, though it is between
angles of less quality than the angle E, and has a common
base B A, is between angles more nearly equal than E,
therefore it will be lighter in F than in E; and it will also
be brighter, because it is nearer to the part which gives

* See chapters 215 and 219.

them light. According to the 6th rule,* which says, that part of the body is to be the lightest which is nearest to the luminary.

219.—*Of the Termination of Reflexes on their Grounds.*

The termination of a reflected light on a ground lighter than that reflex, will not be perceivable; but if such a reflex terminates upon a ground darker than itself, it will be plainly seen; and the more so in proportion as that ground is darker, and *vice versâ.*†

220.—*Of double and treble Reflections of Light.*

Double reflexes are stronger than single ones, and the shadows which interpose between the common light and

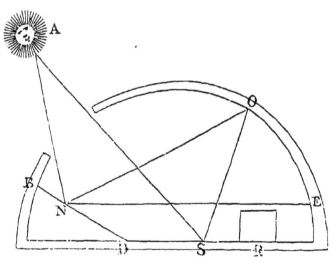

these reflexes are very faint. For instance, let A be the luminous body, A N, A S, are the direct rays, and S N the parts which receive the light from them. O and E are the places enlightened by the reflection of that light in

---

* This was intended to constitute a part of some book of perspective, which we have not; but the rule here referred to will be found in chap. 310 of the present work.

† See chapters 215 and 217.

those parts. A N E is a single reflex, but A N O, A S O
is the double reflex.   The single reflex is that which
proceeds from a single light, but the double reflection is
produced by two different lights.   The single one E is
produced by the light striking on B D, while the double
one O proceeds from the enlightened bodies B D and D R
co-operating together; and the shadows which are between
N O and S O will be very faint.

221.—Reflexes in the Water, and particularly those of the Air.

The only portion of air that will be seen reflected in the
water, will be that which is reflected by the surface of
the water to the eye between equal angles; that is to
say, the angle of incidence must be equal to the angle of
reflection.

COLOURS AND COLOURING

COLOURS.

222.—What Surface is best calculated to receive most Colours.

WHITE is more capable of receiving all sorts of colours than the surface of any body whatever that is not transparent. To prove it, we shall say, that any void space is capable of receiving what another space, not void, cannot receive. In the same manner, a white surface, like a void space, being destitute of any colour, will be fittest to receive such as are conveyed to it from any other enlightened body, and will participate more of the colour than black can do; which latter, like a broken vessel, is not able to contain anything.

223.—What Surface will show most perfectly its true Colour.

That opaque body will show its colour more perfect and beautiful which has near it another body of the same colour.

224.—On what Surfaces the true Colour is least apparent.

Polished and glossy surfaces show least of their genuine colour. This is exemplified in the grass of the fields, and the leaves of trees, which, being smooth and glossy, will reflect the colour of the sun, and the air, where they strike, so that the parts which receive the light do not show their natural colour.

225.—What Surfaces show most of their true and genuine Colour.

Those objects that are the least smooth and polished show their natural colours best; as we see in cloth, and in the leaves of such grass or trees as are of a woolly nature; which, having no lustre, are exhibited to the eye in their true natural colour; unless that colour happen to be confused by that of another body casting on them reflections of an opposite colour, such as the redness of the setting sun, when all the clouds are tinged with its colour.

226.—Of the Mixture of Colours.

Although the mixture of colours may be extended to an infinite variety, almost impossible to be described, I will not omit touching slightly upon it, setting down at first a certain number of simple colours to serve as a foundation, and with each of these mixing one of the others; one with one, then two with two, and three with three, proceeding in this manner to the full mixture of all the colours together; then I would begin again, mixing two of these colours with two others, and three with three, four with four, and so on to the end. To these two colours we shall put three; to these three add three more, and then six, increasing always in the same proportion.

I call those simple colours, which are not composed, and cannot be made or supplied by any mixture of other colours. Black and white are not reckoned among colours; the one is the representative of darkness, the other of light: that is, one is a simple privation of light, the other is light itself. Yet I will not omit mentioning them, because there is nothing in painting more useful and necessary; since painting is but an effect produced by lights and shadows, viz., *chiaro-scuro*. After black and white come blue and yellow, then green and tawny or umber, and then purple and red. These eight colours are all that Nature produces.

With these I begin my mixtures, first black and white, black and yellow, black and red; then yellow and red: but I shall treat more at length of these mixtures, in a separate work,* which will be of great utility, nay very necessary. I shall place this subject between theory and practice.

227.—Of the Colours produced by the Mixture of other Colours, called secondary Colours.

The first of all simple colours is white, though philosophers will not acknowledge either white or black to be colours; because the first is the cause, or the receiver of colours, the other totally deprived of them. But as painters cannot do without either, we shall place them among the others; and according to this order of things, white will be the first, yellow the second, green the third, blue the fourth, red the fifth, and black the sixth. We shall set down white for the representative of light, without which no colour can be seen; yellow for the earth; green for water; blue for air; red for fire; and black for total darkness.

If you wish to see by a short process the variety of all the mixed or composed colours, take some coloured glasses, and, through them, look at all the country round: you will find that the colour of each object will be altered and mixed with the colour of the glass through which it is seen. Observe which colour is made better, and which is hurt by the mixture. If the glass be yellow, the colour of the objects may either be improved, or greatly impaired by it. Black and white will be most altered, while green and yellow will be meliorated. In the same manner you may go through all the mixtures of colours, which are infinite. Select those which are new and agreeable to the sight; and following the same method, you may go on with two glasses, or three, till you have found what will best answer your purpose.

* No such work was ever published, nor, for anything that appears, ever written by Leonardo.

228.—*Of Verdigris.*

This green, which is made of copper, though it be mixed with oil, will lose its beauty, if it be not varnished immediately. It not only fades, but, if washed with a sponge and pure water only, it will detach from the ground upon which it is painted, particularly in damp weather; because verdigris is produced by the strength of salts. which easily dissolve in rainy weather, but still more if washed with a wet sponge.

229.—*How to increase the Beauty of Verdigris.*

If you mix with the verdigris some caballine aloe, it will add to it a great degree of beauty. It would acquire still more from saffron, if it did not fade. The quality and goodness of this aloe will be proved by dissolving it in warm brandy. Supposing the verdigris has already been used, and the part finished, you may then glaze it thinly with this dissolved aloe, and it will produce a very fine colour. This aloe may be ground also in oil by itself, or with the verdigris, or any other colour, at pleasure.

230.—*How to paint a Picture that will last almost for ever.*

After you have made a drawing of your intended picture, prepare a good and thick priming with pitch and brickdust well pounded; after which give it a second coat of white lead and Naples yellow; then, having traced your drawing upon it, and painted your picture, varnish it with clear and thick old oil, and stick it to a flat glass, or crystal, with a clear varnish. Another method, which may be better, is, instead of the priming of pitch and brickdust, take a flat tile well vitrified, then apply the coat of white and Naples yellow, and all the rest as before. But before the glass is applied to it, the painting must be perfectly dried in a stove, and varnished with nut oil and amber, or else with purified nut oil alone, thickened in the sun.*

231.— The Mode of painting on Canvas, or Linen Cloth.

Stretch your canvas upon a frame, then give it a coat of weak size, let it dry, and draw your outlines upon it. Paint the flesh colours first ; and while it is still fresh or moist, paint also the shadows, well softened and blended together. The flesh colour may be made with white, lake, and Naples yellow. The shades with black, umber, and a little lake; you may, if you please, use black chalk. After you have softened this first coat, or dead colour, and let it dry, you may retouch over it with lake and other colours, and gum water that has been a long while made and kept liquid, because in that state it becomes better, and does not leave any gloss. Again, to make the shades darker, take the lake and gum as above, and ink; ‡ and with this you may shade or glaze many colours, because it is transparent; such as azure, lake, and several others. As for the lights, you may retouch or glaze them slightly with gum water and pure lake, particularly vermilion.

---

* The French translation of 1716 has a note on this chapter, saying, that the invention of enamel painting found out since the time of Leonardo da Vinci, would better answer to the title of this chapter, and also be a better method of painting. I must beg leave, however, to dissent from this opinion, as the two kinds of painting are so different that they cannot be compared. Leonardo treats of oil painting, but the other is vitrification. Leonardo is known to have spent a great deal of time in experiments, of which this is a specimen; and it may appear ridiculous to the practitioners of more modern date, as he does not enter more fully into a minute description of the materials, or the mode of employing them. The principle laid down in the text appears to me to be simply this : to make the oil entirely evaporate from the colours by the action of fire, and afterwards to prevent the action of the air by the means of a glass : which in itself is an excellent principle, but not applicable, any more than enamel painting, to large works.

† It is evident that distemper or size painting is here meant.

‡ Indian ink.

232.—*Of lively and beautiful Colours.*

For those colours which you mean should appear beautiful, prepare a ground of pure white. This is meant only
for transparent colours: as for those that have a body, and
are opaque, it matters not what ground they have, and a
white one is of no use. This is exemplified by painted
glasses; when placed between the eye and clear air, they
exhibit most excellent and beautiful colours, which is not
the case when they have thick air, or some opaque body,
behind them.

233.—*Of transparent Colours.*

When a transparent colour is laid upon another of a
different nature, it produces a mixed colour, different from
either of the simple ones which compose it. This is
observed in the smoke coming out of a chimney, which,
when passing before the black soot, appears bluish, but as
it ascends against the blue of the sky, it changes its
appearance into a reddish brown. So the colour lake laid
on blue will turn it to a violet colour; yellow upon blue
turns to green; saffron upon white becomes yellow; white
scumbled upon a dark ground appears blue, and is more
or less beautiful as the white and the ground are more or
less pure.

234.—*In what Part a Colour will appear in its greatest*
Beauty.

We are to consider here in what part any colour will
show itself in its most perfect purity; whether in the
strongest light or deepest shadow, in the demi-tint, or in
the reflex. It would be necessary to determine first, of
what colour we mean to treat, because different colours
differ materially in that respect. Black is most beautiful
in the shades; white in the strongest light; blue and green
in the half-tint; yellow and red in the principal light;
gold in the reflexes; and lake in the half-tint.

235. —*How any Colour without a Gloss, is more beautiful in the Lights than in the Shades.*

All objects which have no gloss, show their colours better in the light than in the shadow, because the light vivifies and gives a true knowledge of the nature of the colour, while the shadows lower and destroy its beauty, preventing the discovery of its nature. If, on the contrary, black be more beautiful in the shadows, it is because black is not a colour.

236.—*Of the Appearance of Colours.*

The lighter a colour is in its nature, the more so it will appear when removed to some distance; but with dark colours it is quite the reverse.

237.—*What Part of a Colour is to be the most beautiful.*

If A be the light, and B the object receiving it in a direct line, E cannot receive that light, but only the reflection from

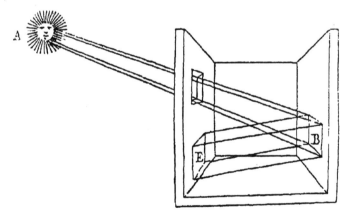

B, which we shall suppose to be red. In that case, the light it produces being red, it will tinge with red the object E; and if E happen to be also red before, you will see that colour increase in beauty, and appear redder than B; but if E were yellow, you will see a new colour, participating of the red and the yellow.

238.—*That the Beauty of a Colour is to be found in the Lights,*

As the quality of colours is discovered to the eye by the light, it is natural to conclude, that where there is most light, there also the true quality of the colour is to be seen; and where there is most shadow, the colour will participate of, and be tinged with, the colour of that shadow. Remember, then, to show the true quality of the colour in the light parts only.*

239.—*Of Colours.*

The colour which is between the light and the shadow will not be so beautiful as that which is in the full light. Therefore the chief beauty of colours will be found in the principal lights.†

240.—*No Object appears in its true Colour, unless the Light which strikes upon it be of the same Colour.*

This is very observable in draperies, where the light folds casting a reflection, and throwing a light on other folds opposite to them, make them appear in their natural colour. The same effect is produced by gold leaves casting their light reciprocally on each other. The effect is quite contrary if the light be received from an object of a different colour.‡

241.—*Of the Colour of Shadows.*

The colour of the shadows of an object can never be pure if the body which is opposed to these shadows be not of the same colour as that on which they are produced. For instance, if in a room, the walls of which are green, I place

---

* This rule is not without exception : see chap. 234.
† See chap. 238.
‡ See chap. 237.

a figure clothed in blue, and receiving the light from another blue object, the light part of that figure will be of a beautiful blue, but the shadows of it will become dingy, and not like a true shade of that beautiful blue, because it will be corrupted by the reflections from the green wall; and it would be still worse if the walls were of a darkish brown.

242.—*Of Colours.*

Colours placed in shadow will preserve more or less of their original beauty, as they are more or less immersed in the shade. But colours situated in a light space will show their natural beauty in proportion to the brightness of that light. Some say, that there is as great variety in the colours of shadows, as in the colours of objects shaded by them. It may be answered, that colours placed in shadow will show less variety amongst themselves as the shadows are darker. We shall soon convince ourselves of this truth, if, from a large square, we look through the open door of a church, where pictures, though enriched with a variety of colours, appear all clothed in darkness.

243.—*Whether it be possible for all Colours to appear alike by means of the same Shadow.*

It is very possible that all the different colours may be changed into that of a general shadow; as is manifest in the darkness of a cloudy night, in which neither the shape nor colour of bodies is distinguished. Total darkness being nothing but a privation of the primitive and reflected lights by which the form and colour of bodies are seen, it is evident that the cause being removed the effect ceases, and the objects are entirely lost to the sight.

244.—*Why White is not reckoned among the Colours.*

White is not a colour, but has the power of receiving all the other colours. When it is placed in a high situation in the country, all its shades are azure; according to the fourth proposition,* which says, that the surface of any opaque body participates of the colour of any other body sending the light to it. Therefore white, being deprived of the light of the sun by the interposition of any other body, will remain white; if exposed to the sun on one side, and to the open air on the other, it will participate both of the colour of the sun and of the air. That side which is not opposed to the sun, will be shaded of the colour of the air. And if this white were not surrounded by green fields all the way to the horizon, nor could receive any light from that horizon, without doubt it would appear of one simple and uniform colour, viz., that of the air.

245.—Of Colours.

The light of the fire tinges everything of a reddish yellow; but this will hardly appear evident, if we do not make the comparison with the daylight. Towards the close of the evening this is easily done; but more certainly after the morning twilight; and the difference will be clearly distinguished in a dark room, when a little glimpse of daylight strikes upon any part of the room, and there still remains a candle burning. Without such a trial the difference is hardly perceivable, particularly in those colours which have most similarity—such as white and yellow, light green and light blue; because the light which strikes the blue, being yellow, will naturally turn it green; as we have said in another place,† that a mixture of blue and yellow produces green. And if to a green colour you add some yellow, it will make it of a more beautiful green.

246.—Of the Colouring of remote Objects

The painter who is to represent objects at some distance from the eye, ought merely to convey the idea of general

* See chapters 247 and 274, in the present work. Probably they were intended to form a part of a distinct treatise, and to have been ranged as propositions in that, but at present they are not so placed.
† See chap. 248.

undetermined masses, making choice, for that purpose, of cloudy weather, or towards the evening, and avoiding, as was said before, to mark the lights and shadows too strong on the extremities; because they would in that case appear like spots of difficult execution, and without grace. He ought to remember, that the shadows are never to be of such a quality as to obliterate the proper colour in which they originated, if the situation of the coloured body be not in total darkness. He ought to mark no outline, not to make the hair stringy, and not to touch with pure white any but those things which in themselves are white; in short, the lightest touch upon any particular object ought to denote the beauty of its proper and natural colour.

247.—The Surface of all opaque Bodies participates of the Colour of the surrounding Objects.

The painter ought to know, that if any white object is placed between two walls, one of which is also white, and the other black, there will be found between the shady side of that object and the light side, a similar proportion to that of the two walls; and if that object be blue, the effect will be the same. Having therefore to paint this object, take some black, similar to that of the wall from which the reflexes come; and to proceed by a certain and scientific method, do as follows: When you paint the wall, take a small spoon to measure exactly the quantity of colour you mean to employ in mixing your tints; for instance, if you have put in the shading of this wall three spoonfuls of pure black and one of white, you have, without any doubt, a mixture of a certain and precise quality. Now, having painted one of the walls white, and the other dark, if you mean to place a blue object between them with shades suitable to that colour, place first on your pallet the light blue, such as you mean it to be, without any mixture of shade, and it will do for the lightest part of your object. After which take three spoonfuls of black, and one of this light blue, for your darkest shades. Then observe whether your object be round or square: if it be square, these two extreme tints of light and shade

H

will be close to each other, cutting sharply at the angle; but if it be round, draw lines from the extremities of the walls to the centre of the object, and put the darkest shade between equal angles, where the lines intersect upon the superficies of it; then begin to make them lighter and lighter gradually to the point N O, lessening the strength of the shadows as much as that place participates of the light A D, and mixing that colour with the darkest shade A B in the same proportion.

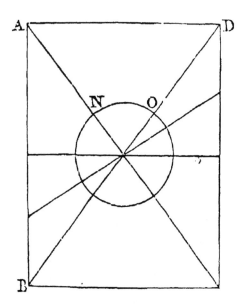

248.—*General Remarks on Colours.*

Blue and green are not simple colours in their nature, for blue is composed of light and darkness; such is the azure of the sky, viz., perfect black and perfect white. Green is composed of a simple and a mixed colour, being produced by blue and yellow.

Any object seen in a mirror, will participate of the colour of that body which serves as a mirror; and the mirror in its turn is tinged in part by the colour of the object it represents; they partake more or less of each other as the colour of the object seen is more or less strong than the colour of the mirror. That object will appear of the strongest and most lively colour in the mirror, which has the most affinity to the colour of the mirror itself.

Of coloured bodies, the purest white will be seen at the greatest distance, therefore the darker the colour, the less it will bear distance.

Of different bodies equal in whiteness, and in distance from the eye, that which is surrounded by the greatest darkness will appear the whitest; and on the contrary, that shadow will appear the darkest which has the brightest white round it.

Of different colours equally perfect, that will appear most excellent which is seen near its direct contrary: a pale colour against red; a black upon white (though neither the one nor the other are colours); blue near a yellow; green near red: because each colour is more distinctly seen, when opposed to its contrary, than to any other similar to it.

Anything white seen in a dense air full of vapours, will appear larger than it is in reality.

The air between the eye and the object seen will change the colour of that object into its own; so will the azure of the air change the distant mountains into blue masses. Through a red glass everything appears red; the light round the stars is dimmed by the darkness of the air, which fills the space between the eye and the planets.

The true colour of any object whatever will be seen in those parts which are not occupied by any kind of shade, and have not any gloss (if it be a polished surface).

I say, that white terminating abruptly upon a dark ground, will cause that part where it terminates to appear darker, and the white whiter.

COLOURS IN REGARD TO LIGHT AND SHADOW.

249.—Of the Light proper for painting Flesh Colour from Nature.

YOUR window must be open to the sky, and the walls painted of a reddish colour. The summer-time is the best when the clouds conceal the sun, or else your walls on the south side of the room must be so high, as that the sunbeams cannot strike on the opposite side, in order that the reflection of those beams may not destroy the shadows.

250.—*Of the Painter's Window.*

The window which gives light to a painting room, ought to be made of oiled paper, without any cross bar, or projecting edge at the opening, or any sharp angle in the inside of the wall, but should be slanting by degrees the whole thickness of it; and the sides be painted black.

251.—*The Shadows of Colours.*

The shadows of any colour whatever must participate of that colour more or less, as it is nearer to, or more remote from, the mass of shadows; and also in proportion to its distance from, or proximity to, the mass of light.

252.—*Of the Shadows of White.*

To any white body receiving the light from the sun, or the air, the shadows should be of a bluish cast; because white is no colour, but a receiver of all colours; and as by the fourth proposition * we learn that the surface of any object participates of the colours of other objects near it, it is evident that a white surface will participate of the colour of the air by which it is surrounded.

* See chap. 274.

253.—*Which of the Colours will produce the darkest Shade.*

That shade will be the darkest which is produced by the whitest surface; this also will have a greater propensity to variety than any other surface; because white is not properly a colour, but a receiver of colours, and its surface will participate strongly of the colour of surrounding objects, but principally of black or any other dark colour, which being the most opposite to its nature, produces the most sensible difference between the shadows and the lights.

254.—*How to manage when a White terminates upon another White.*

When one white body terminates on another of the same colour, the white of these two bodies will be either alike or not. If they be alike, that object which of the two is nearest to the eye, should be made a little darker than the other, upon the rounding of the outline; but if the object which serves as a ground to the other be not quite so white, the latter will detach of itself, without the help of any darker termination.

255.—*On the Backgrounds of Figures.*

Of two objects equally light, one will appear less so if seen upon a whiter ground; and, on the contrary, it will appear a great deal lighter if upon a space of a darker shade. So flesh colour will appear pale upon a red ground and a pale colour will appear redder upon a yellow ground. In short, colours will appear what they are not, according to the ground which surrounds them.

256.—*The Mode of composing History.*

Amongst the figures which compose an historical picture, those which are meant to appear the nearest to the eye must have the greatest force; according to the second proposition* of the third book, which says, that colour will be seen in the greatest perfection which has less air interposed between it and the eye of the beholder; and for that reason the shadows (by which we express the relievo of bodies) appear darker when near than when at a distance, being then deadened by the air which interposes. This does not happen to those shadows which are near the eye, where they will produce the greatest relievo when they are darkest.

257.—*Remarks concerning Lights and Shadows.*

Observe, that where the shadows end, there be always a kind of half-shadow to blend them with the lights. The shadow derived from any object will mix more with the light at its termination, in proportion as it is more distant from that object. But the colour of the shadow will never be simple; this is proved by the ninth proposition,† which says, that the superficies of any object participates of the colours of other bodies, by which it is surrounded, although it were transparent, such as water, air, and the like: because the air receives its light from the sun, and darkness is produced by the privation of it. But as the air has no colour in itself, any more than water, it receives all the colours that are between the object and the eye. The vapours mixing with the air in the lower regions near the earth, render it thick, and apt to reflect the sun's rays on all sides, while the air above remains dark; and because light (that is, white) and darkness (that is, black), mixed

---

* Although the author seems to have designed that this, and many other propositions to which he refers, should have formed a part of some regular work, and he has accordingly referred to them whenever he has mentioned them, by their intended numerical situation in that work, whatever it might be, it does not appear that he ever carried this design into execution. There are, however, several chapters in the present work, viz., 293, 289, 285, 295, in which the principle in the text is recognised, and which probably would have been transferred into the projected treatise, if he had ever drawn it up.

† The note on the preceding chapter is in a great measure applicable to this, and the proposition mentioned in the text is also to be found in chapter 247 of the present work.

together, compose the azure, that becomes the colour of the sky, which is lighter or darker in proportion as the air is more or less mixed with damp vapours.

258.—*Why the Shadows of Bodies upon a white Wall are bluish towards Evening.*

The shadows of bodies produced by the redness of the setting sun, will always be bluish. This is accounted for by the eleventh proposition,* which says, that the super-

ficies of any opaque body participates of the colour of the object from which it receives the light; therefore the white wall, being deprived entirely of colour, is tinged by the colour of those bodies from which it receives the light, which in this case are the sun and sky. But because the sun is red towards the evening, and the sky is blue, the shadow on the wall not being enlightened by the sun, receives only the reflection of the sky, and therefore will appear blue; and the rest of the wall, receiving light immediately from the sun, will participate of its red colour.

* See the note on the chapter next but one preceding. The proposition in the text occurs in chap. 247 of the present work.

259.—*Of the Colour of Faces.*

The colour of any object will appear more or less distinct
in proportion to the extent of its surface. This proposition
is proved, by observing that a face appears dark at a small
distance, because, being composed of many small parts, it
produces a great number of shadows; and the lights being
the smallest part of it, are soonest lost to the sight, leaving
only the shadows, which being in a greater quantity, the
whole of the face appears dark, and the more so if that
face has on the head, or at the back, something whiter.

260.—*A Precept relating to Painting.*

Where the shadows terminate upon the lights, observe
well what parts of them are lighter than the others, and
where they are more or less softened and blended; but
above all, remember, that young people have no sharp
shadings: their flesh is transparent, something like what
we observe when we put our hand between the sun and our
eyes; it appears reddish, and of a transparent brightness.
If you wish to know what kind of shadow will suit the
flesh colour you are painting, place one of your fingers
close to your picture, so as to cast a shadow upon it, and
according as you wish it either lighter or darker, put it
nearer or farther from it, and imitate it.

261.—*Of Colours in Shadow.*

It happens very often that the shadows of an opaque body
do not retain the same colour as the lights. Sometimes
they will be greenish, while the lights are reddish, although
this opaque body be all over of one uniform colour. This
happens when the light falls upon the object (we will
suppose from the east), and tinges that side with its own
colour. In the west we will suppose another opaque body
of a colour different from the first, but receiving the same
light. This last will reflect its colour towards the East,
and strike the first with its rays on the opposite side,
where they will be stopped, and remain with their full

colour and brightness. We often see a white object with red lights, and the shades of a bluish cast; this we observe particularly in mountains covered with snow, at sunset, when the effulgence of its rays makes the horizon appear all on fire.

262.—*Of the Choice of Lights.*

Whatever object you intend to represent is to be supposed situated in a particular light, and that entirely of your own choosing. If you imagine such objects to be in the country, and the sun be overcast, they will be surrounded by a great quantity of general light. If the sun strikes upon those objects, then the shadows will be very dark, in proportion to the lights, and will be determined and sharp; the primitive as well as the secondary ones. These shadows will vary from the lights in colour, because on that side the object receives a reflected light hue from the azure of the air, which tinges that part; and this is particularly observable in white objects. That side which receives the light from the sun, participates also of the colour of that. This may be particularly observed in the evening, when the sun is setting between the clouds, which it reddens; those clouds being tinged with the colour of the body illuminating them, the red colour of the clouds, with that of the sun, casts a hue on those parts which receive the light from them. On the contrary, those parts which are not turned towards that side of the sky, remain of the colour of the air, so that the former and the latter are of two different colours. This we must not lose sight of, that, knowing the cause of those lights and shades, it be made apparent in the effect, or else the work will be false and absurd. But if a figure be situated within a house, and seen from without, such figure will have its shadows very soft; and if the beholder stands in the line of the light, it will acquire grace, and do credit to the painter, as it will have great relief in the lights, and soft and well-blended shadows, particularly in those parts where the inside of the room appears less obscure, because there the shadows are almost imperceptible: the cause of which we shall explain in its proper place.

COLOURS IN REGARD TO BACKGROUNDS.

263.—*Of avoiding hard Outlines.*

Do not make the boundaries of your figures with any other colour than that of the background on which they are placed; that is, avoid making dark outlines.

264.—*Of Outlines.*

The extremities of objects which are at some distance, are not seen so distinctly as if they were nearer. Therefore the painter ought to regulate the strength of his outlines, or extremities, according to the distance.

The boundaries which separate one body from another, are of the nature of mathematical lines, but not of real lines. The end of any colour is only the beginning of another, and it ought not to be called a line, for nothing interposes between them, except the termination of the one against the other, which being nothing in itself, cannot be perceivable; therefore the painter ought not to pronounce it in distant objects.

265.—*Of Backgrounds.*

One of the principal parts of painting is the nature and quality of backgrounds, upon which the extremities of any convex or solid body will always detach and be distinguished in nature, though the colour of such objects, and that of the ground, be exactly the same. This happens, because the convex sides of solid bodies do not receive the light in the same manner with the ground, for such sides or extremities are often lighter or darker than the ground. But if such extremities were to be of the same colour as the ground, and in the same degree of light, they certainly could not be distinguished. Therefore such a choice in painting ought to be avoided by all intelligent and judicious painters; since the intention is to make the object appear

as it were. out of the ground. The above case would produce the contrary effect, not only in painting, but also in
objects of real relievo.

266.—*How to detach Figures from the Ground.*

All solid bodies will appear to have a greater relief, and
to come more out of the canvas, on a ground of an undetermined colour, with the greatest variety of lights and
shades against the confines of such bodies (as will be
demonstrated in its place), provided a proper diminution
of lights in the white tints, and of darkness in the shades,
be judiciously observed.

267.—*Of Uniformity and Variety of Colours upon plain Surfaces.*

The backgrounds of any flat surfaces which are uniform
in colour and quantity of light, will never appear separated
from each other; *vice versâ*, they will appear separated if
they are of different colours or lights.

268.—*Of Backgrounds suitable both to Shadows and Lights.*

The shadows or lights which surround figures, or any
other objects, will help the more to detach them the more
they differ from the objects; that is, if a dark colour does
not terminate upon another dark colour, but upon a very
different one; as white, or partaking of white, but lowered,
and approximated to the dark shade.

269.—*The apparent Variation of Colours, occasioned by the Contrast of the Ground upon which they are placed.*

No colour appears uniform and equal in all its parts,
unless it terminate on a ground of the same colour. This
is very apparent when a black terminates on a white
ground, where the contrast of colour gives more strength
and richness to the extremities than to the middle.

CONTRAST, HARMONY, AND REFLEXES, IN REGARD TO COLOURS.

270.—*Gradation in Painting.*

WHAT is fine is not always beautiful and good: I address this to such painters as are so attached to the beauty of colours, that they regret being obliged to give them almost imperceptible shadows, not considering the beautiful relief which figures acquire by a proper gradation and strength of shadows. Such persons may be compared to those speakers who in conversation make use of many fine words without meaning, which altogether scarcely form one good sentence.

271.—*How to assort Colours in such a Manner as that they may add Beauty to each other.*

If you mean that the proximity of one colour should give beauty to another that terminates near it, observe the rays of the sun in the composition of the rainbow, the colours of which are generated by the falling rain, when each drop in its descent takes every colour of that bow, as is demonstrated in its place.*

If you mean to represent great darkness, it must be done by contrasting it with great light; on the contrary, if you want to produce great brightness, you must oppose to it a very dark shade: so a pale yellow will cause red to appear more beautiful than if opposed to a purple colour.

There is another rule, by observing which, though you do not increase the natural beauty of the colours, yet by bringing them together they may give additional grace to each other, as green placed near red, while the effect would be quite the reverse, if placed near blue.

Harmony and grace are also produced by a judicious arrangement of colours, such as blue with pale yellow or white, and the like; as will be noticed in its place.

* Not in this work.

272.—*Of detaching the Figures.*

Let the colours of which the draperies of your figures are composed, be such as to form a pleasing variety, to distinguish one from the other; and although, for the sake of harmony, they should be of the same nature,* they must not stick together, but vary in point of light, according to the distance and interposition of the air between them. By the same rule, the outlines are to be more precise, or lost, in proportion to their distance or proximity.

273.—*Of the Colour of Reflexes.*

All reflected colours are less brilliant and strong than those which receive a direct light, in the same proportion as there is between the light of a body and the cause of that light.

274.—*What Body will be the most strongly tinged with the Colour of any other Object.*

An opaque surface will partake most of the genuine colour of the body nearest to it, because a great quantity of the species of colour will be conveyed to it; whereas such colour would be broken and disturbed if coming from a more distant object.

275.—*Of Reflexes.*

Reflexes will partake, more or less, both of the colour of the object which produces them, and of the colour of that

---

* I do not know a better comment on this passage than Felibien's Examination of Le Brun's Picture of the Tent of Darius. From this (which has been reprinted, with an English translation by Colonel Parsons, in 1700, in folio,) it will clearly appear, what the chain of connection is between every colour there used and its nearest neighbour, and consequently a rule may be formed from it with more certainty and precision than where the student is left to develop it for himself, from the mere inspection of different examples of colouring.

object on which they are produced, in proportion as this latter body is of a smoother or more polished surface than that by which they are produced.

276.—*Of the Surface of all shadowed Bodies.*

The surface of any opaque body placed in shadow, will participate of the colour of any other object which reflects the light upon it. This is very evident; for if such bodies were deprived of light in the space between them and the other bodies, they could not show either shape or colour. We shall conclude then, that if the opaque body be yellow, and that which reflects the light blue, the part reflected will be green, because green is composed of blue and yellow.

277.—*That no reflected Colour is simple, but is mixed with the nature of the other Colours.*

No colour reflected upon the surface of another body, will tinge that surface with its own colour alone, but will be mixed by the concurrence of other colours also reflected

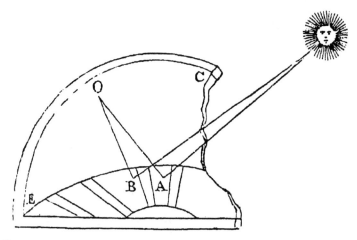

on the same spot. Let us suppose A to be of a yellow colour, which is reflected on the convex C O E, and that the blue colour B be reflected on the same place. I say that a mixture of the blue and yellow colours will tinge the convex surface; and that, if the ground be white, it will produce a green reflection, because it is proved that a mixture of blue and yellow produces a very fine green.

278.—*Of the Colour of Lights and Reflexes.*

When two lights strike upon an opaque body, they can vary only in two ways; either they are equal in strength, or they are not. If they be equal, they may still vary in two other ways, that is, by the equality or inequality of their brightness: they will be equal, if their distance be the same; and unequal, if it be otherwise. The object placed at an equal distance, between two equal lights, in point both of colour and brightness, may still be enlightened by them in two different ways, either equally on each side, or unequally. It will be equally enlightened by them, when the space which remains round the lights shall be equal in colour, in degree of shade, and in brightness. It will be unequally enlightened by them when the spaces happen to be of different degrees of darkness.

279.—*Why reflected Colours seldom partake of the Colour of the Body where they meet.*

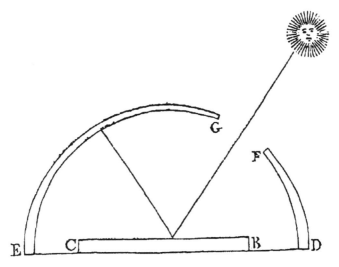

It happens very seldom that the reflexes are of the same colour with the body from which they proceed, or with that upon which they meet. To exemplify this, let the convex body D F G E be of a yellow colour, and the body B C, which reflects its colour on it, blue; the part of the convex surface which is struck by that reflected light will take a green tinge, being B C, acted on by the natural light of the air or the sun.

280.— *The Reflexes of Flesh Colours.*

The lights upon the flesh colours, which are reflected by the light striking upon another flesh-coloured body, are redder and more lively than any other part of the human figure; and that happens according to the third proposition of the second book,* which says, the surface of any opaque body participates of the colour of the object which reflects that light in proportion as it is near to or remote from it, and also in proportion to the size of it; because, being large, it prevents the variety of colours in smaller objects round it, from interfering with, and discomposing the principal colour, which is nearer. Nevertheless, it does not prevent its participating more of the colour of a small object near it, than of a large one more remote. See the sixth proposition † of perspective, which says, that large objects may be situated at such a distance as to appear less than small ones that are near.

281.—*Of the Nature of Comparison.*

Black draperies will make the flesh of the human figure appear whiter than in reality it is ; ‡ and white draperies, on the contrary, will make it appear darker. Yellow will render it higher coloured, while red will make it pale.

---

* See chapters 223, 237, 274, 282, of the present work. We have before remarked, that the propositions so frequently referred to by the author, were never reduced into form, though apparently he intended a regular work in which they were to be included.

† Nowhere in this work.

‡ This is evident in many of Vandyke's portraits, particularly of ladies, many of whom are dressed in black velvet; and this remark will in some measure account for the delicate fairness which he frequently gives to the female complexion.

282.—*Where the Reflexes are seen.*

Of all reflections of the same shape, size, and strength, that will be more or less strong which terminates on a ground more or less dark.

The surface of those bodies will partake most of the colour of the object that reflects it, which receive that reflection by the most nearly equal angles.

Of the colours of objects reflected upon any opposite surface by equal angles, that will be the most distinct which has its reflecting ray the shortest.

Of all colours, reflected under equal angles, and at equal distance upon the opposite body, those will be the strongest which come reflected by the lightest coloured body.

The object will reflect its own colour most precisely on the opposite object, which has not round it any colour that clashes with its own; and consequently that reflected colour will be most confused which takes its origin from a variety of bodies of different colours.

That colour which is nearest the opposed object will tinge it the most strongly; and *vice versâ*: let the painter, therefore, in his reflexes on the human body, particularly on the flesh colour, mix some of the colour of the drapery which comes nearest to it; but not pronounce it too distinctly, if there be not good reason for it.

PERSPECTIVE OF COLOURS.

283.—*A Precept of Perspective in regard to Painting.*

WHEN, on account of some particular quality of the air, you can no longer distinguish the difference between the lights and shadows of objects, you may reject the perspective of shadows, and make use only of the linear perspective, and the diminution of colours, to lessen the knowledge of the objects opposed to the eye; and this, that is to say, the loss of the knowledge of the figure of each object, will make the same object appear more remote.

The eye can never arrive at a perfect knowledge of the interval between two objects variously distant by means of the linear perspective alone, if not assisted by the perspective of colours.

284.—*Of the Perspective of Colours.*

The air will participate less of the azure of the sky, in proportion as it comes nearer to the horizon, as it is proved by the third and ninth proposition,* that pure and subtile bodies (such as compose the air) will be less illuminated by the sun than those of thicker and grosser substance: and as it is certain that the air which is remote from the earth is thinner than that which is near it, it will follow, that the latter will be more impregnated with the rays of the sun, which giving light at the same time to an infinity of atoms floating in this air, renders it more sensible to the eye. So that the air will appear lighter towards the horizon, and darker as well as bluer in looking up to the sky; because there is more of the thick air between our eyes and the horizon, than between our eyes and that part of the sky above our heads.

* These propositions, any more than the others, mentioned in different parts of this work, were never digested into a regular treatise, as was evidently intended by the author, and consequently are not to be found, except perhaps in some of the volumes of the author's manuscript collections.

For instance : if the eye placed in P looks through the air along the line P R, and then lowers itself a little along

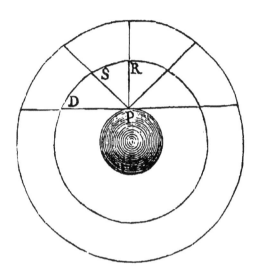

P S, the air will begin to appear a little whiter, because there is more of the thick air in this space than in the first. And if it be still removed lower, so as to look straight at the horizon, no more of that blue sky will be perceived which was observable along the first line P R, because there is a much greater quantity of thick air along the horizontal line P D, than along the oblique P S, or the perpendicular P R.

285.—*The Cause of the Diminution of Colours.*

The natural colour of any visible object will be diminished in proportion to the density of any other substance which interposes between that object and the eye.

286.—*Of the Diminution of Colours and Objects.*

Let the colours vanish in proportion as the objects diminish in size, according to the distance.

287.—Of the Variety observable in Colours, according to their
          Distance or Proximity.

The local colour of such objects as are darker than the
air, will appear less dark as they are more remote; and, on
the contrary, objects lighter than the air will lose their
brightness in proportion to their distance from the eye.
In general, all objects that are darker or lighter than the
air, are discoloured by distance, which changes their
quality so that the lighter appears darker, and the darker
lighter.

288.—At what Distance Colours are entirely lost.

Local colours are entirely lost at a greater or less distance,
according as the eye and the object are more or less elevated
from the earth. This is proved by the seventh proposition,*
which says the air is more or less pure, as it is near to, or
remote from the earth. If the eye, then, and the object
are near the earth, the thickness of the air which interposes, will in a great measure confuse the colour of that
object to the eye. But if the eye and the object are placed
high above the earth, the air will disturb the natural colour
of that object very little. In short, the various gradations
of colour depend not only on the various distances, in
which they may be lost; but also on the variety of lights,
which change according to the different hours of the day,
and the thickness or purity of the air through which the
colour of the object is conveyed to the eye.

289.—Of the Change observable in the same Colour, according
          to its Distance from the Eye.

Among several colours of the same nature, that which
is the nearest to the eye will alter the least; because the
air which interposes between the eye and the object seen,
envelopes, in some measure, that object. If the air which
interposes be in great quantity, the object seen will be

* See chapters 293, 307, 308.

strongly tinged with the colour of that air; but if the air be thin, then the view of that object, and its colour, will be very little obstructed.

290.—*Of the bluish Appearance of remote Objects in a Landscape.*

Whatever be the colour of distant objects, the darkest, whether natural or accidental, will appear the most tinged with azure. By the natural darkness is meant the proper colour of the object; the accidental one is produced by the shadow of some other body.

291.—*Of the Qualities in the Surface which first lose themselves by Distance.*

The first part of any colour which is lost by the distance is the gloss, being the smallest part of it, as a light within a light. The second that diminishes by being farther removed, is the light, because it is less in quantity than the shadow. The third is the principal shadows, nothing remaining at last but a kind of middling obscurity.

292.—*From what Cause the Azure of the Air proceeds.*

The azure of the sky is produced by the transparent body of the air, illumined by the sun, and interposed between the darkness of the expanse above, and the earth below. The air in itself has no quality of smell, taste, or colour, but is easily impregnated with the quality of other matter surrounding it; and will appear bluer in proportion to the darkness of the space behind it, as may be observed against the shady sides of mountains, which are darker than any other object. In this instance the air appears of the most beautiful azure; while on the other side, that receives the light, it shows through that more of the natural colour of the mountain.

293.—*Of the Perspective of Colours.*

The same colour being placed at various distances and equal elevation, the force and effect of its colouring will be according to the proportion of the distance which there is from each of these colours to the eye.   It is proved thus :

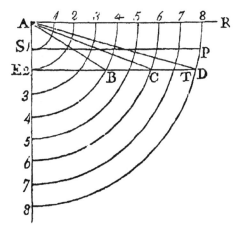

let A B E D be one and the same colour.   The first, E, is placed at two degrees of distance from the eye A; the second, B, shall be four degrees; the third, C, six degrees; and the fourth, D, eight degrees; as appears by the circle which terminate upon and intersect the line A R.   Let us suppose that the space A R, S P, is one degree of thin air, and S P E T another degree of thicker air.   It will follow, that the first colour, E, will pass to the eye through one degree of thick air, E S, and through another degree, S A, of thinner air.   And B will send its colour to the eye in A, through two degrees of thick air, and through two others of the thinner sort.   C will send it through three degrees of the thin, and three of the thick sort, while D goes through four degrees of the one, and four of the other. This demonstrates, that the gradation of colours is in proportion to their distance from the eye.*   But this happens only to those colours which are on a level with

* See chap. 287.

the eye; as for those which happen to be at unequal elevations, we cannot observe the same rule, because they are in
that case situated in different qualities of air, which alter
and diminish these colours in various manners.

294.—*Of the Perspective of Colours in dark Places.*

In any place where the light diminishes in a gradual
proportion, till it terminates in total darkness, the colours
also will lose themselves and be dissolved in proportion as
they recede from the eye.

295.—*Of the Perspective of Colours.*

The principal colours, or those nearest to the eye, should
be pure and simple; and the degree of their diminution
should be in proportion to their distance, viz., the nearer
they are to the principal point, the more they will possess
of the purity of those colours, and they will partake of the
colour of the horizon in proportion as they approach to it.

296.—*Of Colours.*

Of all the colours which are not blue, those that are
nearest to black will, when distant, partake most of the
azure; and, on the contrary, those will preserve their
proper colour at the greatest distance, that are most
dissimilar to black.

The green, therefore, of the fields will change sooner into
blue than yellow or white, which will preserve their
natural colour at a greater distance than that, or even red.

297.—*How it happens that Colours do not change, though placed in different Qualities of Air.*

The colour will not be subject to any alteration when the
distance and the quality of air have a reciprocal proportion.
What it loses by the distance it regains by the purity of
the air, viz., if we suppose the first or lowest air to have
four degrees of thickness, and the colour to be at one

degree from the eye; and the second air above to have
three degrees; the air having lost one degree of thickness, the colour will acquire one degree upon the distance.
And when the air still higher shall have lost two degrees
of thickness, the colour will acquire as many upon the
distance; and in that case the colour will be the same at
three degrees as at one.   But to be brief, if the colour be
raised so high as to enter that quality of air which has lost
three degrees of thickness, and acquired three degrees of
distance, then you may be certain that that colour which
is high and remote, has lost no more than the colour which
is below and nearer; because in rising it has acquired
those three degrees which it was losing by the same
distance from the eye; and this is what was meant to be
proved.

298.—*Why Colours experience no apparent Change, though placed in different Qualities of Air.*

It may happen that a colour does not alter, though
placed at different distances, when the thickness of the air
and the distance are in the same inverse proportion.   It is
proved thus:—let A be the eye, and H any colour what-

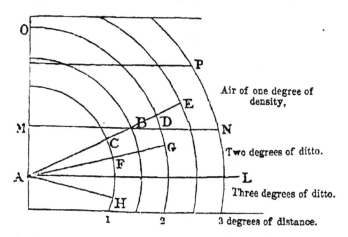

ever, placed at one degree of distance from the eye, in a
quality of air of four degrees of thickness; but because the

second degree above, A M N L, contains a thinner air by one-half, which air conveys this colour, it follows that this colour will appear as if removed double the distance it was at before, viz., at two degrees of distance, A F and F G, from the eye; and it will be placed in G. If that is raised to the second degree of air A M N L, and to the degree O M, P N, it will necessarily be placed at E, and will be removed from the eye the whole length of the line A E, which will be proved in this manner to be equal in thickness to the distance A G. If in the same quality of air the distance A G interposed between the eye and the colour occupies two degrees and a half, it is sufficient to preserve the colour G, when raised to E, from any change, because the degree A C and the degree A F being the same in thickness, are equal and alike, and the degree C D, though equal in length to the degree F G, is not alike in point of thickness of air; because half of it is situated in a degree of air of double the thickness of the air above: this half degree of distance occupies as much of the colour as one whole degree of the air above would, which air above is twice as thin as the air below, with which it terminates; so that by calculating the thickness of the air, and the distances, you will find that the colours have changed places without undergoing any alteration in their beauty. And we shall prove it thus: reckoning first the thickness of the air, the colour H is placed in four degrees of thickness, the colour G in two degrees, and E at one degree. Now let us see whether the distances are in an equal inverse proportion; the colour E is at two degrees and a half of distance, G at two degrees, and H at one degree. But as this distance has not an exact proportion with the thickness of the air, it is necessary to make a third calculation in this manner: A C is perfectly like and equal to A F; the half degree C B, is like but not equal to A F, because it is only half a degree in length, which is equal to a whole degree of the quality of the air above; so that by this calculation we shall solve the question. For A C is equal to two degrees of thickness of the air above, and the half degree C B is equal to a whole degree of the same air above; and one degree more is to be taken in, viz., B E, which makes the fourth. A H has four degrees of thickness of air, A G also four, viz., A F two in value, and F G also two, which taken together make four. A E has also four, because A C contains two, and C D one, which is the half of A C, and in the same quality of air; and there is a whole degree above in the thin air, which altogether make four. So that if A E is not double the distance A G, nor four times the distance A H, it is equivalent by the half degree C B of thick air, which is equal to a whole degree of thin air above. This proves the truth of the proposition, that the colour H G E does not undergo any alteration by these different distances.

299.—*Contrary Opinions in regard to Objects seen afar off.*

Many painters will represent the objects darker, in proportion as they are removed from the eye; but this cannot be true, unless the objects seen be white; as shall be examined in the next chapter.

300.—*Of the Colour of Objects remote from the Eye.*

The air tinges objects with its own colour more or less in proportion to the quantity of intervening air between it and the eye, so that a dark object at the distance of two miles (or a density of air equal to such distance), will be more tinged with its colour than if only one mile distant.

It is said, that, in a landscape, trees of the same species appear darker in the distance than near; this cannot be true, if they be of equal size, and divided by equal spaces. But it will be so if the first trees are scattered, and the light of the fields is seen through and between them, while the others which are farther off, are thick together, as is often the case near some river or other piece of water: in this case no space of light fields can be perceived, but the trees appear thick together, accumulating the shadow on each other. It also happens, that as the shady parts of plants are much broader than the light ones, the colour of the plants, becoming darker by the multiplied shadows, is preserved, and conveyed to the eye more strongly than that of the other parts; these masses, therefore, will carry the strongest parts of their colour to a greater distance.

301.—*Of the Colour of Mountains.*

The darker the mountain is in itself, the bluer it will appear at a great distance. The highest part will be the darkest, as being more woody; because woods cover a great many shrubs, and other plants, which never receive any light. The wild plants of those woods are also naturally of a darker hue than cultivated plants; for oak, beech, fir, cypress, and pine trees are much darker than olive and other domestic plants. Near the top of these mountains, where the air is thinner and purer, the darkness of the woods will make it appear of a deeper azure than at the bottom, where the air is thicker. A plant will detach very little from the ground it stands upon, if that ground be of a colour something similar to its own; and, *vice versá*, that part of any white object which is nearest to a dark one, will appear the whitest, and the less so as it is removed from it; and any dark object will appear darker, the nearer it is to a white one; and less so, if removed from it.

302.—*Why the Colour and Shape of Objects are lost in some Situations apparently dark, though not so in Reality.*

There are some situations which, though light, appear dark, and in which objects are deprived both of form and colour. This is caused by the great light which pervades the intervening air; as is observable by looking in through a window at some distance from the eye, when nothing is seen but a uniform darkish shade; but if we enter the house, we shall find that room to be full of light, and soon distinguish every small object contained within that window. This difference of effect is produced by the great brightness of the air, which contracts considerably the pupil of the eye, and by so doing diminishes its power. But in dark places the pupil is enlarged, and acquires as much in strength as it increases in size. This is proved in my second proposition of perspective.*

* This book on perspective was never drawn up.

303.—*Various Precepts in Painting.*

The termination and shape of the parts in general are very little seen, either in great masses of light, or of shadows; but those which are situated between the extremes of light and shade are the most distinct.

Perspective, as far as it extends in regard to painting, is divided into three principal parts; the first consists in the diminution of size according to distance; the second concerns the diminution of colours in such objects; and the third treats of the diminution of the perception altogether of those objects, and of the degree of precision they ought to exhibit at various distances.

The azure of the sky is produced by a mixture composed of light and darkness;[*] I say of light, because of the moist particles floating in the air, which reflect the light. By darkness, I mean the pure air, which has none of these extraneous particles to stop and reflect the rays. Of this we see an example in the air interposed between the eye and some dark mountains, rendered so by the shadows of an innumerable quantity of trees; or else shaded on one side by the natural privation of the rays of the sun: this air becomes azure, but not so on the side of the mountain which is light, particularly when it is covered with snow.

Among objects of equal darkness and equal distance, those will appear darker that terminate upon a lighter ground, and *vice versâ*.[†]

That object which is painted with the most white and the most black, will show greater relief than any other; for that reason I would recommend to painters to colour and dress their figures with the brightest and most lively colours; for if they are painted of a dull or obscure colour, they will detach but little, and not be much seen, when the picture is placed at some distance, because the colour of every object is obscured in the shades; and if it be represented as originally so all over, there will be but little difference between the lights and the shades, while lively colours will show a striking difference.

* See chap. 292.   † See chapters 212, 248, 255.

AERIAL PERSPECTIVE.

304.—*Aerial Perspective.*

THERE is another kind of perspective, called aerial, because by the difference of the air it is easy to determine the distance of different objects, though seen on the same line; such, for instance, as buildings behind a wall, and appearing all of the same height above it. If in your picture you want to have one appear more distant than another, you must first suppose the air somewhat thick; because, as we have said before, in such a kind of air the objects seen at a great distance, as mountains are, appear bluish like the air, by means of the great quantity of air that interposes between the eye and such mountains. You will then paint the first building behind that wall of its proper colour; the next in point of distance, less distinct in the outline, and participating, in a greater degree, of the bluish colour of the air; another, which you wish to send off as much farther, should be painted as much bluer; and if you wish one of them to appear five times farther removed beyond the wall, it must have five times more of the azure. By this rule, these buildings which appeared all of the same size, and upon the same line, will be distinctly perceived to be of different dimensions, and at different distances.

305.—*The Parts of the smallest Objects will first disappear in Painting.*

Of objects receding from the eye the smallest will be first lost to the sight; from which it follows, that the largest will be the last to disappear. The painter, therefore, ought not to finish the parts of those objects which are very far off, but follow the rule given in the sixth book.*

How many, in the representation of towns, and other

* There is no work of this author to which this can at present refer, but the principle is laid down in chapters 274, 306, of the present treatise.

objects remote from the eye, express every part of the
buildings in the same manner as if they were very near.
It is not so in Nature, because there is no sight so powerful
as to perceive distinctly at any great distance the precise
form of parts or extremities of objects.   The painter, therefore, who pronounces the outlines, and the minute distinction of parts, as several have done, will not give the
representation of distant objects, but by this error will
make them appear exceedingly near.   Again, the angles
of buildings in distant towns are not to be expressed (for
they cannot be seen), considering that angles are formed
by the concurrence of two lines into one point, and that a
point has no parts ; it is therefore invisible.

306.—*Small Figures ought not to be too much finished.*

Objects appear smaller than they really are when they
are distant from the eye, and because there is a great deal
of air interposed, which weakens the appearance of forms,
and, by a natural consequence, prevents our seeing distinctly the minute parts of such objects.   It behoves the
painter, therefore, to touch those parts slightly, in an unfinished manner; otherwise it would be against the effect
of Nature, whom he has chosen for his guide.   For, as we
said before, objects appear small on account of their great
distance from the eye; that distance includes a great
quantity of air, which, forming a dense body, obstructs
the light, and prevents our seeing the minute parts of
the objects.

307.—*Why the Air is to appear whiter as it approaches nearer to the Earth.*

As the air is thicker nearer the earth, and becomes
thinner as it rises, look, when the sun is in the east,
towards the west, between the north and south, and you
will perceive that the thickest and lowest air will receive
more light from the sun than the thinner air, because its
beams meet with more resistance.

If the sky terminate low, at the end of a plain, that part of it nearest to the horizon, being seen only through the thick air, will alter and break its natural colour, and will appear whiter than over your head, where the visual ray does not pass through so much of that gross air, corrupted by earthy vapours. But if you turn towards the east, the air will be darker the nearer it approaches the earth; for the air being thicker, does not admit the light of the sun to pass so freely.

308.—*How to paint the distant Part of a Landscape.*

It is evident that the air is in some parts thicker and grosser than in others, particularly that nearest to the earth; and as it rises higher, it becomes thinner and more transparent. The objects which are high and large, from which you are at some distance, will be less apparent in the lower parts; because the visual ray which perceives them, passes through a long space of dense air; and it is easy to prove that the upper parts are seen by a line, which, though on the side of the eye it originates in a thick air, nevertheless, as it ascends to the highest summit of its object, terminates in an air much thinner than that of the lower parts; and for that reason the more that line or visual ray advances from the eye, it becomes, in its progress from one point to another, thinner and thinner, passing from a pure air into another which is purer; so that a painter who has mountains to represent in a landscape, ought to observe, that from one hill to another, the tops will appear always clearer than the bases. In proportion as the distance from one to another is greater, the top will be clearer; and the higher they are, the more they will show their variety of form and colour.

309.—*Of precise and confused Objects.*

The parts that are near in the foreground should be finished in a bold determined manner; but those in the distance must be unfinished, and confused in their outlines.

310.—*Of distant Objects.*

That part of any object which is nearest to the luminary from which it receives the light, will be the lightest.

The representation of an object in every degree of distance, loses degrees of its strength; that is, in proportion as the object is more remote from the eye it will be less perceivable through the air in its representation.

311.—*Of Buildings seen in a thick Air.*

That part of a building seen through a thick air, will appear less distinct than another part seen through a thinner air. Therefore the eye N, looking at the tower

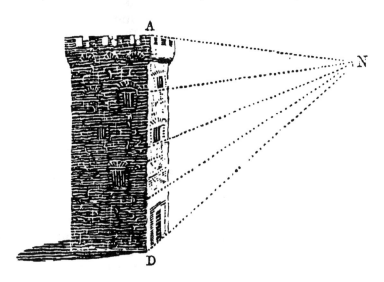

A D, will see it more confusedly in the lower degrees, but at the same time lighter; and as it ascends to the other degrees it will appear more distinct, but somewhat darker.

312.—*Of Towns and other Objects seen through a thick Air.*

Buildings or towns seen through a fog, or the air made thick by smoke or other vapours, will appear less distinct

the lower they are; and, *vice versâ*, they will be sharper
and more visible in proportion as they are higher. We
have said in chapter 321 that the air is thicker the
lower it is, and thinner as it is higher. It is demonstrated
also by the cut, where the tower A F is seen by the eye

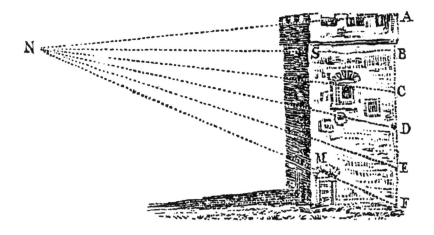

N, in a thick air, from B to F, which is divided into four
degrees, growing thicker as they are nearer the bottom.
The less the quantity of air interposed between the eye and
its object is, the less also will the colour of the object
participate of the colour of that air. It follows, that the
greater the quantity of air interposed between the eye and
the object seen is, the more this object will participate of
the colour of the air. It is demonstrated thus: N being
the eye looking at the five parts of the tower A F, viz.
A B C D E, I say, that if the air were of the same thickness, there would be the same proportion between the
colour of the air at the bottom of the tower and the colour
of the air that the same tower has at the place B, as there
is in length between the line M and F. As, however, we
have supposed that the air is not of equal thickness, but,
on the contrary, thicker as it is lower, it follows, that the
proportion by which the air tinges the different elevations
of the tower B C F exceeds the proportion of the lines;
because the line M F, besides its being longer than the line

ᴋ

S B, passes by unequal degrees through a quality of air which is unequal in thickness.

313.—*Of the inferior Extremities of distant Objects.*

The inferior or lower extremities of distant objects are not so apparent as the upper extremities. This is observable in mountains and hills, the tops of which detach from the sides of other mountains behind. We see the tops of these more determined and distinctly than their bases; because the upper extremities are darker, being less encompassed by thick air, which always remains in the lower regions, and makes them appear dim and confused. It is the same with trees, buildings, and other objects high up. From this effect it often happens that a high tower, seen at a great distance, will appear broad at top, and narrow at bottom; because the thin air towards the top does not prevent the angles on the sides and other different parts of the tower from being seen, as the thick air does at the bottom. This is demonstrated by the seventh proposition,* which says, that the thick air interposed between the eye and the sun is lighter below than above, and where the air is whitish it confuses the dark objects more than if such air were bluish or thinner, as it is higher up. The battlements of a fortress have the spaces between equal to the breadth of the battlement, and yet the space will appear wider; at a great distance the battlements will appear very much diminished, and being removed still farther, will disappear entirely, and the fort show only the straight wall, as if there were no battlements.

314.—*Which Parts of Objects disappear first by being removed farther from the Eye, and which preserve their Appearance.*

The smallest parts are those which, by being removed, lose their appearance first. This may be observed in the gloss upon spherical bodies, or columns, and the slender

* See chapters 307, 322.

parts of animals; as in a stag, the first sight of which does not discover its legs and horns so soon as its body, which, being broader, will be perceived from a greater distance. But the parts which disappear the very first, are the lines which describe the members, and terminate the surface and shape of bodies.

315.—*Why Objects are less distinguished in proportion as they are farther removed from the Eye.*

This happens because the smallest parts are lost first; the second, in point of size, are also lost at a somewhat greater distance, and so on successively; the parts by degrees melting away, the perception of the object is diminished; and at last all the parts, and the whole, are entirely lost to the sight.* Colours also disappear on account of the density of the air interposed between the eye and the object.

316.—*Why Faces appear dark at a distance.*

It is evident that the similitude of all objects placed before us, large as well as small, is perceptible to our senses through the iris of the eye. If through so small an entrance the immensity of the sky and of the earth is admitted, the faces of men (which are scarcely anything in comparison of such large objects), being still diminished by the distance, will occupy so little of the eye, that they become almost imperceptible. Besides, having to pass through a dark medium from the surface to the *Retina* in the inside, where the impression is made, the colour of faces (not being very strong, and rendered still more obscure by the darkness of the tube), when arrived at the focus appears dark. No other reason can be given on that point, except that the speck in the middle of the apple of the eye is black, and, being full of a transparent fluid like

* See chapters 116, 121, 305.

air, performs the same office as a hole in a board, which on looking into it appears black; and that those things which are seen through both a light and dark air, become confused and obscure.

317.—Of Towns and other Buildings seen through a Fog in the Morning or Evening.

Buildings seen afar off in the morning or in the evening, when there is a fog or thick air, show only those parts distinctly which are enlightened by the sun towards the horizon; and the parts of those buildings which are not turned towards the sun remain confused and almost of the colour of the fog.

318.—Of the Height of Buildings seen in a Fog.

Of a building near the eye the top parts will appear more confused than the bottom; because there is more fog between the eye and the top than at the base. And a square tower, seen at a great distance through a fog, will appear narrower at the base than at the summit. This is accounted for in chapter 313, which says, that the fog will appear whiter and thicker as it approaches the ground; and, as it is said before,* that a dark object will appear smaller in proportion as it is placed on a whiter ground. Therefore, the fog being whiter at bottom than at top, it follows that the tower (being darkish) will appear narrower at the base than at the summit.

319.—Why Objects which are high, appear darker at a Distance than those which are low, though the Fog be uniform, and of equal Thickness.

Amongst objects situated in a fog, thick air, vapour, smoke, or at a distance, the highest will be the most distinctly seen: and amongst objects equal in height,

* See chapters 313 and 323.

that placed in the darkest fog, will be most confused and dark. As it happens to the eye H, looking at A B C,

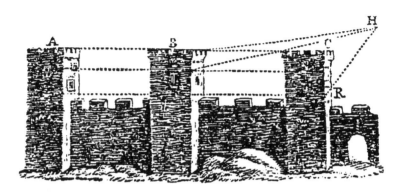

three towers of equal height: it sees the top C as low as R, in two degrees of thickness; and the top B, in one degree only; therefore the top C will appear darker than the top of the tower B.

320.—*Of Objects seen in a Fog.*

Objects seen through a fog will appear larger than they are in reality, because the aerial perspective does not agree with the linear, viz., the colour does not agree with the magnitude of the object;* such a fog being similar to the

---

* To our obtaining a correct idea of the magnitude and distance of any object seen from afar, it is necessary that we consider how much of distinctness an object loses at a distance (from the mere interposition of the air), as well as what it loses in size; and these two considerations must unite before we can decidedly pronounce as to its distance or magnitude. This calculation, as to distinctness, must be made upon the idea that the air is clear; as if by any accident it is otherwise, we shall (knowing the proportion in which clear air dims· a prospect) be led to conclude this farther off than it is, and, to justify that conclusion, shall suppose its real magnitude correspondent · with the distance, at which from its degree of distinctness it appears to be. In the circumstance remarked in the text there is, however, a great deception; the fact is, that the colour and the minute parts ·of the object are lost in the fog, while the size of it is not diminished in proportion; and the eye being accustomed to see objects diminished in size at a great distance, supposes this to be farther off than it is, and consequently imagines it larger.

thickness of air interposed between the eye and the horizon
in fine weather. But in this case the fog is near the eye,
and though the object be also near, it makes it appear as
if it were as far off as the horizon; where a great tower
would appear no bigger than a man placed near the eye.

321.—Of those Objects which the Eyes perceive through a Mist or thick Air.

The nearer the air is to water, or to the ground, the
thicker it becomes. It is proved by the nineteenth proposition of the second book,* that bodies rise in proportion
to their weight; and it follows, that a light body will
rise higher than another which is heavy.

322.—Miscellaneous Observations.

Of different objects equal in magnitude, form, shade,
and distance from the eye, those will appear the smaller
that are placed on the lighter ground. This is exemplified
by observing the sun when seen behind a tree without
leaves: all the ramifications seen against that great light
are so diminished that they remain almost invisible. The
same may be observed of a pole placed between the sun
and the eye.

Parallel bodies placed upright, and seen through a fog,
will appear larger at top than at bottom. This is proved
by the ninth proposition,† which says, that a fog or thick
air, penetrated by the rays of the sun, will appear whiter
the lower they are.

Things seen afar off will appear out of proportion,
because the parts which are the lightest will send their
image with stronger rays than the parts which are darkest.
I have seen a woman dressed in black, with a white veil
over her head, which appeared twice as large as her
shoulders covered with black.

---

* This proposition, though undoubtedly intended to form a part of
some future work, which never was drawn up, makes no part of the
present.

† See chap. 307.

MISCELLANEOUS OBSERVATIONS.

LANDSCAPE.

323.—*Of Objects seen at a Distance.*

ANY dark object will appear lighter when removed to some distance from the eye. It follows, by the contrary reason, that a dark object will appear still darker when brought nearer to the eye. Therefore the inferior parts of any object whatever, placed in thick air, will appear farther from the eye at the bottom than at the top; for that reason the lower parts of a mountain appear farther off than its top, which is in reality the farthest.

324.—*Of a Town seen through a thick Air.*

The eye which, looking downwards, sees a town immersed in very thick air, will perceive the top of the buildings darker, but more distinct than the bottom. The tops detach against a light ground, because they are seen against the low and thick air which is beyond them. This is a consequence of what has been explained in the preceding chapter.

325.—*How to draw a Landscape.*

Contrive that the trees in your landscape be half in shadow and half in the light. It is better to represent

them as when the sun is veiled with thin clouds, because
in that case the trees receive a general light from the sky,
and are darkest in those parts which are nearest to the
earth.

326.—Of the Green of the Country.

Of the greens seen in the country, that of trees and
other plants will appear darker than that of fields and
meadows, though they may happen to be of the same
quality.

327.—What Greens will appear most of a bluish Cast.

Those greens will appear to approach nearest to blue
which are of the darkest shade when remote. This is
proved by the seventh proposition,* which says, that blue
is composed of black and white seen at a great distance.

328.—The Colour of the Sea from different Aspects.

When the sea is a little ruffled it has no sameness of
colour; for, whoever looks at it from the shore, will see
it of a dark colour, in a greater degree as it approaches
towards the horizon, and will perceive also certain lights
moving slowly on the surface like a flock of sheep. Whoever looks at the sea from on board a ship, at a distance
from the land, sees it blue. Near the shore it appears
darkish, on account of the colour of the earth reflected by the
water, as in a looking-glass; but at sea the azure of the air
is reflected to the eye by the waves in the same manner.

329.—Why the same Prospect appears larger at some Times than at others.

Objects in the country appear sometimes larger and
sometimes smaller than they actually are, from the circumstance of the air interposed between the eye and the
horizon happening to be either thicker or thinner than
usual.

* Vide chapters 292, 303.

Of two horizons equally distant from the eye, that which is seen through the thicker air will appear farther removed; and the other will seem nearer, being seen through a thinner air.

Objects of unequal size, but equally distant, will appear equal if the air which is between them and the eye be of proportionable inequality of thickness, viz., if the thickest air be interposed between the eye and the smallest of the objects. This is proved by the perspective of colours,* which is so deceitful that a mountain which would appear small by the compasses, will seem larger than a small hill near the eye; as a finger placed near the eye will cover a large mountain far off.

330.—*Of Smoke.*

Smoke is more transparent, though darker, towards the extremities of its waves than in the middle.

It moves in a more oblique direction in proportion to the force of the wind which impels it.

Different kinds of smoke vary in colour, as the causes that produce them are various.

Smoke never produces determined shadows, and the extremities are lost as they recede from their primary cause. Objects behind it are less apparent in proportion to the thickness of the smoke. It is whiter nearer its origin, and bluer towards its termination.

Fire appears darker, the more smoke there is interposed between it and the eye.

Where smoke is farther distant, the objects are less confused by it.

It encumbers and dims all the landscape like a fog. Smoke is seen to issue from different places, with flames at the origin and the most dense part of it. The tops of mountains will be more seen than the lower parts, as in a fog.

331.—*In what part Smoke is lightest.*

Some which is seen between the sun and the eye will be lighter and more transparent than any other in the land-

* See chap. 298

scape. The same is observed of dust, and of fog; while, if you place yourself between the sun and those objects, they will appear dark.

332.—*Of the Sunbeams passing through the Openings of Clouds.*

The sunbeams which penetrate the openings interposed between clouds of various density and form, illuminate all the places over which they pass, and tinge with their own colour all the dark places that are behind: which dark places are only seen in the intervals between the rays.

333.—*Of the Beginning of Rain.*

When the rain begins to fall, it tarnishes and darkens the air, giving it a dull colour, but receives still on one side a faint light from the sun, and is shaded on the other side, as we observe in clouds; till at last it darkens also the earth, depriving it entirely of the light of the sun. Objects seen through the rain appear confused and of undetermined shape, but those which are near will be more distinct. It is observable, that on the side where the rain is shaded, objects will be more clearly distinguished than where it receives the light; because on the shady side they lose only their principal lights, whilst on the other they lose both their lights and shadows, the lights mixing with the light part of the rain, and the shadows are also considerably weakened by it.

334.—*The Seasons are to be observed.*

In autumn you will represent the objects according as it is more or less advanced. At the beginning of it the leaves of the oldest branches only begin to fade—more or less, however, according as the plant is situated in a fertile or barren country. And do not imitate those who represent trees of every kind (though at equal distance) with the same quality of green. Endeavour to vary the colour of meadows, stones, trunks of trees, and all other objects, as much as possible, for Nature abounds in variety *ad infinitum.*

335.—*The Difference of Climates to be observed.*

Near the sea-shore, and in southern parts, you will be careful not to represent the winter season by the appearance of trees and fields, as you would do in places more inland, and in northern countries, except when these are covered with evergreens, which shoot afresh all the year round.

336.—*Of Dust.*

Dust becomes lighter the higher it rises, and appears darker the less it is raised, when it is seen between the eye and the sun.

337.—*How to represent the Wind.*

In representing the effect of the wind, besides the bending of trees, and leaves twisting the wrong side upwards, you will also express the small dust whirling upwards till it mixes in a confused manner with the air.

338.—*Of a Wilderness.*

Those trees and shrubs which are by their nature more loaded with small branches, ought to be touched smartly in the shadows, but those which have larger foliage will cause broader shadows.

339.—*Of the Horizon seen in the Water.*

By the sixth proposition,* the horizon will be seen in the water as in a looking-glass, on that side which is opposite the eye. And if the painter has to represent a spot covered with water, let him remember that the colour of it cannot be either lighter or darker than that of the neighbouring objects.

---

* This was probably to have been a part of some other work, but it does not occur in this.

340.—*Of the Shadow of Bridges on the Surface of the Water.*

The shadows of bridges can never be seen on the surface of the water, unless it should have lost its transparent and reflecting quality, and become troubled and muddy; because clear water ·being polished and smooth on its surface, the image of the bridge is formed in it as in a looking-glass, and reflected in all the points situated between the eye and the bridge at equal angles; and even the air is seen under the arches. These circumstances cannot happen when the water is muddy, because it does not reflect the objects any longer, but receives the shadow of the bridge in the same manner as a dusty road would receive it.

341.—*How a Painter ought to put in Practice the Perspective of Colours.*

To put in practice that perspective which teaches the alteration, the lessening, and even the entire loss of the very essence of colours, you must take some points in the country at the distance of about sixty-five yards* from each other; as trees, men, or some other remarkable objects. In regard to the first tree, you will take a glass, and having fixed that well, and also your eye, draw upon it, with the greatest accuracy, the tree you see through it; then put it a little on one side, and compare it closely with the natural one, and colour it, so that in shape and colour it may resemble the original, and that by shutting one eye they may both appear painted, and at the same distance. The same rule may be applied to the second and third tree at the distance you have fixed. These studies will be very useful if managed with judgment, where they may be wanted in the offscape of a picture. I have observed that the second tree is less by four-fifths than the first, at the distance of thirteen yards

* Cento braccia, or cubits. The Florence braccio is one foot ten inches seven-eighths, English measure.

342.—*Various Precepts in Painting.*

The superficies of any opaque body participates of the colour of the transparent medium interposed between the eye and such body, in a greater or less degree, in proportion to the density of such medium and the space it occupies.

The outlines of opaque bodies will be less apparent in proportion as those bodies are farther distant from the eye.

That part of the opaque body will be the most shaded, or lightest, which is nearest to the body that shades it, or gives it light.

The surface of any opaque body participates more or less of the colour of that body which gives it light, in proportion as the latter is more or less remote, or more or less strong.

Objects seen between lights and shadows will appear to have greater relievo than those which are placed wholly in the light, or wholly in shadow.

When you give strength and precision to objects seen at a great distance, they will appear as if they were very near. Endeavour that your imitation be such as to give a just idea of distances. If the object in nature appear confused in the outlines, let the same be observed in your picture.

The outlines of distant objects appear undetermined and confused, for two reasons: the first is, that they come to the eye by so small an angle, and are therefore so much diminished, that they strike the sight no more than small objects do, which though near can hardly be distinguished, such as the nails of the fingers, insects, and other similar things: the second is, that between the eye and the distant objects there is so much air interposed, that it becomes thick; and, like a veil, tinges the shadows with its own whiteness, and turns them from a dark colour to another between black and white, such as azure.

Although, by reason of the great distance, the appearance of many things is lost, yet those things which receive the light from the sun will be more discernible, while the rest remain enveloped in confused shadows. And because the air is thicker near the ground, the things which are lower will appear confused; and *vice versâ.*

When the sun tinges the clouds on the horizon with red, those objects which, on account of their distance, appear bluish, will participate of that redness, and will produce a mixture between the azure and red, which renders the prospect lively and pleasant; all the opaque bodies which receive that light will appear distinct, and of a reddish colour; and the air, being transparent, will be impregnated with it, and appear of the colour of *lilies.**

The air which is between the earth and the sun when it rises or sets, will always dim the objects it surrounds more than the air anywhere else, because it is whiter.

It is not necessary to mark strongly the outlines of any object which is placed upon another. It ought to detach of itself.

If the outline or extremity of a white and curved surface terminate upon another white body, it will have a shade at that extremity, darker than any part of the light; but if against a dark object, such outline, or extremity, will be lighter than any part of the light.

Those objects which are most different in colour will appear the most detached from each other.

Those parts of objects which first disappear in the distance, are extremities similar in colour, and ending one upon the other, as the extremities of an oak tree upon another oak similar to it. The next to disappear at a greater distance are, objects of mixed colours, when they terminate one upon the other, as trees, ploughed fields, walls, heaps of rubbish or of stones. The last extremities of bodies that vanish are those which, being light, terminate upon a dark ground; or being dark, upon a light ground.

Of objects situated above the eye, at equal heights, the farthest removed from the eye will appear the lowest; and if situated below the eye, the nearest to it will appear the

---

* Probably the author here means yellow lilies, or *fleurs de lis.*

lowest. The parallel lines situated sidewise will concur to one point.*

Those objects which are near a river or a lake in the distant part of a landscape, are less apparent and distinct than those that are remote from them.

Of bodies of equal density, those that are nearest to the eye will appear thinnest, and the most remote thickest.

A large eye-ball will see objects larger than a small one. The experiment may be made by looking at any of the celestial bodies, through a pin-hole, which being capable of admitting but a portion of its light, it seems to diminish and lose of its size in the same proportion as the pin-hole is smaller than the usual apparent size of the object.

A thick air interposed between the eye and any object, will render the outlines of such object undetermined and confused, and make it appear of a larger size than it is in reality; because the linear perspective does not diminish the angle which conveys the object to the eye. The aerial perspective carries it farther off, so that the one removes it from the eye, while the other preserves its magnitude.†

When the sun is in the west the vapours of the earth fall down again and thicken the air, so that objects not enlightened by the sun remain dark and confused, but those which receive its light will be tinged yellow and red, according to the sun's appearance on the horizon. Again, those that receive its light are very distinct, particularly public buildings and towns in houses and villages, because their shadows are dark; and it seems as if those parts which are plainly seen were coming out of confused and undetermined foundations, because at that time everything is of one and the same colour, except what is enlightened by the sun.‡

Any object receiving the light from the sun, receives also the general light; so that two kinds of shadows are produced: the darkest of the two is that which happens to have its central line directed towards the centre of the sun. The central lines of the primitive and secondary lights are

---

* That point is always found in the horizon, and is called the point sight, or the vanishing point.
† See chap. 320.   ‡ See chap. 317.

the same as the central lines of the primitive and secondary shadows.

The setting sun is a beautiful and magnificent object when it tinges with its colour all the great buildings of towns, villages, and the top of high trees in the country. All below is confused and almost lost in a tender and general mass; for, being only enlightened by the air, the difference between the shadows and the lights is small, and for that reason it is not much detached. But those that are high are touched by the rays of the sun, and, as was said before, are tinged with its colour; the painter therefore ought to take the same colour with which he has painted the sun, and employ it in all those parts of his work which receive its light.

It also happens very often, that a cloud will appear dark without receiving any shadow from a separate cloud, according to the situation of the eye; because it will see only the shady part of the one, while it sees both the enlightened and shady parts of the other.

Of two objects at equal height, that which is the farthest off will appear the lowest. Observe the first cloud in the cut, though it is lower than the second, it appears as if it were higher. This is demonstrated by the section of the pyramidical rays of the low cloud at M A, and the second

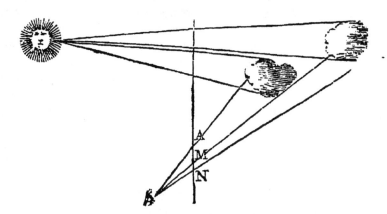

(which is higher) at N M, below M A. This happens also when, on account of the rays of the setting or rising sun a dark cloud appears higher than another which is light.

343.—*The Brilliancy of a Landscape.*

The vivacity and brightness of colours in a landscape will never bear any comparison with a landscape in Nature when illumined by the sun, unless the picture be placed so as to receive the same light from the sun itself.

MISCELLANEOUS OBSERVATIONS.

344.—*Why a painted Object does not appear so far distant as a real one, though they be conveyed to the Eye by equal Angles.*

If a house be painted on the pannel B C, at the apparent distance of one mile, and by the side of it a real one be

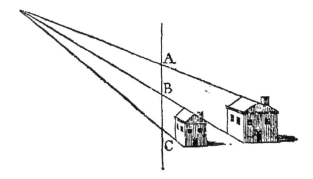

perceived at the true distance of one mile also; which objects are so disposed, that the pannel, or picture, A C, intersects the pyramidical rays with the same opening of angles; yet these two objects will never appear of the same size, nor at the same distance, if seen with both eyes.*

* This position has been already laid down in chapter 124 (and will also be found in chapter 348) ; and the reader is referred to the note on that passage, which will also explain that in the text, for further illustration. It may, however, be proper to remark, that though the Author has here supposed both objects conveyed to the eye by an angle of the same extent, they cannot, in fact, be so seen, unless one eye be shut; and the reason is this : if viewed with both

L

345.—*How to draw a Figure standing upon its Feet, to appear forty Braccia* * *high, in a Space of twenty Braccia, with proportionate Members.*

In this, as in any other case, the painter is not to mind what kind of surface he has to work upon; particularly if his painting is to be seen from a determined point, such as a window, or any other opening. Because the eye is not

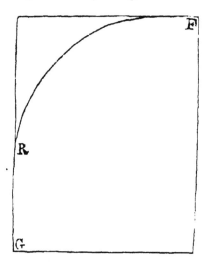

to attend to the evenness or roughness of the wall, but only to what is to be represented as beyond that wall; such as a landscape, or anything else. Nevertheless a curved surface, such as F R G, would be the best, because it has no angles.

346.—*How to draw a Figure twenty-four Braccia high, upon a Wall twelve Braccia high.*

(Plate 22.)

Draw upon part of the wall M N half the figure you mean to represent; and the other half upon the cove above,

eyes, there will be two points of sight, one in the centre of each eye; and the rays from each of these to the objects must of course be different, and will consequently form different angles.

* The braccio is one foot ten inches and seven-eighths English measure.

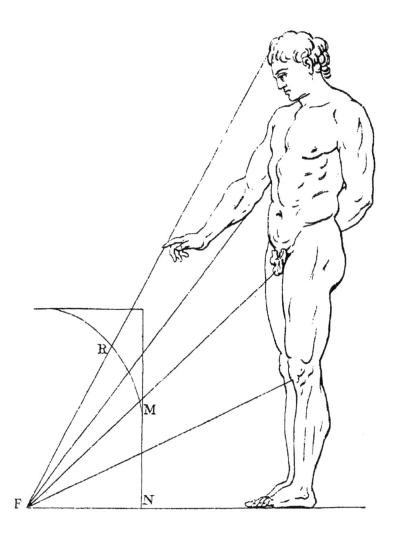

R

M

F N

Plate 22.

Chap. 340.

M R. But before that, it will be necessary to draw upon a flat board, or a paper, the profile of the wall and cove, of the same shape and dimension, as that upon which you are to paint. Then draw also the profile of your figure, of whatever size you please, by the side of it; draw all the lines to the point F, and where they intersect the profile M R, you will have the dimensions of your figure as they ought to be drawn upon the real spot. You will find, that on the straight part of the wall M N, it will come of its proper form, because the going off perpendicularly will diminish it naturally; but that part which comes upon the curve will be diminished upon your drawing. The whole must be traced afterwards upon the real spot, which is similar to M N. This is a good and safe method.

347.—*Why, on measuring a Face, and then painting it of the same Size, it will appear larger than the natural one.*

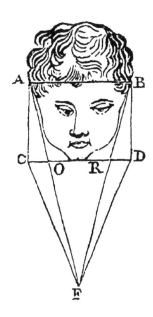

A B is the breadth of the space, or of the head, and it is placed on the paper at the distance C F, where the cheeks

are, and it would have to stand back all A C, and then the
temples would be carried to the distance O R of the lines
A F, B F; so that there is the difference C O and R D.
It follows that the line C F, and the line D F, in order to
become shorter,* have to go and find the paper where the
whole height is drawn, that is to say, the lines F A, and
F B, where the true size is ; and so it makes the difference,
as I have said, of C O, and R D.

348.—*Why the most perfect Imitation of Nature will not appear to have the same Relief as Nature itself.*

If Nature is seen with two eyes, it will be impossible
to imitate it upon a picture so as to appear with the same
relief, though the lines, the lights, shades, and colour, be
perfectly imitated.† It is proved thus : let the eyes A B,

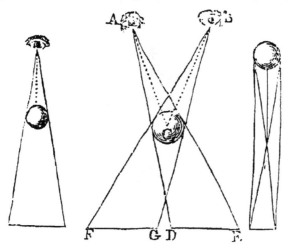

look at the object C, with the concurrence of both the
central visual rays A C and B C. I say, that the sides of
the visual angles (which contain these central rays) will
see the space G D, behind the object C. The eye A will
see all the space F D, and the eye B all the space G E.
Therefore the two eyes will see behind the object C all the

* *i.e.* To be abridged according to the rules of perspective.
† See chap. 122.

space F E; for which reason that object C becomes as it were transparent, according to the definition of transparent bodies, behind which nothing is hidden. This cannot happen if an object were seen with one eye only, provided it be larger than the eye. From all that has been said, we may conclude, that a painted object, occupying all the space it has behind, leaves no possible way to see any part of the ground, which it covers entirely by its own circumference.*

349.—Universality of Painting; a Precept.

A painter cannot be said to aim at universality in the art, unless he love equally every species of that art. For instance, if he delight only in landscape, his can be esteemed only as a simple investigation; and, as our friend Botticello † remarks, is but a vain study; since, by throwing a sponge impregnated with various colours against a wall, it leaves some spots upon it, which may appear like a landscape. It is true also, that a variety of compositions may be seen in such spots, according to the disposition of mind with which they are considered; such as heads of men, various animals, battles, rocky scenes, seas, clouds, woods, and the like. It may be compared to the sound of bells, which may seem to say whatever we choose to imagine. In the same manner also, those spots may furnish hints for

* The whole of this chapter, like the next but one preceding, depends on the circumstance of there being in fact two points of sight, one in the centre of each eye, when an object is viewed with both eyes. In natural objects the effect which this circumstance produces is, that the rays from each point of sight, diverging as they extend towards the object, take in not only that, but some part also of the distance behind it, till at length, at a certain distance behind it, they cross each other; whereas, in a painted representation, there being no real distance behind the object, but the whole being a flat surface, it is impossible that the rays from the points of sight should pass beyond that flat surface; and as the object itself is on that flat surface, which is the real extremity of the view, the eyes cannot acquire a sight of anything beyond.

† A well-known painter at Florence, contemporary with Leonardo da Vinci, who painted several altar-pieces and other public works.

compositions, though they do not teach us how to finish any particular part; and the imitators of them are but sorry landscape-painters.

350.—*In what Manner the Mirror is the true Master of Painters.*

When you wish to know if your picture be like the object you mean to represent, have a flat looking-glass, and place it so as to reflect the object you have imitated, and compare carefully the original with the copy. You see upon a flat mirror the representation of things which appear real; Painting is the same. They are both an even superficies, and both give the idea of something beyond their superficies. Since you are persuaded that the looking-glass, by means of lines and shades, gives you the representation of things as if they were real; you being in possession of colours which in their different lights and shades are stronger than those of the looking-glass, may certainly, if you employ the rules with judgment, give to your picture the same appearance of Nature as you admire in the looking-glass. Or rather, your picture will be like Nature itself seen in a large looking-glass.

This looking-glass (being your master) will show you the lights and shades of any object whatever. Amongst your colours there are some lighter than the lightest part of your model, and also some darker than the strongest shades; from which it follows, that you ought to represent Nature as seen in your looking-glass, when you look at it with one eye only; because both eyes surround the objects too much, particularly when they are small.*

351.—*Which Painting is to be esteemed the best.*

That painting is the most commendable which has the greatest conformity to what is meant to be imitated. This kind of comparison will often put to shame a certain description of painters, who pretend they can mend the works of Nature; as they do, for instance, when they pretend to

* See chapters 224 and 348.

represent a child twelve months old, giving him eight heads in height, when Nature in its best proportion admits but five. The breadth of the shoulders also, which is equal to the head, they make double, giving to a child a year old the proportions of a man of thirty. They have so often practised, and seen others practise these errors, that they have converted them into habit, which has taken so deep root in their corrupted judgment, that they persuade themselves that Nature and her imitators are wrong in not following their own practice.*

352.—*Of the Judgment to be made of a Painter's Work.*

The first thing to be considered is, whether the figures have their proper relief, according to their respective situations, and the light they are in: that the shadows be not the same at the extremities of the groups, as in the middle; because being surrounded by shadows, or shaded only on one side, produces very different effects. The groups in the middle are surrounded by shadows from the other figures, which are between them and the light. Those which are at the extremities have the shadows only on one side, and receive the light on the other. The strongest and smartest touches of shadows are to be in the interstice between the figures of the principal group where the light cannot penetrate.†

Secondly, that by the order and disposition of the figures they appear to be accommodated to the subject, and the true representation of the history in question.

Thirdly, that the figures appear alive to the occasion which brought them together, with expressions suited to their attitudes.

353.—*How to make an imaginary Animal appear natural.*

It is evident that it will be impossible to invent any animal without giving it members, and these members must individually resemble those of some known animal.

If you wish, therefore, to make a chimera, or imaginary

---

* See chap. 10.   † See chap. 201.

animal, appear natural (let us suppose a serpent); take the head of a mastiff, the eyes of a cat, the ears of a porcupine, the mouth of a hare, the brows of a lion, the temples of an old cock, and the neck of a sea tortoise.*

354.—*Painters are not to imitate one another.*

One painter ought never to imitate the manner of any other; because in that case he cannot be called the child of Nature, but the grandchild. It is always best to have recourse to Nature, which is replete with such abundance of objects, than to the productions of other masters, who learnt everything from her.

355.—*How to judge of one's own Work.*

It is an acknowledged fact, that we perceive errors in the works of others more readily than in our own. A painter, therefore, ought to be well instructed in perspective, and acquire a perfect knowledge of the dimensions of the human body; he should also be a good architect, at least as far as concerns the outward shape of buildings, with their different parts; and where he is deficient, he ought not to neglect taking drawings from Nature.

It will be well also to have a looking-glass by him, when he paints, to look often at his work in it, which, being seen the contrary way, will appear as the work of another hand, and will better show his faults. It will be useful also to quit his work often, and take some relaxation, that his judgment may be clearer at his return; for too great application and sitting still is sometimes the cause of many gross errors.

356.—*Of correcting Errors which you discover.*

Remember, that when, by the exercise of your own judgment, or the observation of others, you discover any errors in your work, you immediately set about correcting them, lest, in exposing your works to the public, you expose

---

* Leonardo was remarkably fond of this kind of inventions, and is accused of having lost a great deal of time in this way.

your defects also. Admit not any self-excuse, by persuading yourself that you shall retrieve your character, and that by some succeeding work you shall make amends for your shameful negligence; for your work does not perish as soon as it is out of your hands, like the sound of music, but remains a standing monument of your ignorance. If you excuse yourself by saying that you have not time for the study necessary to form a great painter, having to struggle against necessity, you yourself are only to blame; for the study of what is excellent is food both for mind and body. How many philosophers, born to great riches, have given them away, that they might not be retarded in their pursuits!

357.—*The best Place for looking at a Picture.*

Let us suppose, that A B is the picture, receiving the light from D; I say, that whoever is placed between C and E will see the picture very badly, particularly if it be painted in oil, or varnished; because it will shine, and will

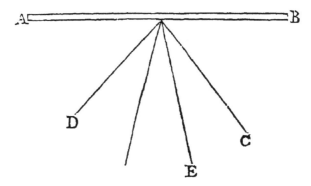

appear almost of the nature of a looking-glass. For these reasons, the nearer you go towards C, the less you will be able to see, because of the light from the window upon the picture, sending its reflection to that point. But if you place yourself between E D, you may conveniently see the picture, and the more so as you draw nearer to the point D, because that place is less liable to be struck by the reflected rays.

358.—*Of Judgment.*

There is nothing more apt to deceive us than our own judgment, in deciding on our own works; and we should derive more advantage from having our faults pointed out by our enemies, than by hearing the opinions of our friends, because they are too much like ourselves, and may deceive us as much as our own judgment.

359.—*Of Employment anxiously wished for by Painters.*

And you, painter, who are desirous of great practice, understand, that if you do not rest it on the good foundation of Nature, you will labour with little honour and less profit; and if you do it on a good ground, your works will be many and good, to your great honour and advantage.

360.—*Advice to Painters.*

A painter ought to study universal Nature, and reason much within himself on all he sees, making use of the most excellent parts that compose the species of every object before him. His mind will by this method be like a mirror, reflecting truly every object placed before it, and become, as it were, a second Nature.

361.—*Of Statuary.*

To execute a figure in marble, you must first make a model of it in clay, or plaster, and when it is finished, place it in a square case, equally capable of receiving the block of marble intended to be shaped like it. Have some peg-like sticks to pass through holes made in the sides, and all round the case; push them in till every one touches the model, marking what remains of the sticks outwards with ink, and making a countermark to every stick and its hole, so that you may at pleasure replace them again. Then having taken out the model, and placed the block of marble in its stead, take so much out of it, till all the pegs go in at the same holes to the marks you had made. To facilitate the work, contrive your frame so that every part of it, separately, or all together, may be lifted up, except the bottom, which must remain under the marble. By this method you may chop it off with great facility.*

362.—*On the Measurement and Division of Statues into Parts.*

Divide the head into twelve parts, each part into twelve degrees, each degree into twelve minutes, and these minutes into seconds.†

363.—*A Precept for the Painter.*

The painter who entertains no doubt of his own ability, will attain very little. When the work succeeds beyond the judgment, the artist acquires nothing; but when the judgment is superior to the work, he never ceases improving, if the love of gain do not retard his progress.

364.—*On the Judgment of Painters.*

When the work is equal to the knowledge and judgment of the painter, it is a bad sign; and when it surpasses the judgment, it is still worse, as is the case with those who wonder at having succeeded so well. But when the judgment surpasses the work, it is a perfectly good sign; and the young painter who possesses that rare disposition, will, no doubt, arrive at great perfection. He will produce few works, but they will be such as to fix the admiration of every beholder.

* The method here recommended, was the general and common practice at that time, and continued so with little, if any variation, till lately. But about thirty years ago, the late Mr. Bacon invented an entirely new method, which, as better answering the purpose, he constantly used, and from him others have also adopted it into practice.

† This may be a good method of dividing the figure for the purpose of reducing from large to small, or *vice versâ*; but it not being the method generally used by the painters for measuring their figures, as being too minute, this chapter was not introduced amongst those of general proportions.

365.—That a Man ought not to trust to himself, but ought to consult Nature.

Whoever flatters himself that he can retain in his memory all the effects of Nature, is deceived, for our memory is not so capacious: therefore consult Nature for everything.

GENERAL INDEX.

The number at the end of each Title refers to the corresponding Chapter in the original edition in Italian.

DRAWING.

PROPORTION.

ANATOMY.

MOTION AND EQUIPOISE OF FIGURES.

INVENTION OR COMPOSITION.

M

LIGHT AND SHADOW.

COLOURS AND COLOURING.

COLOURS

COLOURS IN REGARD TO LIGHT AND SHADOW.

COLOURS IN REGARD TO BACKGROUNDS.

AERIAL PERSPECTIVE.

MISCELLANEOUS OBSERVATIONS.

LANDSCAPE.

MISCELLANEOUS OBSERVATIONS.

APPENDIX.

---·◦·---

I. MANUSCRIPTS OF LEONARDO DA VINCI.

II. CLASSIFIED CATALOGUE OF HIS PRINCIPAL PAINTINGS.

III. DRAWINGS AND SKETCHES.

I.

MANUSCRIPTS OF LEONARDO DA VINCI.

THE history of these Manuscripts has been investigated by so many learned men * that we are able to trace the most important of them through all their vicissitudes during the last three and a half centuries; and the account of their various travels is both curious and interesting.

Leonardo gave by his will " to Messer Francisco da Melzi, gentleman, of Milan, in gratitude for the services he has rendered him in times past, all and every one of the books that the said testator now possesses, and other instruments and drawings concerning his art and the profession of painter." Melzi, who was Leonardo's sole executor, took his treasures to his home at Vaprio, on the banks of the Adda, where he guarded them piously until his death. His heirs, however, seem to have had but small regard for them, and allowed a certain Lelio Gavardi to take away fourteen volumes. These were afterwards recovered by Signor Gian Ambrogio Mazenta, who returned them to the Melzi family. But Signor Orazio, then the head of the family, " marvelled much," says Mazenta, " that I should have taken so much trouble," and courteously presented the re-

* Venturi, Amoretti, Gaye, Uzielli, Govi, and many others.

covered volumes to him, adding—"There are many more drawings by the same hand lying in the garret of my country house."

About the year 1594, Pompeo Leoni, a sculptor of Arezzo, obtained possession of a few of these volumes, and sold some of the drawings (which are now at Windsor) to the Earl of Arundel, and the rest to Count Galeazzo Arconati, who, on January 21, 1637, presented them to the Ambrosian Library at Milan.

We may suppose that Arconati collected all the volumes he could procure, for at the end of the next century there were certainly not less than thirteen volumes of Leonardo's works in the Ambrosian, including the "Codice Atlantico," a book of large size, containing many hundred important drawings which had been collected and bound up by Leoni, whose name appears in an inscription on the cover.

When Bonaparte entered Milan, in 1796, he, with his usual rapacity, seized these volumes and sent them to the Bibliothèque de l'Institut at Paris, where they all remained until the peace of 1815, when the "Codice Atlantico" was returned to Milan; while the other twelve were most unaccountably left behind in Paris, where they still remain.

At the present time we can trace the following twenty volumes, or collections, of Leonardo's Manuscripts:—

Twelve in the Bibliothèque de l'Institut at Paris, marked in large Roman letters—A to L. (See page 230.)

One in the Ambrosian Library at Milan, known as the "Codice Atlantico," which has lately been thoroughly investigated by Signor Govi, in his "Saggio delle Opere di Leonardo di Vinci." (See page 228.)

One in the possession of the Trivulzio family at Milan, known as the "Codicetto Trivulziano." This volume was sold to Don Carlo Trivulzio about 1750, by Don Gaetano Caccia of Novara.

One, a Treatise on the flight of birds, in the possession of Count Manzoni of Lugo.

One in the Arundel collection in the British Museum (No. 263). This is a rough book of observations and demonstrations on subjects chiefly of mixed mathematics; being unconnected notes written by him at different times, commencing 22nd March, 1508, on the mechanical powers of forces, percussion, gravity, motion, optics, astronomy, etc., with various arithmetical and geometrical propositions in Italian. Several memoranda occur in this volume (noticed in the Catalogue of the Arundel MSS., p. 79), particularly the death of his father Pietro da Vinci. (See page 232).

One in the Royal collection at Windsor Castle, originally purchased by the Earl of Arundel from Pompeo Leoni, and purchased by Charles 1., at the sale of the Arundel collection. Many of these drawings, engraved by Bartolozzi and others, were published by John Chamberlaine, the King's Librarian, in 1796. (See Catalogue on page 233.)

Two in the Ashburnham collection, made up, it has been asserted, from the volumes in the Bibliothèque de l'Institut.

One in the possession of the Earl of Leicester, at Holkham, on the weight and motive power of water.

And scattered drawings, accompanied with the usual annotations, are to be found in the Public Libraries at Vienna, Venice, Florence, Turin, and Paris. (See pages 231, 232.)

The following volumes have been lost:—

One presented by Mazenta to the painter, Ambrozio Figini, who bequeathed it to Ercole Bianchi. This was subsequently purchased by Consul Smith, of Venice, but all trace of it has now disappeared.

One presented by Mazenta to Duke Carlo Emmanuele, of Savoy. This was possibly burned in one of the fires which took place in the Royal Library of Turin, in 1667 or 1679.

Leonardo's writings are quickly recognized. It is said that he was left-handed, and this may be one reason for the curious fact that nearly all his manuscripts are written backwards, from right to left, and cannot be easily read without the aid of a mirror.

Venturi says that they contain speculations in those branches of natural philosophy nearest allied to geometry; that they are first sketches and occasional notes, the author always intending afterwards to compose from them complete treatises. The spirit of geometry guided him throughout, whether it were in the art of analyzing a subject in the connexion of the discourse, or the care of always generalizing his ideas. As to natural philosophy, he never was satisfied on any proposition if he had not proved it by experiment.

The same author has likewise given extracts from Da Vinci's Manuscripts, arranged under the following heads:—

I. *Of the descent of heavy bodies, combined with the rotation of the Earth.*—Copernicus did not draw up his law of gravitation and rotation until forty years later.

II. *Of the Earth divided into particles.*—Leonardo supposes that fragments of the earth fell from above the atmosphere, and arrived at a centre where they oscillated like a stone suspended from a thread.

III. *Of the Earth and the Moon.*—He discovers that the scintillation of a star is not in the star itself, but in our eyes. And that the earth, receiving the light of the sun, is an earth to the moon itself and reflects the rays of the sun.

IV. *Of the action of the Sun on the Sea.*—Leonardo thinks that in consequence of this action, the level of the sea at the equinox raises itself, and that the waters, falling back again from the poles restore the equilibrium.

V. *Of the ancient state of the Earth.*—His speculations on this subject do not appear to have any important value.

VI. *Of Flame and Air.*—Flame, he says, like an animal, is nourished by air, and dies when air is wanting; and he accounts for the smoke from the fact that the air has not penetrated there. Leonardo therefore discovered the theory of combustion three centuries before modern physicists.

VII. *Of Statics.*—He shows by diagrams the action of the lever, more particularly of the oblique lever.

VIII. *Of the descent of heavy bodies on inclined planes.*—He discourses on the easiest method of moving heavy bodies.

IX. *Of the Water which is supplied from a canal.*—Leonardo remarks on the various causes which vary the supply of the water.

X. *Of Whirlpools.*—In a vortex, he says, there is a mass of water which rests suspended, and in the midst a vacuum; and he carefully analyzes this phenomenon.

XI. *Of Vision.*—Leonardo has written on vision at some length, both in his "Treatise on Painting," and his "Treatise on Perspective," as well as in his "Notes on Light and Cloud." He does not absolutely mention the camera-obscura, but he describes its action so well, that it is evident the discovery of the camera may be attributed to him.

XII. *On various Instruments.*—He describes several instruments:—Proportional compasses on a movable centre, by which an oval can be traced; apparatus to indicate the density of the air; a machine for measuring the humidity of the air.

Leonardo also designed a helmet, communicating with the air, for the pearl-fishers in the Indian seas; apparatus to help swimmers; a machine suggested by the wings of a bat, by means of which men could fly; a press to squeeze the oil from olives; a measure for ribbons; a machine to twist thread; a new method

N

of casting medals; and he certainly knew the immense power of steam. In fact, there was scarcely a subject connected with science or art, upon which he did not contribute some addition to the knowledge of his day.

Notwithstanding all the researches that have been made, it is still uncertain whether the first edition of the "Trattato della Pittura" was printed from Leonardo's own manuscripts, or from notes gathered by one of his disciples from the scattered volumes. It is possible that an examination of the twelve volumes now in Paris might set this question at rest.

The only other published work of Leonardo is the "Trattato del Moto e Misura dell' Aqua" (On the motion and power of water).

II.

A CLASSIFIED AND DESCRIPTIVE CATALOGUE OF THE PRINCIPAL PAINTINGS OF LEONARDO DA VINCI.

PART I.—HOLY FAMILY—MADONNA—CHRIST.

*** *Except when the authority is named, the criticisms contained in the following Catalogue must be taken as the opinions of M. Arsène Houssaye, from whose work it has been chiefly compiled.*

1.—THE BAPTISM OF CHRIST.

In the Gallery of the Academy of Fine Arts, Florence.

LEONARDO DA VINCI painted nothing more than the angel in this picture, which was the composition of his master, Andrea Verocchio. Tradition affirms that this was the last work ever executed by Andrea, for that, on seeing the angel painted by his pupil, he threw down his palette for ever.

Verocchio drew correctly, but his figures are stiff and spiritless; the angel of Leonardo has been aptly termed a "brilliant stain" on his picture—a ray of sunlight on a faded page.

Engraved in Rosini's "Storia della Pittura Italiana."

2.—MADONNA OF VAPRIO.

Painted in fresco on a wall.

LEONARDO lived at Vaprio for four years in a house near the Adda, the neighbour of his landlord Melzi, who dwelt in the adjoining villa. On the wall overlooking the court-yard of this villa is painted a picture of the Madonna and Infant Saviour. It is of colossal size, the head of the Virgin being not less than six *palmi*, or about four feet six inches, in height. In the year 1796 some soldiers of the Republic bivouacked in this court, lit a fire against the wall of Leonardo's house, and blackened the fresco like the funnel of a chimney. The heads, fortunately, were comparatively uninjured. The whole has since been repainted.

Passavant believes that Leonardo made the cartoon for this picture, but that the fresco itself was the work of Francesco Melzi. We may conclude, however, that Leonardo did more than the sketch. The Virgin has a beautiful though severe countenance, and the Child wears that smile of gracious expression which Leonardo, and perhaps he alone, knew how to represent.

Engraved in Fumagalli's " Scuola di Leonardo."

3.—THE VIRGIN AMONG THE ROCKS. (*La Vierge aux Rochers.*)
In the Gallery of the Louvre.

THIS is possibly a copy. Waagen says that this painting cannot have been the work of Leonardo, " for, in opposition to the remarkable and poetical style of composition, characterizing the epoch when the talents of this painter had attained their highest perfection, there are certain parts, such as the heads of the angel and of the Virgin, which are without expression, and display a surprising feebleness of design; the folds of the drapery, moreover, have a false and stiff appearance."

M. Passavant hazards the following conjecture : " We cannot suppose that Leonardo was content with executing merely the sketch for this composition : we believe that a picture, formerly in the Chapel of the Conception in the Church of the Franciscans at Milan, which is mentioned in the ' Treatise on Painting,' by Lomazzo (p. 171-212), and also in the ' Passeghi de Scanelli et Lormanni,' (1751, Milan), and which was sold in 1796 for thirty ducats to the painter Hamilton because it was thought to be a copy, was really by Leonardo himself. It afterwards passed into the collection of the Duke of Suffolk; two angels which were formerly at either side of the principal picture are at present in the gallery of the Duke de Melzi, and attest by their brilliancy the authenticity of the work of which they once formed a part. The picture in the Louvre is doubtless a copy."

The Duke of Devonshire possesses a drawing of very great beauty, representing a head of the Virgin with her hair falling on both sides of the face, which is turned a little to the right. On the same page is a head of the Holy Child, three quarters seen. These two studies are in black chalk, relieved with white, on blue paper. M. Passavant, who has given this description, adds: "This drawing, of extraordinary beauty and well preserved, appears to be a study for the 'Vierge aux Rochers' of the Louvre."

In the Museum at Nantes there is a duplicate of the "Vierge aux Rochers" (No. 199), and the catalogue affirms that it is the original: this statement cannot be depended on.

"The aspect of the Virgin in the 'Vierge aux Rochers,'" says Théophile Gautier, "is mysterious and charming. A grotto of basaltic rocks shelters the divine group, who are sitting on the margin of a clear spring, in the transparent depths of which we see the pebbles of its bed. Through the arcade of the grotto, we discover a rocky landscape, with a few scattered trees, and crossed by a stream, on the banks of which rises a village. All this is of a colour as indefinable as those mysterious countries one traverses in a dream, and accords marvellously with the figures. What more adorable type than that of the Madonna; it is especially Leonardo's; and does not in any way recall the Virgins of Perugino or Raphael. Her head is spherical in form! the forehead well-developed; the fine oval of her cheeks is gracefully rounded so as to enclose a chin most delicately curved; the eyes with lowered eyelids encircled with shadow, and the nose, not in a line with the forehead, like that of a Grecian statue, but still finely shaped; with nostrils tenderly cut, and trembling, as though her breathing made them palpitate; the mouth a little large, it is true, but smiling with a deliciously enigmatic expression that Da Vinci gives to his female faces, a tiny shade of mischief mingling with the purity and goodness. The hair is long, loose, and silky, and falls in crisp meshes around the shadow-softened cheeks, according with the half-tints with incomparable grace."

This picture was formerly in the possession of Francis I. It was originally painted on wood, but was transferred to canvas some years since, and has been retouched to such an extent, that, at first sight, it is difficult to pronounce any opinion upon it.

In the Exhibition of Works of the Old Masters at the Royal Academy in 1870, the Earl of Suffolk exhibited his " Vierge aux Rochers," which Waagen says is " most probably the original."

Engraved in line by Desnoyers.

4.—The Virgin seated on the knees of St. Anne.
In the Gallery of the Louvre.

" In the picture of the Virgin seated on the knees of St. Anne," —we quote Théophile Gautier,—" the shadows are more subdued than in ' La Vierge aux Rochers ;' the painter has certainly not employed in this picture that dark tint which has marred his other paintings; the colouring is lighter and cooler. In a landscape strewn with rocks and little trees, of which you may count the leaves, St. Anne holds on her knees the Virgin, who gracefully leans towards the Infant Jesus. The Child is playing with a little lamb, which He holds gently by the ear, with a charmingly infantile action which takes nothing from the nobility of the composition. A few slight lines cross the forehead and cheeks of St. Anne, but do not detract from her beauty; for Leonardo shrank from the representation of sadness, and would not afflict the eye by a spectacle of decrepitude. The head of the Virgin is exquisitely fine in outline; her face beams with virginal grace and maternal love; her eyes are bathed in tenderness, and her half-smiling mouth has that indefinable expression of which Leonardo alone knew the secret."

M. Taine also speaks of this painting, giving us, as it were, a page of music : " In the little Jesus of the picture of St. Anne, a shoulder, a cheek, a temple, alone emerge from the shadowy depth. Leonardo da Vinci was a great musician. Perhaps he found in that gradation and change of colour, in that vague yet charming magic of chiaroscuro, an effect resembling the crescendos and decresendos of grand musical works."

The authenticity of this picture has often been called in

question. Waagen attributes it to a pupil of Leonardo, "so much," he says, "is the usual smile of his figures here exaggerated and affected." Rosini says that it may be the work of Salaï, but that it had perhaps been re-touched by Leonardo, unless, indeed, it be by Bernardino de Luini. M. Delécluze is of the same opinion as M. Rosini. Passavant, however, affirms that it is an original picture, for, says he, "none of the pupils of Leonardo had a touch so spiritual, or that firmness of expression so much to be admired in this work."

There are many existing copies; the greater number of which have claimed to be the original, but it is acknowledged now that many of these are much inferior to the painting in the Louvre. Even though the blue garment of the Virgin is effaced, though the left leg has certainly been re-painted, yet we think this is the work of Leonardo da Vinci, or else a masterpiece by Bernardino de Luini.

A sketch for this picture, according to M. Rigollot, is in the collection belonging to the Plattenberg family, in Westphalia. Among the copies may be cited: one which was for some time in the collection at the sacristy of San Celso at Milan, but is now in the Leuchtenberg Gallery at Munich. It is by Salaï; D'Argenville has, however, attributed it to Leonardo himself. Another, which is in the Royal Gallery at Florence, the Catalogue of 1844 attributes to Salaï. This was bought at Vienna, according to Lanzi, by the Grand-Duke of Tuscany, Ferdinand III. Viardot, speaking of another copy at the Ambrosian Library at Milan, gives it as his opinion that it is by Luini. Kugler mentions one in the Brera Gallery; "it is," says he, "the work of Andrea Salaino, for one can recognize the hand of this master by the warm and transparent red of his flesh-tints."

The Royal Museum of Madrid also possesses a copy, or a sketch of an inferior kind, of the St. Anne of the Louvre.

Engraved by Langier; by Cantini; and in Landon's "Vies et Œuvres des Peintres."

5.—THE HOLY FAMILY OF ST. PETERSBURG.

In the Gallery of the Hermitage.

THE history of this picture reads like an old legend. Amoretti, the Abbé Lanzi, and M. de Gallenberg all repeat the same story.

The painting was lost when the palace of the Dukes of Mantua was pillaged by the Germans. It disappeared for a long time, and at length fell into the possession of the Abbé Salvadori, one of the secretaries of the Count Firmian. Salvadori also concealed the picture, believing that the Count, who was Governor of Mantua, would make him return it to the palace whence it had been stolen. After the death of Salvadori, the picture was sent to the village of Mori, in the Trent district, where it was sold by the heirs of the Abbé to the agents of Catherine II.

Passavant says of this picture that "all those who have seen it in the Gallery of the Hermitage are convinced that it is a superb work, worthy of the great Florentine master."

Pagavi thought it so beautiful, and so nearly like the work of Raphael, that he marked it with the monogram of Leonardo, in order to prevent its being attributed to the Prince of Painters.

Henri Beyle likewise speaks of this painting with enthusiasm, saying that "Leonardo never painted anything better or more sublime."

There is also a long description of it in the "Histoire de la Peinture en Italie" by the same author. "Mary," he says, "is seen full-face; she gazes on her son with pride, and is one of the grandest figures of the mother of our Saviour that was ever painted; the Child, full of gaiety and life, embraces her; behind them, to the left of the spectator, is a young woman reading. This figure is frequently named St. Catherine, but it is probably the portrait of the sister-in-law of Leo X., wife of Giulio de' Medici, to whom she was married in January, 1515; this picture being, according to Beyle, of a date subsequent to that event. On the opposite side is St. Joseph, whose head is the most original one in the picture; he looks down smilingly upon the Holy Child with a graceful expression of playful humour. This is Leonardo's own idea; for it was far from the spirit of that age to introduce any gaiety into a sacred subject; in this respect he was the precursor of Correggio."

M. Viardot, on the contrary, says, in his "Musées d'Allemagne et de Russe," that this is "a defective work, in which two women, Mary and Catherine, are drawn one above another, where all is ugly, ungraceful, and grotesque (!)."

Kugler indicates many copies or replicas of this "Holy Family." The best known is the "Vierge au Bas-relief," in the possession of Lord Monson; others are in England or Milan.

The St. Petersburg picture bears the signature "L. D. V."; this alone would not prove it to be the work of Leonardo da Vinci, were the touch of the master not otherwise plainly visible on this beautiful painting.

Engraved in the "Galerie de l'Hermitage, avec descriptions," by Camille de Genève.

6.—THE INFANT JESUS.
At Bologna.

VASARI speaks of a picture of the Holy Child, that Leonardo painted for Baldassare Turini. It is, perhaps, this statement of Vasari that has caused Lanzi to cite as authentic, "a Child Jesus lying in a rich cradle, ornamented with pearls, which is at Bologna, in the apartments of the Gonfaloniere at the palace."

This picture exhibits the Holy Infant clothed, with the exception of the head, which is crowned with light, and recalls the luminous effect of the portrait of Lucrezia Crivelli in the Louvre.

Henri Beyle says that he believes it to be by Leonardo, but in his early manner; he adds that it shows nothing of his customary style. According to Vasari, this Holy Child was "marvellously beautiful and graceful."

7.—CHRIST DISPUTING WITH THE DOCTORS.
In the National Gallery, London.

THIS picture, which formerly belonged to the Carr Collection, was originally the property of the Aldobrandini family. Its authenticity has been much disputed. Rigollot is of opinion that Leonardo made the original drawing, but that the picture itself was painted by Bernardino Luini. Others critics agree in assigning the work to this distinguished pupil of Leonardo.

In the fifteenth and sixteenth centuries, scholars followed closely on the steps of their instructors. It was not until after the publication of the Abbé Lanzi's "Storia Pittorica" that we began to concern ourselves much with many painters of the

second order, the names, the merits, and the works of whom he
revealed. He it was who first restored to fame Luini, Salaï,
Solario, Oggione, Cesare da Sesto, Beltraffio, and other pupils
of Leonardo da Vinci.

"We have now," says Waagen, "learned how to detect the
peculiarities of each of these artists, and in what authentic work
of Leonardo can be found that warm flesh tint so brilliant in all
its parts, and those local tints of blue and red draperies, so pure,
so uniform, and so well painted? But however beautiful may
be the features of Christ, although they recall in general the
well-known type of the school of Leonardo, although there is a
slight tinge of melancholy, the face lacks that depth of character,
that grandeur, which Leonardo usually imprinted on his works.
The composition and the drawing are much too feeble to be his
work, if indeed it could be recognized through the unfortunate
restorations which this picture has undergone. The forehead,
the cheeks, and the hands of Christ have above all suffered from
the method of Italian restorers, which consists in retouching the
flesh tints with a coloured varnish: a process which may satisfy
the uncritical crowd, but which vexes the true connoisseur, who
seeks in vain for the original touch of the painter's pencil."

D'Agincourt says that though this picture has been attributed
to Bernardino Luini, he believes it to be really Leonardo's. In
his "Histoire de l'Art" he thus speaks of it:—"The subject of
this painting is confused and badly arranged; the figures are
half length. The Saviour is represented with his face towards
us; his expression is sweet and noble, but rather feminine, in
spite of his growing beard; he wears a garment of silk covered
with jewels."

In the opinion of Herr Passavant, "This splendid picture is
most carefully finished, and in parts finely coloured, especially
the hands of the Christ; it is in good preservation, apparently
one of Leonardo's later productions, more fulness and roundness
of form being perceptible than in his earlier works. The colours
are also laid on in full body, although with much tenderness."

A fine copy of this picture is in the Spada Palace at Rome.

Engraved by Felsing; by Ghigi; by Leonelli; and in Landon's
"Vies et Œuvres des Peintres."

8—Christ Bearing His Cross.

In the possession of Sir Thomas Proctor Beauchamp.

THIS painting was shown at the Exhibition of Works of the Old Masters at the Royal Academy in 1871.

9—Heads of Christ.

IN his "Catalogue of the King's Pictures" (Paris 1754), Lépicié mentions a half-length figure of Christ, carrying the globe in His left hand and in the attitude of blessing it with His right. He notes this as being very feeble. This picture was etched by Wenceslaus Hollar, in 1650. The "Magasin Pittoresque" of the year 1849 published a wood engraving of it after a drawing by Granville. A notice by M. de Chenevières-Pointel accompanies this engraving.

M. Passavant states that he found several different heads or busts of Christ in profile, either bearing the cross or holding the globe: but he considers these as nothing more than the productions of Leonardo's pupils.

Engraved also by Felsing.

"Never," says M. G. d'Adda (*Gazette des Beaux-Arts*, August, 1868), "has sentiment inspired by dignity and truth of religion been carried farther than in the head of Christ in the Gallery of the Brera." Must we apply to this also the decision of M. Passavant, just quoted, that all the heads of Christ attributed to Leonardo are the work of his pupils? Gault de St.-Germain mentions a head of the Saviour as being in the possession of Prince Lichtenstein, at Vienna, which is regarded by Winckelmann as one of the most remarkable productions of genius, a sublime work of the highest type of manly beauty.

In the Cathedral at Antwerp is a head of Christ, attributed to Leonardo; we know not on what authority.

10.—The Madonna of Lucca.

In the Casa Buonvisi at Lucca.

THIS small picture is regarded as a very early work of Leonardo's, and, according to Beyle, in his first style. M. de Rumohr, in his "*Italienische Forschungen*," says, "Here may be found traces of those strivings after intense expression so peculiar to this master; and at the same time a certain similarity to the Florentine painters of the time of Ghirlandajo."

11.—The Virgin of San Onofrio.

In the Convent of San Onofrio, at Rome.

D'Agincourt mentions this picture as being painted in fresco on a window frame of the Convent of San Onofrio. The Virgin is represented holding a flower, which she offers to the Infant Jesus. It has been restored by Palmaroli, on a gold background. A bust seen behind is supposed by d'Agincourt to represent the donor.

As far as can be judged, after the repainted portions of Palmaroli and the marks left by time, this picture much resembles in subject, and even in execution, the works of Lorenzo di Credi, one of Leonardo's fellow-students. But M. Rumohr concludes that "it is a work of Leonardo's youth, done during his sojourn at Rome, before leaving it for the court of Lodovico Sforza, at Milan." If, however, Leonardo did not go to Rome, for the first time, earlier than 1514, this fresco would according to chronology, be a work of his third "epoch," which would seem more than doubtful.

12.—The Cartoon of St. Anne.

In the Royal Academy of Arts, London.

The early history of this Cartoon is much complicated. Vasari recounts many details, and describes the work with great admiration, at some length, but, after Vasari, a cloud hangs over its history. Lanzi believes that it was lost; Lomazzo, in his "Trattato della Pittura," says that it may be found in the possession of the painter Aurelio Laurino, at Milan, after it had been seen in France.

In any case, the description Vasari has left us closely corresponds with the picture in London; which does full justice to the genius of the master, who has stamped this work with the imprint of his power. "It excited," says Vasari, "general admiration when it was exhibited in Florence, in the year 1502." It is a drawing in black and white chalk; the heads are rather less than life-size; the perfection of the design is admirable, though incomplete; the extremities and the drapery of the virgin are scarcely indicated; and the whole work is much faded.

The Virgin holds the Infant Christ upon her knees, and the child is gazing at the little St. John playing with a lamb. St. Anne, seated by the side of the Virgin, is looking at her daughter with ecstasy, while with her left hand she points heavenward. "Her smile," says Vasari, "indicates the excess of her joy in seeing her offspring raised to celestial rank."

Herr Passavant says, "This is a unique and beautiful cartoon. Through what various hands it passed, previous to its arrival in England, I have not been able to discover. It is now treated as a precious relic, and kept under glass in the keeper's room. It is drawn in black chalk and highly finished. In style of treatment, as far as regards a greater attention to effect of light than to strict symmetry of form, it resembles the sketch of the Adoration of the Kings, in the Florence Gallery. It is in good preservation."

Engraved by Anker Smith. (*A Photograph of this cartoon is published in Mrs. C. Heaton's "Life of Leonardo."*)

13.—THE VIRGIN OF MUNICH.

In the Pinacothek.

VASARI recounts that he saw at the house of Signor Giulio Torini a small picture by Leonardo, "representing the Madonna with her son in her arms." This had been painted with extreme care, but was already much altered. Leonardo is said to have painted it while at Peschia, when on his way from Milan to Rome, for Signor Baldassare Torini, for whom also he executed an Infant Christ of marvellous beauty and grace.

It has been suggested that this description probably refers to the picture now numbered 567, in the Pinacothek at Munich, in which the Virgin, seated in an open cave, surrounded by a landscape, holds with her right arm the infant, who is couching by her side beneath her mantle. It much resembles the "Vierge aux Rochers" of the Louvre.

In his book on "l'Art en Allemagne," M. Fortoul mentions

this picture; he attributes it to Leonardo, and extols its
"delicious colouring;" a praise which some may think calculated rather to cast a doubt on its authenticity.

14.—The Virgin "au Bas-Relief."

Formerly Lord Monson's, now in the possession of the Countess of
Warwick, at Gatton Park.

This Holy Family, which appears to be nearly a repetition of
the picture at the Hermitage, was, in 1835, the property of Mr.
Woodburn, a picture-dealer in London, who sold it to Lord
Monson. M. Passavant says of this picture, "it is one of the
best-preserved works of Leonardo; the drawing is exquisite,
and the colours still fresh: it is altogether an admirable and
original picture." Other critics, however, decline to regard it
as undoubtedly authentic, and suggest that it may be an
extremely skilful copy of a sketch by Leonardo. The figures
are rounded, the tones warm yet brilliant, but the expressions
of the countenances are not quite those associated with
Leonardo's style.

This group is composed of the Virgin, the Infant Jesus, the
youthful St. John, Joseph, and Zacharias.

At Milan, in the gallery of the Duke de Melzi, there is a Holy
Family comprising the same personages. It is attributed to
Cesare da Sesto, whose "Adoration of the Magi," in the gallery
at Naples, has also for its principal group a Holy Family much
resembling it.

The collection of Cardinal Feschi contains another copy of
this picture, which is generally known as the "Vierge au Bas-
relief," although the bas-relief from which the name is taken is
nothing more than one of the smaller accessories.

In the Fitz-William Museum, there is a fine copy, on a
reduced scale.

Engraved by Förster.

15.—The Holy Family of Madrid.

We owe our acquaintance with this picture, this "famous
work," to M. Viardot, who, in his book, "Musées d'Espagne,
d'Angleterre, et de Belgique," has spoken of this Holy Family in
terms of exaggerated laudation.

The solidity and the perfect preservation so especially dwelt on by M. Viardot tend to cast a doubt on the originality of this picture; Leonardo's paintings are not usually either solid or in good preservation.

M. Kugler has not mentioned it in his catalogue of the principal works in the "Museo del Rey," included in volume ii. of his "Handbuch der Geschichte der Malerei."

M. Viardot says that this "Holy Family" is painted in the manner of "Modesty and Vanity," in the Sciarra Palace, which latter picture he also highly praises. However, M. de Rumohr attributes the work in question to Salaï, and Fumagalli believes it to have been painted by Luini.

16.—The Virgin of the Esterhazy Gallery.

The Virgin in this painting is between St. Catherine and St. Barbara, and supports in her arms the Holy Child, who is looking at a book on the table before Him. M. Passavant says "that it is agreed to attribute it to Luini."

The group is shown at half length, and, according to M. Viardot, recalls the Holy Family of Madrid, which he considers it nearly equals in importance and beauty. He goes on, however, to point out that the heads of the three women singularly resemble each other, and are of the same type, scarcely varied.

Probably this picture was sketched by the great master himself, and finished by Luini.

Engraved by Steinmüller.

17.—Virgin, with the Donor.
In the Brussels Gallery. (?)

Lépicié gives the following description of this Virgin in his Catalogue Raisonné of the pictures belonging to the King of France : "Virgin holding the Infant Christ. The Holy Mother, in a simple and graceful attitude, bears in her arms the Holy Child, near whom may be seen the little St. John.

"In the foreground of this picture, the artist has placed the figure of a kneeling man, in the act of adoration. The background is partly formed by a curtain.

"Independently of the grand character of the design, there

may here be found that grace and fidelity of expression which Leonardo gives his figures."

This picture was presented to the Museum of Brussels in the year xi. of the first French Republic.

18.—VIRGIN.

Belonging to Lord Ashburton.

AN angel is seen raising the cover of a bed on which the Divine Infant is sleeping in the arms of His mother; while the little St. John and an angel watch by Him.

The figures are half the size of nature.

This picture, which was formerly in the Prior's chamber of the Escurial, subsequently formed part of the collection of General Sebastiani.

Dr. Waagen says it is by Luini. At present it belongs to Lord Ashburton, who, on the authority of many critics, believes it to be genuine.

19.—VIRGIN OF THE ALBANI PALACE.

Rome.

BOTH Lanzi and Raphael Mengs speak of this picture; the former says that its grace is impossible to describe, and the latter goes so far as to assert, that it is the most valuable work in that gallery; on the other hand, Passavant simply refers to it as " perhaps by Luini, or one of the same school."

The Virgin is represented as though asking for a branch of lilies with which her Infant Jesus is playing, while he shrinks away as unwilling to part with them. It is altogether a very graceful composition.

Engraved by Martinet.

20.—THE VIRGIN AT ALTON TOWERS.

Earl of Shrewsbury.

HERR PASSAVANT (in " Kunstreise durch England und Belgien ") mentions a small picture by Leonardo, preserved at Alton Towers, the seat of the Earl of Shrewsbury. " It shows the Virgin with the Infant Christ upon her breast; the Child stretches out his hand for a pink which she holds in her hand. The background represents a landscape, with the Lake of Como in the distance and in the foreground is a garden; the mother wears a black dress and yellow mantle."

21.—THE VIRGIN OF THE POURTALÈS GALLERY.

THE "Bulletin de l'Alliance des Arts," vol. i. page 30, refers to this painting, and attributes it to Leonardo. It was once in the possession of the Royal Family of Spain, and was bought for a work of Luini, at the Pourtalès sale. "In it the Virgin is shown bending towards her Infant Son, as she offers Him a flower."

22.—THE VIRGIN OF ANDREA SOLARIO.
In the Louvre.

THIS picture, signed "Andreas de Solario fec.," although it vividly recalls the manner of G. Ferrari, his master, is most probably founded on a design by Leonardo, "for," says Passavant, "there is still existing in the collection at the Ambrosian Library, a drawing in red chalk by this master, half-length life size, which has served as a basis for many of the pictures painted at Milan by the pupils or the imitators of Leonardo's school; these are, however, all inferior to that at the Louvre. This drawing by Leonardo has been engraved by Gerli."

So Andrea Solario must nevertheless be awarded a great share in the praise due to this admirable picture, which, with its lightness, its inimitable charm, its transparency and brilliant colouring, belongs entirely to the Lombard school.

23.—THE VIRGIN OF THE BRERA GALLERY.
Milan.

THIS also has been pointed out to us by Passavant. "The Virgin and the Child Jesus are in a landscape; the picture is incomplete. It was formerly in the possession of the Archbishop of Milan, and is at present in the Brera Gallery. The design is too feeble to be Leonardo's; but it may be by Salaino."

24.—THE HOLY FAMILY OF BRESCIA.

AGAIN our information rests on the authority of Passavant: "The Holy Family, in an open tent, surrounded by a landscape with a river, on which there are two swans. This picture, executed with great care, has passed from the collection of Sigismund Belluso, of Mantua, to that of the Count Theodore Lecchi, at Brescia; it is evidently a work by one of Da Vinci's pupils."

25.—The Madonna of Milan.

"The Virgin is holding the Holy Child with both hands, and He strokes her chin as though He were about to embrace her, meanwhile turning His head towards the spectators. The picture is very charming, and most highly finished." Kugler thus describes this work, which he found in the Casa Aracœli, at Milan.

Is it really by Leonardo, and is it still at Milan? M. Charles Clément refers to a Madonna in the Litta Palace of the same city. "The Virgin," says he, "is seen in profile, as she inclines her head towards the Infant Christ. The drawing is of great beauty, and displays a grandeur, amplitude, and roundness, which are of a truly extraordinary character.

"The face of the Virgin is painted in a somewhat dry manner, denoting the influence of Flemish art.

"The authenticity of this picture has been contested, but it is nevertheless an admirable piece of painting."

Engraved in the selection of Fumagalli

26.—The Virgin with the Scales.
In the Gallery of the Louvre.

The drawing of this picture is somewhat undecided; it has been supposed that it was painted by Leonardo during a period of depression. Waagen attributed it to Marco d'Oggione, while Passavant names Salaino as the probable painter; the catalogue of the Louvre, however, unhesitatingly gives it to Leonardo.

The name of this work was derived from the scales of the Last Judgment, which St. Michael is represented as offering to the Infant Jesus seated on the knees of His mother; but neither Mary nor her son appear to pay any attention to him, for they are occupied with watching the little St. John, who is toying with a lamb beside his mother, St. Elizabeth.

Engraved in Landon's "Vies et Œuvres des Peintres."

27.—THE HOLY FAMILY.

In the Gallery of the Louvre.

IN this the Infant Christ is seated on a cushion, His mother supports Him, and assists in taking a cross of reeds from the hands of the little St. John the Baptist.

Waagen, and after him Passavant, refer this picture to the Roman school; the former says, "That from its composition, its agreeable character, and the warmth of its colouring, which is slightly gloomy in the shadows, he recognizes a work of Pierino del Vago." At the Louvre, however, it is attributed to Leonardo.

28.—MATER DOLOROSA.

FUMAGALLI, in his "Recueil," gives the drawing for a bust of the "Mater Dolorosa." "It is," says Kugler, "of remarkable grandeur and nobility, and evidently is the design for a completed work." Where it is now to be found is uncertain.

29.—ASSUMPTION OF THE VIRGIN.

THIS picture is mentioned by il Padre Gattico, who, in a manuscript history of the Convent of Santa Maria delle Grazie at Milan, says that Leonardo painted over the door of the convent church an Assumption of the Virgin, which was executed on canvas; "there may be seen, in a glory formed by numberless little angels, St. Dominic and the Duke Lodovico Sforza on the one side, and on the other St. Peter Martyr and the Duchess Beatrice. The picture was in the form of a lunette; it was transferred to the sacristy in 1726, where it has been copied in fresco." All these details do not interfere with the fact that the authenticity of this picture has been doubted by the greater number of historians on art; they even insinuate that the Dominican Gattico, in his too great anxiety to enhance the glory of his convent, has not hesitated to depart from strict truth.

30.—VIRGIN SURROUNDED BY SAINTS.

THIS is known to M. Millin only, who, in his "Voyage dans le Milanais," states that the church of the Brera possesses a Virgin by Leonardo da Vinci.

"She is surrounded by three bishops and a cardinal, the donor, his wife, and their children; two angels are placing a crown upon her head."

31.—THE VIRGIN OF POMMERSFELD.

COUNT SCHÖNBORN possesses in the gallery of his castle of Pommersfeld a Virgin represented with the Holy Child upon her knees, on a cushion. The virgin is supported by a pedestal, and the Child points to a vase on a table.

Kugler says that this Virgin and Child are the portraits of a beautiful woman and her son known to Leonardo; but a little further on he attributes the picture to Solario.

On comparing the Virgin at Pommersfeld with the work numbered 1228 in the Louvre, known as the "Virgin of Andrea Solario," "there may be found," says Dr. Rigollot, "the same amiable expression in the faces, the same well-drawn forms, so fine and so rounded, and the same excellent fore-shortening of the limbs of the child with its softened contours, and the rosy tone of the toes and the elbows; one may recognize also the clear flesh tints, with their delicate blue half-tones and transparent shadows, though these last are rather dark, the beautiful blue colouring of the mantle, and the red dress with its white lights and orange shadows; in fact, in the soft work of the pencil, in the manner in which the colours are grounded and diffused, the handiwork of the pupil of Gaudenzio Ferrari may readily be discovered." This picture was at first attributed to Raphael, but wrongly; it is doubted whether it is more rightly referred to Solario.

Granted that this picture has a sufficiently original appearance to account for many copies having been made, it is nevertheless doubtful if it is the work of Leonardo. The features of the Virgin "with a short nose," the elaborate nature of the painting, and the superficial expression of her face, are not in any way characteristic of Leonardo da Vinci.

Among the copies which have been made of this Virgin of Pommersfeld, Waagen refers to a painting in the Gallery at Berlin; which is stated in the catalogue to have been painted after a composition by Leonardo.

32.—The Virgin and Infant Jesus.

M. G. de Moulins, the owner of this picture, published, in 1848, a pamphlet "On the Illustrious Leonardo da Vinci and his Immortal Works," informing us of its being in his possession, and that he was prepared to dispose of it on remunerative terms. He also affirmed in the same pamphlet that it had never been out of his family since the time when it was given to François de Moulins, who was Grand Almoner of France, and once tutor to Francis I., and died in 1535. Besides his own statement, he gives no other confirmation of the fact than a phrase from Félibien: "There is in the cabinet of M. de Sourdis a Virgin holding a little Jesus in her arms." This M. de Sourdis was a near relative and intimate friend of the De Moulins family.

The picture is painted on wood; the figures are larger than life size; the Virgin supports her cheek against the head of her Child, whom she holds upon her lap; she is clothed in a red dress, and a mantle of azure blue lined with orange silk falls from her shoulders; the Child is unclothed.

Part II.—SACRED HISTORICAL SUBJECTS.

33.—The Last Supper.

In the Convent of Santa Maria delle Grazie, Milan.

This, the greatest work of Leonardo, has already been so fully described in this volume (see page xxxv.), that further notice is not needed.

Engraved by Raphael Morghen; Thouvenet; and many others.

Herr Passavant gives the following criticism on the copy at the Royal Academy:—"A copy in oils, by Marco Uggione, from Leonardo's celebrated painting in Sta. Maria delle Grazie in Milan, is of the same size as the original.

" The united efforts of ignorance and destruction having now rendered the splendid fresco a mere shadow of what it was, this copy by one of Leonardo's best pupils assumes a proportionate value. It is also in itself a fine performance, preserving the character of the heads most completely, all that is wanting being that delicacy of finish which particularly distinguished the original. The beauty of the old painting in this respect is further proved by the ten original heads which formerly belonged to the Ambrosian Library, and which are now in England.* They were purloined from the library during the period of the French Revolution, fell into the hands of Sir Thomas Baring, and afterwards passed into the collection of Sir Thomas Lawrence, at whose sale they came into the possession of Mr. Woodburn, in whose gallery I had the advantage of seeing them. These ten heads are of extraordinary beauty, and in tolerable preservation; drawn in black chalk, with a slight tint of colour, and altogether well worthy of the great master. It seems as if Leonardo had devoted his chief efforts to the heads, leaving the rest of the figure only slightly expressed. In the sloping, almost horizontal strokes, we recognize the peculiar signs of Leonardo's pencil, while the great delicacy of the drawing and perfect gradation of tone are incontrovertible proofs of his excellence. The copy now before us, by Marco Uggione, formerly embellished the refectory of the Chartreuse at Pavia, but was stolen during the troubles of the revolution by a Frenchman, who brought it to Milan, and having there taken up a sum of money upon it, absconded, and was no more heard of. In the meantime the picture remained unnoticed and unreclaimed till the year 1815, when the Treaty of Paris being concluded and every nation striving to regain her own, this copy, for better security, was brought over and publicly exhibited in England. Sir Benjamin West, at that time President of the Royal Academy, made a most favourable report of its merits, but purchasers were few in number, and the Academy subsequently obtained it at a low price."

34.—St. John the Baptist.
In the Gallery of the Louvre.

Dr. Kugler says, in his " Handbuch der Kunstgeschichte," that " this St. John, the portrait of Lucrezia Crivelli, and that of

---

* Eight of these heads are in the Gallery of the Hermitage.

Mona Lisa, which are in the Louvre, can alone be regarded as thoroughly authenticated works of Leonardo's most brilliant period, since nearly all references relate either to these or to incomplete or missing works." If it were not for the cross in the hand of the saint, the radiancy of his face, and the impassioned expression of his mouth and eyes, and the gesture with which he points towards heaven, it might lead one to mistake him for a Bacchus—he seems to be crying "Evoe" to Jupiter after his first vintage. The beauty of the modelling and the flesh-tones mingled with the shadows, which are almost opaque, the clear spaces brilliant with metallic-like reflection, are all characteristic of the hand of Leonardo.

Unhappily, the head alone has been left as he painted it; a number of retouches have defaced this *chef-d'œuvre*, this companion to the Mona Lisa.

The entire history of this picture is not known, but it is certain that Louis XIII. made it a present to Charles I. of England, who, in exchange, gave him a portrait of Erasmus by Holbein, and a Holy Family by Titian. It is probable that Cromwell once had it in his possession. By a series of unknown adventures, Leonardo's painting fell into the hands of the amatuer Jabach, from whom it was obtained for the Louvre. The Ambrosian Collection at Milan possesses a copy of this work.

35.—THE ADORATION OF THE MAGI.

In the Uffizi Gallery, Florence.

THIS was doubtless painted before Leonardo left Florence, about 1480, for the Figures, above all that of the Virgin, are not of that type which he afterwards adopted at Milan.

His constant aim was to master the effects of light; he may claim to be regarded as the inventor of that difficult science which is called " chiaroscuro."

" This picture," says Rumohr, in his " Italienische Forschungen," " in which the distribution and composition are of a studied simplicity, in which the numerous persons are arranged in groups, bound together by skilful disposition of masses, and where all the figures, though placed in a common obscurity, are made visible by the reflections of feeble and broken lights, is the most complete example that Leonardo has left to painters who, like Fra Bartolomeo, have devoted themselves to the art of distributing light, and combining the composition of their pictures by the use of shade on shade."

Engraved in Rosini's " Storia della Pittura Italiana.

36.—BUST OF ST. JOHN.

THE Italian, Conca, mentions "a head of the youthful St. John in the palace of the King of Spain." Mengs speaks of a head of St. John the Baptist in his youth, as belonging to the Princess of the Asturias. These two are probably identical.

Félibien, in his " Entretiens sur les Peintres," says that " there was in the Hôtel de Condé, in the cabinet of M. le Prince, a head of St John the Baptist." It had been painted, he thinks, at Florence, about 1513, by Leonardo da Vinci, for a gentleman of the court of the Duke of Florence, called Camille degli Albizzi. Lanzi, who had seen many pictures of St. John the Baptist, says that they cannot be safely attributed to Leonardo.

Herr Passavant has not given any opinion, neither has Dr. Rigollot. It is probable, however, that Mengs was not deceived; and considering the high eulogy that he gives to the picture of St. John the Baptist in the possession of the Princess of the Asturias, we may readily believe that Leonardo had a hand in " that grand study of chiaroscuro."

37.—ST. JEROME PENITENT.

In the Collection of Cardinal Feschi

THIS is nothing more than a rough sketch, like the Adoration of the Magi. St. Jerome is on his knees in a grotto, with a lion by his side; the head only of the Saint is finished.

38.—HEAD OF ST. JOHN.

At Milan.

HERR PASSAVANT says, in his manuscript notes, " The severed head of St. John is on a plate. The picture is very finely executed, but appears to have been done by a pupil of Leonardo's after his design. It was found in the Ambrosian Collection at Milan. The lights in the hair are heightened by gold, which is not found on any other of the works of this master."

This head of St. John, which has been noticed by few critics, ought to be put among the most doubtful pages of the great book Leonardo has left us.

39.—PICTURES OF HERODIAS.

At Florence.

AN "Herodias" which has for a long time passed as the work of Leonardo still exists in the Tribune of the Uffizj at Florence. It is now almost decided by all art-critics to be a masterpiece of Bernardino Luini, pupil and imitator of Leonardo, the greater number of whose pictures have been attributed to his master; and they are in many cases worthy of that honour. The Herodias of Florence is assuredly one of the most beautiful creations of art. The figures are half-length. Herodias seizes the head of the saint, which the executioner is bringing forward; a serving-maid is standing near.

There are in this picture an energy of expression and a skilfulness of workmanship which are very remarkable. The Royal Palace of Hampton Court possesses a picture of Herodias, attributed to Leonardo da Vinci, but Dr. Waagen thinks that it is more likely to be the work of Beltraffio. There is mention also of an Herodias in the collection of M. Collot, formerly Director of the Mint, Paris, but this is a reproduction of the one at Hampton Court. "If it is not by Leonardo, it is worthy to be so," says a French critic. It is of a very clear tone, more transparent and fine than that of the copy at Hampton Court.

The catalogue of the pictures in the Imperial Gallery at Vienna attributes three pictures of Herodias to Leonardo da Vinci, but none of these three pictures are by the hand of the master. They are all the work of his school. It is difficult, however, to find the signature of any well-known pupil on them. Passavant thinks that one of these may be Cesare da Sesto.

In the Orleans Gallery there is a copy of the Herodias of

Vienna, and the Dresden Gallery also possesses another, but in a bust only. No. 1227 of the Louvre is "Salome," the daughter of Herodias, by Andrea Solario. This has been often attributed to Leonardo, but it is certain that it was bought by Louis XIV., on the understanding that it was a work of Solario. It is one of the good pictures due to the influence of Leonardo. This, according to the "Notices des Tableaux recueillis en Lombardie," once belonged to the Cardinal Richelieu.

Dr. Rigollot found at Amiens, in the collection of an amateur, a fine picture, having for its subject Herodias holding a dish, in which the executioner places the head of St. John the Baptist. An old woman, whose head is covered with a turban, responds with a gesture to the glances of Herodias; two figures are seen in the background. "This picture came from the sale of M. Lafontaine, who, it is believed, had it from George IV., in exchange for some Dutch and Flemish pictures for which the king had a desire. According to the catalogue of the sale, it is believed that it once formed part of the collection of Charles I. It has been attributed to Leonardo, but wrongly.

At the Leeds Exhibition, in 1868, Colonel Markham exhibited a painting by Leonardo—"The Daughter of Herodias receiving the head of St. John."

The picture in the Gallery at Florence has been engraved by Volpato and in Landon's Selection.

40.—SAINT CATHERINE.

LÉPICIÉ, in his "Catalogue des Tableaux du Roi," mentions a half-length of St. Catherine crowned with jessamine, and holding in her right hand an open book, the pages of which she is apparently turning with her left; she is accompanied by two angels, one of whom holds a palm, and the other her instrument of martyrdom. "This picture," adds Lépicié, "is vigorous in colour; the details of the draperies astonish us by their finish; Leonardo has left nothing neglected that may truthfully render the different characters of the materials which drape the principal figure." It is now at Compiègne, and the catalogue refers to it under the erroneous title of "The Holy Family;" it is numbered 139.

There are many St. Catherines attributed to Leonardo; among others one was formerly at Modena, in the gallery of the D'Este family. M. Rigollot mentions another at Milan, in the possession of the painter Appiani.

The Royal Gallery at Copenhagen flatters itself that it possesses the original of all the Saint Catherines attributed to Leonardo; Herr Passavant believes, however, that this is a vain assertion, and that the much-vaunted work is more probably by Luini.

Gault de Saint-Germain speaks of an original St. Catherine in Germany: he probably refers to the painting at Nuremberg, which was engraved by H. C. Müller.

At the Leeds Exhibition of Works of the Old Masters, in 1868, a "St. Catherine and Two Angels" (from the Corsi Gallery, Florence) was lent by Mr. P. F. Howard.

41.—MAGDALENES.

VASARI possessed a drawing by Leonardo representing a Magdalene, the head of whom "was full of grace and expression." This drawing is now preserved in the gallery at Florence. Conca speaks of a "Magdalene with her hair falling loosely about her, which was found in the Cathedral of Burgos, and which skilful connoisseurs attribute to Leonardo." Lanzi mentions two pictures of the Magdalene as attributed to Leonardo, one at the Pitti Palace at Florence, the other at the Aldobrandini, at Rome; but believes that both of these are most likely the work of Luini.

Herr Passavant, in a notice referred to by M. Rigollot, says that the Magdalene of the Aldobrandini Palace was subsequently at Vienna, in the hands of the Counsellor Adamowich.

42.—SAINT SEBASTIAN.

In the Gallery of the Hermitage, St. Petersburg.

M. CHARLES BLANC has narrated the history of this picture in the "Gazette des Beaux-Arts" of the 15th of January, 1861. " It was," says he, " bought by the famous merchant Dubois, at Turin, towards the commencement of the Empire. Charged to compose a nucleus for a gallery by an Italian prince, he collected

a vast number of paintings, and among them was this St.
Sebastian, which he valued at a hundred thousand francs, as he
declared it to be by Leonardo."

The Italian prince died young; his collection was sold, and the
Saint Sebastian fell into the hands of the Chevalier Bistoli, who
some time afterwards gave this painting in pledge, and it was,
after his death, sold to M. Wolsey-Moreau, who exhibited it in
Paris, where negotiations for its purchase and removal to the
Louvre were opened; but in 1860, the Grand Duchess Marie,
attracted by its beauty, induced the Emperor of Russia to buy
it for sixty thousand francs, that it might be included among
the collection at the Hermitage Gallery in St. Petersburg.

The Saint, tied to a tree by means of red and black ribbons,
points with his left hand to an arrow which has pierced his
heart, and with his right to an inscription.   It is evident, as
M. Charles Blanc remarks, that this is an emblematical portrait
of some grand personage of Milan.

Part III.—CLASSICAL SUBJECTS.

43—Bacchus.

In the Gallery of the Louvre.

Waagen says that the landscape in this picture appears to him
to be the work of Bernazzano, "who often painted backgrounds
for Cesare da Sesto." He dwells "on the local tone, which is
red, on the hardness of the contours, on the awkwardness of
the gradations of shadow." Passavant, on the contrary, extols
the head, the feet, and parts of the scenery, as being entirely
beautiful; "the remainder," he says, "seems never to have
been finished, and has suffered much," but he attributes the
painting to Leonardo without any doubt.

All that can be said with any reasonable pretension to certainty is, that Leonardo painted this picture, but that inex-
perienced hands have tampered with the work in attempting to
restore it.

Passavant truly observes that the vine-leaves and grapes are

of a crude green colour which Leonardo has not employed in
the rest of the picture; he believes that this "Bacchus" is really
meant for St. John the Baptist in the Desert, and recalls the fact
that in the church of St. Eustorgio, at Milan, there is a copy of
this work which is there named St. John the Baptist.

It is not improbable that some purist, scandalized by the
pagan expression of the Saint, was convinced that Leonardo
intended his figure for a Bacchus, and most conscientiously
added the vivid green vine-leaves and grapes. If so, this
"Bacchus" is nothing more than a travesty of Leonardo's work.

M. Giuseppe Campori refers to a volume of manuscript poetry
by Flavio-Antonio Giraldi, in the Public Library of Ferrara, in
which he found a distich alluding to a "Bacchus" attributed to
Leonardo. It runs thus :

"BACCHUS LEONARDI VINCII.

"Tergeminum posthac, mortales, credite Bacchum :
Me peperit doctâ Vincius ille manu."

Does this mean the Bacchus of the Louvre?

Gault de Saint-Germain, in his Catalogue, mentions this
picture as being by some attributed to Lorenzo di Credi. But
why not ascribe it to Leonardo without further discussion?

44.—HEAD OF THE MEDUSA.

In the Uffizi at Florence.

VASARI speaks of a Medusa as belonging to the Duke Cosimo de'
Medici; and it is believed to be the same that is now in the
Uffizj. It is a death-like head, of a fantastic yet realistic type,
and marvellously drawn. The glassy eyes extinguish themselves in rolling in their orbits; the mouth is distorted with
agony, and the hair, which seems bristling with horror, is
composed of hideous green snakes, which Leonardo has rendered
with an extreme fineness of touch; they extend themselves as if
fearfully hissing, even as though they shrunk from the fatal
breath that escapes from that terrible mouth. M. de Rumohr
does not think that this famous head is really a work of Leonardo's youth, and believes that the picture at Florence is no
more than a copy, painted towards the middle of the seventeenth

century, of the Medusa mentioned by Vasari. Passavant remarks that the colour is more thickened than was usual with Leonardo. Notwithstanding these criticisms it is probable that the head in the Gallery at Florence is the same as that which belonged to the Duke Cosimo; it is evidently the work of a youth, incomplete, but bearing unmistakable signs of the powerful touch of a master.

Photographed by Messrs. Alinari of Florence.

45.—Vanity and Modesty.
In the Barberini Palace, Rome.

Piranesi and d'Agincourt have engraved an allegorical picture entitled "Vanity and Modesty," from a work attributed to Leonardo in the Barberini Gallery at Rome. The Giustiniani Collection contained a painting of the same subject, also ascribed to Leonardo, and in the Sciarra Palace at Rome there is a third representation of this allegory, of which M. Viardot says: "This picture is in a most elevated style, and its admirable beauty is such that it does not permit me to raise any doubts of its authenticity." It has, however, been doubted if any one of the three is really by Leonardo. That first mentioned is generally attributed to Luini, and is supposed to have been painted by him over his master's drawing; and that which M. Viardot refers to has also been attributed to Luini by Fumagalli; but M. Rumohr thinks it may be a painting by Salaï.

Engraved by Campanella; by Troyen; and in Landon's Selection.

46.—Leda.
At the Hague.

There is more than one picture of Leda attributed to Leonardo; the chief is that at the Royal Gallery of the Hague. It is a beautiful composition, but has been subjected to many transformations and changes. Too pagan in character for some into whose hands it fell, this picture was re-named "Charity,' and by a process as simple as barbarous, the nude portions of the figures were covered; in this disguise it was the glory of the

Gallery at Hesse-Cassel, after which it was for some years at Malmaison, whence it was taken, no doubt by indirect means, to the Royal Gallery at the Hague, where it has been restored almost to its primitive state.

In this picture Leda is represented with a child on her arm, and one knee on the ground, in the position of a person rising slowly; with her left hand she points to the twins, Pollux and Helen, who are emerging from the mythological egg; a child seated on the other side near a part of the shell appears to regard the principal group with great attention.

The scene passes on the banks of a river, where the grass is mingled with reeds; the river traverses the whole of the background: at one side extends a breadth of country strewn with towers, and on the horizon a chain of mountains loses itself in clouds; to the left an amazon and two cavaliers gallop swiftly along on horseback.

M. de Rumohr has frequently spoken of this picture; he believes it was painted at Milan, on account of its violet tone and rather dingy flesh tints, which recall the painting of the portraits of the Duke and Duchess of Milan; but he finds certain defects in the treatment of the nude portions, which would seem to indicate the date of the picture to be more closely associated with Leonardo's youth.

Passavant says that the composition certainly emanated from Leonardo, "for there exists a drawing, published by Gerli, evidently intended as a sketch for it, but the picture itself, the drawing of which is heavy, is executed by one of his pupils."

Is this the Leda to which Théophile Gautier refers? "Singular to note," says he, "that Leonardo da Vinci, who possessed so profound a knowledge of the science of anatomy, scarcely ever painted a nude figure; for our part, we do not know any other example but the Leda; she is shown at full length in an equilibric pose worthy of the great and beautiful Grecian statues, to which, however, she bears no other resemblance, for Da Vinci, original in everything, draws his ideas from the source of nature alone. At the feet of Leda, which are noble and pure as if they were carved in marble, are two children playing among the shell-chips of their broken egg, the lovely offspring of the celestial swan; the young mother wears that expression of sprightly gaiety which is, as it were, the seal of Leonardo; her eyes sparkle with laughing malice beneath their lightly coupled brows, and the mouth is drawn back at the corners, creasing the dimples of the cheeks with sinuosities so soft, so voluptuous, and at the same time so arch, that her look is almost perfidious."

In the Royal Collection of England there is an original drawing in pen and ink representing Leda standing beside a swan. Herr Passavant, in his notes, says: "This is a composition by Raphael; but it appears that Leonardo once possessed the drawing, or, at all events, his scholars made many copies of it. In the Borghese Gallery at Rome there may be seen an example of this; another was engraved at Paris, by Leroux, in 1835."

In spite of Passavant's positive assertion, the standing Leda is not by Raphael; perhaps, however, the great painter of Urbino may have made the original drawing, which is in England, after a composition of Leonardo's; it is known that in his youth Raphael studied at one time the cartoons of Leonardo and Michael Angelo.

Speaking of Michael Angelo, we must, according to Passavant, restore to him the sketch of Leda which was at Fontainebleau, and of which Lomazzo speaks; this last opinion of Passavant is perhaps more reasonable; the sketch, which is now at Berlin, bears the impress of Michael Angelo rather than that of Leonardo.

Engraved by Leroux.

47.—FLORA.

THIS picture once formed part of the collection belonging to Marie de' Medici; it was afterwards in the Orleans Gallery, at the sale of which it was bought by M. Udney, who re-sold it to the King of the Netherlands. It is finished with all the care usually bestowed on a portrait, and indeed it was for a long time, and not without reason, believed to be a portrait of Diana of Poictiers, or of one of the mistresses of Francis I.

The Dutch have given it the names of Frivolity or Vanity, for what reason none but a German professor of æsthetics can philosophically explain. The figure is simply a charming young woman holding a flower, with her right breast uncovered. In a catalogue of the pictures belonging to Charles I. of England, there is mention of a painting representing a half-length figure of a laughing woman holding a flower, which was referred to a pupil of Leonardo.

M. Passavant speaks of "an old copy, in which the entire figure is nude," and which was at Stratton, the residence of Sir T. Caring; he thinks it is the one indicated in the catalogue above named.

There is in London another picture of the same subject, also attributed by Dr. Waagen to Leonardo. The woman is clothed in a blue mantle and a blue-tinted white robe, and holds a flower in her left hand; her posture is charming; the head recalls the most beautiful of Leonardo's faces, and the execution is of great purity. "But," says Dr. Wagen, "the features are here of a particularly fine character: the delicate nature of the amber flesh tones, and, above all, the manner in which the colours are grounded, seem to proclaim this the work of Andrea Solario."

May not this last-mentioned example be the half-length laughing figure referred to in the catalogue of King Charles? It is now in the gallery of the Duke of Sutherland, at Stafford House.

Another Flora attributed to Francis Melzi, and said to be designed by Leonardo, was a few years ago in the possession of Signor Lancelloti at Naples.

Lithographed by J. Linnell.

PART IV.—HISTORICAL SUBJECTS.

48.—CARTOON OF THE BATTLE OF ANGHIARI.
(Battle of the Standard.)

THE Battle of Anghiari was fought against Niccolò Piccinino near Florence, in 1440; it was by no means terrible, since but one man was killed in it, and even he, not from wounds received in the fight, but because he fell beneath the horses' feet and was trampled to death.

A special decree of the Republic had charged Leonardo to represent this battle in a large picture on the walls of the council

P

chamber; he commenced his sketch in the hall at Santa Maria Novella, and made it of such large proportions that he was obliged to call in the aid of his engineering science in designing a machine to elevate and lower his work with ease. Vasari speaks of the cartoon with enthusiasm, above all extolling a group of cavaliers disputing about the possession of a standard or flag; but he says that Leonardo was forced to renounce his intention of painting the picture in oils, on account of the imperfect method then followed for the preparation of colours. In the " Carteggio inedito d' artisti dei secoli xiv. xv. xvi." by Doctor Gaye, we read that some parts of this work were indeed begun in 1504, that Leonardo was assisted by Raphael, Antonio di Biago, and by Ferrando l'Espagnol, and that so much as they then did was still to be seen in 1513.

The original design of Leonardo is lost. Passavant says that the group of soldiers engraved by Edelinck, after a drawing by Rubens, and that reproduced in Plate 39 of vol. i. of L'Etruria Pittrice," are neither of them taken from the original sketch, which does not exist, but from a reduced copy believed to be the work of Bronzino, or from a drawing in the Ruccellai Palace at Florence.

The "Battle of the Standard" was engraved by Bertrand Edelinck.

Part V.—PORTRAITS.

49.—Portrait of Leonardo.
In the Gallery of the Uffizi at Florence.

This portrait of Leonardo, painted by himself, is the one which is so well known through the engravings of Raphael Morghen, Campiglia, and others. He was sixty years of age.

Engraved also by Laguillermie.

50.—Portrait of Leonardo *(drawn in profile)*.
In the Royal Collection at Windsor Castle.

This was published in 1796, in a selection entitled " Imitations of Original Designs by Leonardo da Vinci, consisting of various drawings, published by John Chamberlaine." The stippled engraving by Bartolozzi, in imitation of red chalk, is a profile. The countenance shines with a light which seems to come from on high; the head of so beautiful a type in the original, is rendered with a singularly delicate exactitude. A copy of this is in the Ambrosian Library. It is said that this is the portrait of which Vasari speaks as in the possession of Francesco Melzi.

The Museum of the Louvre once contained a profile portrait of Leonardo, a drawing in red chalk which came from the collection at Modena.

Photographed in Mrs. C. Heaton's "Life of Leonardo."

51.—PORTRAIT OF LEONARDO. (*Full face.*)
At Venice.

IN the collection at the Academy of Fine Arts at Venice may be seen a superb head, almost full face, drawn in red, which is very probably a portrait of Leonardo in his advanced age. Bossi has engraved it in his " Cenacolo," and there is a copy in black chalk among the drawings belonging to the King of the Netherlands.

52.—PORTRAIT OF LEONARDO.
In the Esterhazy Gallery at Vienna.

THIS portrait represents Leonardo holding a letter in his hand, on which is written : " A Maria Ant della Torre Leonardo di Piero da Vinci manda il ritratto." It ought to be—A Marc-Ant. M. Viardot declares this portrait to be absolutely authentic; but Count Gallemberg has not even spoken of it in his work composed at Vienna in 1833, and published in 1834 under the title of " Leonardo da Vinci."

53.—PORTRAIT OF LEONARDO.
At Milan.

"THIS is indeed," says M. Viardot, " the beautiful and venerable head of the patriarch-artist."

It is drawn in profile on paper with red chalk, and may possibly be a copy of that in the Royal Collection at Windsor.

54.—PORTRAIT OF LEONARDO.

At Vaprio.

COUNSELLOR PAGAVI, in his manuscript memoirs, refers to a portrait of Leonardo painted by himself, as being in a house known as La Canonica di Vavro (or Vaprio), situated on the Adda.

This house belonged to the Melzi family, whom Leonardo often visited there, they being among his most intimate friends.

The old Canonica d' Aprio has resisted the destroying influences of wind and rain. There are, however, no traces of this painting discoverable therein. It has probably either perished or been removed elsewhere.

55.—PORTRAIT OF FRANCIS I.

IN this picture, which belongs to Mr. Pocock, the king is represented as St. John the Baptist.

The frame bears the date 1518. Leonardo had ceased to paint at the later period of his life, which this date would indicate; it may, however, have been added after his death.

Lithographed by Day and Haghe.

56.—PORTRAIT OF MONA LISA. (LA GIOCONDA.)

In the Gallery of the Louvre.

THIS masterpiece, which has been called "the despair of painters," is an enigma of beauty. It is a portrait of the wife of Francesco del Giocondo; and Vasari, although an Italian, and speaking in that flowery language, could not find terms sufficiently laudatory in which to express his enthusiasm.

Francis 1. bought this grand work for 4000 gold crowns of the currency of his time, and equal to 20,000 of our present coinage. "La Joconde" might now be sold for that sum and yet be considered cheap.

After the "Last Supper," this is the most admirable work of Leonardo's that remains to us; but like it, it is a work which each day becomes more mysterious and more effaced. The background—a charming landscape, where the blue sea is bordered by picturesque mountains—is half invisible to our eyes, but we can yet contemplate this delightfully pure drawing, we can still admire these finely ideal forms so delicately rendered, we can still feel enraptured before the ineffable gaze of these lucidly dewy eyes; we can still, like the contemporaries of Francis I., fall into a dream before the infinitely mysterious smile; but where now are the warm tones and life-like flesh-tints, the vivid carnations that once enchanted Vasari? It is with difficulty that we can bring ourselves to be astonished now at the hands—"hands without parallel even up to our own time"—which are of irreproachable beauty in form, but the colour of which has almost vanished into night.

Félibien, whom modern critics seem to regard with disdain, but who will keep his place among art historians, had never seen anything more finished or better expressed than "La Gioconda." "It has so much grace, and such sweetness in the eyes and the features, that it appears almost living; and it seems to one who sees this portrait, that it is of a woman who takes pleasure in being admired." This is concisely and comprehensively written.

" The work of Leonardo is a marvel, a thing more divine than human." Thus spoke Vasari, and justly. In the presence of so wonderful a painting one endeavours to calculate the time that was consumed in its execution; it may be, one thinks, that the artist yielded to the fascination he so well displayed, and that he prolonged at pleasure the luxury of a *tête-à-tête* with this charming woman; it may be that he had, in fact, great difficulty in expressing the proud serenity and provocation contained in this face, the smile of which sometimes appears almost unearthly, and seems to magnetize us with its voluptuous attraction. We fancy that after having finished the drawing with much delicacy, and shaded it off into almost imperceptible obscurity, and having thus approached and then withdrawn, as it were, the artist had wished to follow into mystery his recoiling half-tints, to hide from our eyes in a veil of mist the lovely figure, until it appears at last as a dream in the midst of a fairy land, surrounded by small blue rocky mountains, pointed sharply and carved in crystal, like stalactites reversed towards the sky.

The Royal Museum of Madrid possesses a copy of this portrait, in which the background is formed of a dark curtain. It is said that this copy is by Leonardo himself; but he rarely copied anything, much more his own pictures; moreover, this copy of Madrid is too well preserved to have been painted by Leonardo. There are others, in England, in Germany, and elsewhere, which are quite as beautiful as that at Madrid, but which are not from the hand of the master himself.

Passavant mentions two copies, "one which may be found in the Hermitage Gallery, and another forming part of the collection of Cardinal Fesch," in which Mona Lisa is represented unclothed.

Engraved by Fanchey; by Massard; and in Landon's Selection.

57.—LA MONACA.

In the Pitti Palace, Florence.

THIS half-length figure of a nun or young girl wearing a hood is of strange beauty and fascination, and shines vividly amid the many masterpieces which fill the galleries of the Pitti Palace.

It has been said that this is not the work of Leonardo, but of one of his scholars. Oltrocchi, however, suggests that it is a painting which is recorded to have been given in 1536 to Cardinal Salviati by a brother-in-law of Leonardo. It was found in the collection of the Marquis Niccolini, and, notwithstanding the doubt that has been expressed, those who see it feel that it is one of the most poetic creations of the master.

58.—PORTRAITS OF LODOVICO SFORZA AND HIS FAMILY.

IT was towards 1495 that Leonardo painted the family of Lodovico il Moro kneeling on a mountain, representing Calvary, which may still be seen in the Convent Delle Grazie at Milan; but while the landscape, said to have been painted by Montorfano, is well preserved, the figures of Leonardo have vanished.

Vasari says that nothing was more beautiful than the heads of the young princes Maximilian and Francesco, who stood near their mother the Duchess Beatrice. Now one can scarcely distinguish anything of these three figures, any more than that of the Duke Lodovico Sforza; the whole group is even more faded than the "Last Supper," which is on the opposite wall.

The mediocre work survives, the work of genius has perished.

Would that Leonardo, the chemist, had been content with the common oils which Montorfano employed!

59.—PORTRAIT OF GIAN GALEAZZO SFORZA.
At Milan.

THERE is a three-quarter length portrait in the Ambrosian Library at Milan, representing the Duke while still in his youth. This, which has for a long time been thought to have been intended for Lodovico, is one of the best portraits by Leonardo. Passavant, in his "Kunstreise durch England," refers to a portrait of Lodovico Sforza drawn in black chalk, of great natural beauty, as preserved at Oxford; this also is attributed to Leonardo, but Passavant believes it to be "by one of his best pupils."

60.—PORTRAIT OF ISABELLA OF ARAGON, WIFE OF GALEAZZO SFORZA.
At Milan.

THIS portrait is also in the Ambrosian Library at Milan. It is a fine profile study, after the manner of Holbein or Van Eyck.

Dr. Burckhardt in his "Cicerone" says, "This profile picture is beyond all description beautiful and charming, and of a perfection in the execution which precludes the possibility of any artist but Leonardo."

61.—PORTRAITS OF THE DUKE MAXIMILIAN SFORZA.

Two portraits of the eldest son of "Il Moro" are attributed to Leonardo; one is in the Ambrosian Library, the other in the possession of the Melzi family.

62.—PORTRAIT OF A WOMAN.
In the Royal Gallery at Augsburg.

THIS is surely a sister of Mona Lisa, a sister in artistic beauty and perfection, and in its presence, as in that of "La Gioconda," the eternal ideal of this great seeker after the perfection of female beauty seems nearly attained. The portrait shows her in full face; the mouth above all is of great delicacy and charm;

the eyes appear to have been retouched, they have not their former expression; the hair and the breast are only sketched out.

63.—PORTRAIT OF LUCREZIA CRIVELLI. ("LA BELLE FERRONNIÈRE.")

In the Gallery of the Louvre.

LE PÈRE DAN, in his "Trésor des Merveilles de Fontainebleau" (1642), calls this a portrait of a Duchess of Mantua. M. Delécluze, in "L'Artiste," says that it is a portrait of Ginevra Benci. For a long time, and even now sometimes, it has also been named La Bella Ferronnière; but according to the most trustworthy historians, the mistress of Francis I., to whom tradition has given that name, was either dead or past an attractive age at the time of Leonardo's arrival in France.

Quite different from La Gioconda, but still as attractive in its somewhat stern placidity, is the portrait of Lucrezia Crivelli, which for so long passed for that of La Belle Ferronnière.

In the *Codex Atlanticus*, an autograph manuscript of Leonardo da Vinci, may be read three Latin epigrams on Lucrezia Crivelli, the mistress of the Duke Lodovico Sforza. It is known, moreover, that Leonardo on arriving at Milan painted a portrait of this lady. The general opinion is, therefore, that this picture in the Louvre is really a portrait of Lucrezia, purchased by Francis I.

It is a beautiful figure, painted in the Florentine manner, before the Milanese type had become Leonardo's ideal. She is represented in three-quarters length, with soft silky hair, and a forehead encircled by a black band fastened with a diamond, thus giving cause for the popular name of La Bella Ferronnière. This beautiful head is full of light, and has an expression of pride mingled slightly with melancholy. The tone of colour is warm and brilliant, and the whole drawing tells of Leonardo in each of its soft, pure lines; the shadows, too, are warm, and almost transparent. Dr. Waagen says that it is the most beautiful picture by Leonardo that the Louvre possesses.

Le Père Dan speaks of five pictures by Leonardo which he saw in the Gallery of Paintings at Fontainebleau:

"1. A figure of the Virgin with a little Jesus, who is supported by an angel, all seated in a pleasant landscape.

"2. St. John the Baptist in the desert.

"3. A half-length figure of Christ.

"4. The portrait of a Duchess of Mantua.

"5. The fifth in number but the first in value, a marvel of painting, is the portrait of a virtuous Italian lady named Mona Lisa."

No. 1 is unknown; No. 2 is the St. John the Baptist of the Louvre; No. 3 is mentioned in the catalogue of Lépicié, but is not now found; No. 4 is the portrait of Lucrezia Crivelli, and No. 5 is Mona Lisa, which the good father counts the first in value, as a work of marvellous skill.

Engraved by Bridoux; Lacroix; and in Landon's Selection.

64.—PORTRAIT OF A YOUNG MAN.
In the Gallery at Florence.

BOTTARI believes that in this he recognizes a portrait of Raphael. The catalogue of 1655 declares positively that it is from the hand of Leonardo: thus—" Ritratto in tavola di un giovane, di mano di Lionardo da Vinci."

According to Passavant, "the colours of this picture are laid on very thickly, and in this respect it resembles the head of the Medusa. It may probably be one of Leonardo's early works."

65.—PORTRAIT OF GINEVRA BENCI.
In the Gallery at Florence.

GINEVRA BENCI was a graceful and charming girl, the daughter of Amerigo Benci, who was Leonardo's landlord, and with whom was found a sketch for the picture of the Adoration of the Magi. Ghirlandajo and Leonardo were often inspired by the beauty and naïveté of the young girl. Ghirlandajo painted her portrait among others, in the fresco that he executed for the church of Santa Maria Novella, towards 1484. Vasari says that Leonardo also painted her: " Ritrasse la Ginevra d'Amerigo Benci, cosa bellissima, ed abbandonò il lavoro a' frati."

This portrait of Ginevra was in the Niccolini Gallery; it was bought by the Duke of Tuscany, and by him placed in the Pitti Palace. It is a lovely work in Leonardo's first manner; it seems as though one could detect the caresses of the brush on those charming eyes, and lips that open with an arch smile—that smile which Leonardo so often gives to his women, even to his Virgins, to render them the more attractive. But this portrait has been "*cleaned*," and with the varnish many of the beauties of its first state have disappeared.

The historian of Italian painting, Rosini, is said to possess an original portrait of Ginevra Benci by Leonardo. It is a charming figure, in a pure style. He has given a representation of it, together with one of the portraits by Ghirlandajo, in his work called "Storia della pittura Italiana, esposta coi monumenti."

Palmerini has engraved a portrait under the name of Laura, which he believes to be also of Ginevra Benci and by Sandro Botticelli. The same portrait has been reproduced in 1824 in a Florentine edition of the works of Raphael Morghen illustrated by Palmerini.

66.—Portrait of Cæsar Borgia.

This portrait is spoken of by M. le Comte de Betz, who had seen it at Bologna in 1845, in the Corazza Collection. The catalogue of pictures in this collection affirms that it is a portrait of Cæsar Borgia painted by Leonardo; but we know that the statements of catalogues must be accepted with reservations. M. de Betz, however, says that he fully recognized in this portrait, which is very beautiful, the manner of Leonardo, and that the eyes have been painted by no one else; they have that strange power of expression which he alone could give, and which retains one so long before his portraits.

67.—Portrait of an Old Man.

At Windsor Castle.

This is a beautiful head of an old man, beardless, drawn with great delicacy and brilliancy. It is attributed to Leonardo. Passavant, however, doubts its authenticity.

68.—PORTRAIT OF CHARLES VIII., OR CHARLES D'AMBOISE.

In the Louvre.

THIS picture was at first designated a portrait of Charles VIII.; afterwards of Louis XII.; and now, on the authority of M. le Blanc, it is said to represent Charles d'Amboise, de Chaumont, Maréchal of France, and Governor of the Duchy of Milan. This favourite of Louis XII. died in 1511, at the age of thirty-nine; he entered Milan with the king in 1509, and it is suggested that this portrait was painted between that time and 1511.

Both Waagen and Passavant think that this portrait ought to be attributed to Jean-Antoine Beltraffio, one of Leonardo's best pupils. In 1846 Hillemacher published an etching of it, with the inscription, " Charles VIII. roy de France."

69.—PORTRAIT OF A MAN, FULL FACE. [BY HOLBEIN.]

In the Dresden Gallery.

THIS picture, which Jacob Folkema has engraved so well under the title of " Portrait d'un guerrier, vu de face," is, according to Lomazzo, the portrait of Giovanni Giacomo Trivulzio, painted after the battle of Agnadel, in which General Trivulzio then sixty-four years of age, commanded the vanguard.

According to other critics this is a portrait of Duke Lodovico; according to Passavant, of Mr. Morett, goldsmith and jeweller to Henry VIII. of England. In support of this latter opinion, it is affirmed that Hollar engraved the picture in question in 1647 with Morett's name attached to it; it was then in the collection of Lord Arundel. It may be remarked that the Comte de Betz refers to a portrait in the Pitti Palace numbered 207, in the gallery called the Saloon of the Iliad, representing a man, which is attributed to Leonardo, and called " L'Orefice." May not this be the portrait that was engraved by Hollar? But if there is no agreement on the subject of the name of the personage represented in the portrait of the Dresden Gallery, neither is there any certainty with regard to the name of its painter, some declaring it to be by Leonardo da Vinci, others by Hans Holbein. M. Viardot, in his " Musées d'Allemagne," says that the merits of this picture are equal to those of·La Gioconda; but other art critics incline to the opinion that it is more like the work of Holbein; and if it be a portrait of Henry the Eighth's goldsmith, they are probably correct. [There is now no doubt but that this portrait is by Holbein.]

Engraved in "The Dresden Gallery."

70.—PORTRAIT OF A WOMAN.
At Antwerp.

M. RIGOLLOT says that he has seen this portrait in the collection of an amateur at Antwerp. It represents a woman seated, and a little less than half life-size. The owner of this picture attributes it to Leonardo, and believes it to be a portrait of a duchess of Milan or Mantua. He was so strongly convinced of its authenticity that he had refused to sell it for 60,000 francs, and would not take less than 100,000. But M. Rigollot refrains from giving us his own opinion.

71.—PORTRAIT OF MARC ANTONIO DELLA TORRE.
At Milan.

MARC ANTONIO DELLA TORRE, professor of anatomy, was the master, the idol, and the friend of Leonardo. It is not then without reason that his portrait is said to have been painted by his great pupil. But can it be that the portrait preserved at the Ambrosian Library is that of the celebrated professor, who died of the plague in 1512? Nothing can prove this assertion, and, as Passavant says, "the picture is too feeble in design and drawing, the drapery too stiff, to allow of its being attributed to Leonardo; it is in oil, and has been entirely repainted."

72.—PORTRAIT OF A MAN IN RED.
In the Dulwich Gallery.

IN his "Kunstwerke und Künstler in England," Dr. Waagen speaks of this portrait, which is attributed to Leonardo, as being, in his opinion, the work of Beltraffio.

73.—HEAD OF A WOMAN.
In the Orleans Gallery.

AMONG the plates published by Conché, in 1786, under the title of "Galerie du Palais Royal," may be found a head of a woman after the Flora of Leonardo, and said to be by the same master. But the original of the "Head of a Woman" is really in the possession of Lord Egerton. It is attributed to Luini, that pupil of Leonardo who has so often deceived one into thinking his work the work of his master.

74.—PORTRAIT OF JEANNE D'ARAGON.

QUEEN JEANNE died in 1435; it therefore appears little probable that the portrait in the Doria Gallery, or that which has been discovered at Rome—both being attributed to Leonardo, on the authority of Amoretti—have any chance of being rightly named.

There is not much to confirm the opinion of Passavant, who asserts that the portrait in the Doria Gallery actually represents the Queen whose name it bears, and that it is also a copy of Raphael's picture in the Louvre, which he thinks was made by one of Leonardo's pupils, who had evidently taken care to give the face that "smiling expression peculiar to the school of his master." "The head is likewise," added he, "very well drawn, as much so as the rest of the picture is stiff in design and dry in colour." How far does this last observation prove this to be a copy by a pupil of Leonardo? Raphael was much younger than Leonardo; how then could he have painted the original portrait of Jeanne d'Aragon, who died before the former was born?

75.—PORTRAIT OF THE CHANCELLOR MORONI.

BUT little faith can be placed in the portraits of his contemporaries which are attributed to Leonardo; it is certain that the greater number are of questionable authenticity. Leonardo painted slowly and was choice about his models, not seeking for sitters beyond his patrons, except in the case of the most beautiful. There is mention of two copies of the portrait of Moroni; they represent, it is true, a personage clothed in the robes of a chancellor, but Geronimo Moroni was not appointed to the chancellorship by Duke Maximilian until after 1512, when Leonardo was no longer at Milan.

These two so-called portraits of Moroni are, the one at Parma in the hands of Count Sauritali, the other at Milan with the

Duke Scotti Gallerati. The first came from the collection of the Duke Modena, and I believe it to be wrongly attributed to Leonardo. As for the second, there is no doubt of its being quite unauthentic.

76.—PORTRAIT OF A WOMAN.

LÉPICIÉ, in the "Catalogue Raisonné," speaks thus of this portrait—"Item.—A head of a woman in profile, commonly called 'La Belle Ferronnière.' She wears a 'toque' of red velvet, bordered with a kind of embroidery in gold, and finished off at the side by a row of pearls; a black veil is fixed to the 'toque,' and falls upon her shoulders. The dress is of some dark blue stuff. The profile is drawn with astonishing precision, and leaves nothing to desire in the finish of the execution." So says Lépicié of the "Belle Ferronnière." Is it really the original, or is it an improved copy? According to M. E. Soulié, assistant-keeper of the Museum at the Louvre, "this portrait is still preserved there, although but little valued, it being estimated in the inventory at 150 francs, and at the time of the last classification it was judged unworthy of a place among the *chefs-d'œuvre* of the Galleries." But the new catalogue, under the number 488, attributes this portrait to the school of Leonardo.

77.—A LAUGHING BOY WITH A TOY.

A PICTURE bearing this title, and attributed to Leonardo, was sold in England, in 1801, to Sir William Hamilton for £1365. We can find no traces of this painting.

PART VI.—PICTURES LOST OR MISSING.

WE may now say a few words on the missing pictures of Leonardo da Vinci, some of which are of great importance and interest.

1.—A Roundel.
(*Rotella del Fico.*)

Vasari narrates that Leonardo, while a youth, painted on a round piece of wood "reptiles and hideous animals, which had a most frightful effect." This is said to have been bought by the Duke of Milan for three hundred ducats; but it is entirely lost.

2.—Adam and Eve.

Vasari refers to this sketch as belonging in his time to Ottavio de' Medici; it was a work of Leonardo's youth, which he had drawn in black and white with the brush, and representing Adam and Eve in the earthly Paradise. It was intended as a design for some tapestry for the King of Portugal.

3.—The Nativity of Our Lord.
(*Probably an Altar-piece.*)

The Duke of Milan, Lodovico Sforza, presented this to the Emperor Maximilian on the occasion of his marriage to Blance-Maria Sforza, the duke's niece. It was one of the most beautiful of all the gems which the Emperor then received.

4.—An Angel.

According to Vasari, Duke Cosimo de' Medici possessed a figure of an angel painted by Leonardo da Vinci. " The angel comes towards you with uplifted arms, which show a most admirable knowledge of foreshortening, in the drawing from the shoulder to the elbow." What has become of this picture, probably the Archangel St. Michael ? M. Rigollot says that after having been perhaps banished to some villa during the regency of the grand-duchesses of Tuscany, it was most likely sold by auction to a broker with the inferior works which were put away in the garrets of the Pitti Palace, and after having been restored, resold to a Russian or an Englishman.

Passavant, in his manuscript notes, says, " The Grand-Duke of Tuscany, having learnt all these circumstances desired to buy this picture back again, but as the price demanded was excessive, he refused to make the purchase."

5.—Two Children playing with a Lamb

This is what Raphael Mengs calls a " picture which is unfinished, but certainly in Leonardo's best style. Besides the merits of the chiaroscuro, there is a grace in the agreeable movements of the figures which recalls the manner of Correggio." Conca also mentions this work: "It is," says he, "a beautiful thing." Mengs had seen it in the cabinet of the Princess of the Asturias, and Conca says that it was in the Royal Palace at Madrid. May it not be the picture of the Aguado Gallery, described as "No. 341. Two children playing on a green sward enamelled with flowers?" This picture was bought for 4000 francs at the sale of that gallery in 1843, but by whom is not known.

6.—Conception of the Virgin.

This painting was found in the church of San Francesco at Milan, according to Lomazzo, who says, "The celestial character of virginity imparted to the Madonna is much admired." It is said that this work is now in England. Professor Mussi formerly possessed the sketch for the head; it was in black chalk, touched with the pencil and heightened the lights. ("Leonardo da Vinci," von Hugo, Grafen von Gallemberg," pp. 225 and 230.)

Luini, perhaps, was the painter of the "Conception," the sketch for which belonged to M. Mussi. Vasari was deceived more than once: this makes it probable that Lomazzo was also.

7.—Virgin Suckling the Infant Jesus.

In the edition of Vasari's works published at Sienna in 1794 there is a note by G. della Valle: "There is a picture of the Virgin suckling the Holy Child, by Leonardo, in the church of Madonna di Campagna at Piacenza, which was bought by Prince Belgiojoso, but is now at Milan, in the collection of the Duke Litta Visconti Aresi." "The execution and the style of the picture," says Passavant, "is that of the school of Van Eyck, which appears to have had some influence over Leonardo during his residence in Milan. The work has been damaged, but re-touched in parts. It was engraved in 1828 by Jacopo Bernardi." Lanzi speaks of a Madonna in the palace of the Belgiojoso d'Este family, "which certainly came from the hand of Leonardo." Perhaps this is the one of which Della Valle makes mention in the note above referred to, and it may be the same as that indicated by l'Anonyme de Morelli, who saw at the house of Michael Contarini, at Venice, in 1543, a picture of the Virgin suckling her child, by Leonardo da Vinci.

Waagen says, "There is a little oval picture of the same subject at Blenheim Palace, in which the Virgin has a sad expression, though full of nobility. This work is treated with much delicacy, but has been greatly defaced; it is attributed to Leonardo, yet I think it must be the production of Beltraffio." ("Kunst und Kunstwerke in England," v. 2.)

8.—NEPTUNE.

VASARI mentions that in his time, Messer Giovanni Gaddi possessed a drawing by Leonardo representing Neptune surrounded by sea-gods. This drawing was made for Antonio Segui, and is also missing.

9.—POMONA.

ACCORDING to Lomazzo, there was at Fontainebleau a picture of Pomona, which was said to be by Leonardo. It was especially famous for the execution of the triple veil with which she is covered.

It is not known what has become of it, for there is no mention of such a work in the catalogues of the various royal galleries of France.

10.—VIRGIN OF PARMA.

LANZI says that this picture, which he saw at Parma in the house of Count Sanvitali, was marked with the monogram L. V., and, according to Gallemberg, one may read: "Leonardo Vinci fece, 1492." It represents the Virgin, the Holy Child, St. John, and St. Michael the Archangel. What has become of this work the authenticity of which appears certain?

11.—Portrait of Cecilia Gallerani.

Cecilia Gallerani was a mistress of Lodovico Sforza, and married Count Pergamino; but history, or a chronicle, affirms that the duke did not cease to love her on that account. Leonardo painted her portrait when he was at the court of Milan; and poets made sonnets in honour of the duke, his mistress, and, above all, of the painter. The Florentine Bellincioni is distinguished among all the others by his poetic laudations. Of all this, however, there remains no more than the doubtful copies of the portrait and the sonnet by Bellincioni. It is said that the original portrait of the beautiful Cecilia was, during the last century, in the possession of the Marquis Boursane at Milan. But where is it now? There was formerly an ancient copy at the Ambrosian Library; and in the Pinacothek at Munich there is a Saint Cecilia which had previously been the property of Professor Franchi, and passes for a copy by one of Leonardo's pupils of the very un-saintlike Cecilia Gallerani. There is also a second original portrait of Cecilia, preserved by the Pallavicini family of San Calocero, and painted at the height of her glory.

12.—Madonna of the Rose.

Leonardo painted this Madonna for the same mistress of Lodovico Sforza. In it the Virgin is represented urging the Infant Jesus to bless a rose. Perhaps this is an allegory, a madrigal in painting; and this rose may be emblematic of the beautiful Cecilia. Why not? In the time of the Duke Lodovico, the sacred and profane went hand in hand.

The "Madonna of the Rose" might have been seen at the house of a wine merchant named Giuseppe Radici; but it is strange that from the duke's palace it should have passed behind the counter. At what time, and how far has it gone now? It is reckoned as one of the most marvellously executed of Leonardo's pictures; the frame bears the following inscription: *Per Cecilia, qual te orna, lauda, e adora, El tuo unico figliolo, o beata Virgine, exora.* A canon of Milan named Foglia possesses a copy of this Madonna.

Rio says that a portrait of Cecilia Gallerani, as St. Cecilia, was at Milan, in the possession of Professor Franchi, and that another was preserved by the Pallavicini of San Calocero.

13.—TEN FIGURES OF AGED PEOPLE.

ACCORDING to M. E. Soulié, a manuscript inventory made in 1709 or 1710, by Bailly, keeper of the King's pictures, refers, among others mentioned by Lépicié, to " a picture by Leonardo da Vinci, representing eight figures of men and women at half-length, surrounding the figures of an old man and woman apparently caressing one another ; all of about 54 centimetres in height, on a surface 90 centimetres in width, painted on wood in a gilded frame." This picture is not now to be found in any French gallery.

14.—BUST OF A SAINT.

M. DE CHENNEVIÈRES has informed us that " in the catalogue of the pictures of M. Crozat, Baron de Thiers, which were sold to the Empress of Russia, there is mention of a *Buste de Saint* attributed to Leonardo."

15.—MADONNA DELLA CARAFFA.

THIS is known to us principally from the praises which Leonardo has bestowed upon it, speaking with enthusiasm of the vase containing flowers sprinkled with dew, " so fresh that one could believe them the work of nature."

This picture is one of those painted during Leonardo's youth, before he had quitted Florence ; it formerly belonged to Clement VIII., and was once in the Borghese Palace at Rome—whence it has disappeared since 1846. D'Argenville, in his " Vies des Peintres," says it was at the Vatican.

16.—THE VIRGIN AND CHILD.

A PICTURE thus designated is mentioned in the historical and chronological catalogue of the works collected at the National depôts for French Antiquities, by Alexander Lenoir, as a work of Leonardo da Vinci ; it is numbered 7 in the list addressed to the Committee of Public Instruction, with the following note appended; "Originally the property of some Dominicans, afterwards transferred to the Museum; it represents the Virgin and Jesus, and is painted on copper, silvered by a preparation much used among artists of the Florentine school, but which has the disadvantage of causing the painting to turn black and peel off after a certain time; of this the picture we are speaking of is an example."

17.—MADONNAS AT FLORENCE.

ACCORDING to Gaye and Bottari, Leonardo painted two Madonnas when he was at Florence, and these were said to be almost finished in 1507; they are now apparently lost.

III.

DRAWINGS AND SKETCHES.

THERE are several collections of drawings by Leonardo da Vinci. The most important are in the Ambrosian Library, Milan; the Gallery of the Louvre, Paris; the Royal Gallery, Florence; the Albertina Gallery, Vienna; the Academy, Venice; the Print Room, British Museum; the Royal Library, Windsor Castle; Christ Church College, Oxford; the Duke of Devonshire's Library; the Earl of Warwick's Collection; and that of Mr. Malcolm, of Poltalloch.

THE AMBROSIAN LIBRARY, MILAN

contains, among the more important drawings, the following Twenty-four Subjects selected from the "Codice Atlantico" to illustrate the SAGGIO DELLE OPERE DI LEONARDO DA VINCI.[1]

1. Fac-simile of the autograph letter sent by Leonardo to Lodovico il Moro, about 1483.

[1] Milan, 1872.

2. Rough sketch and map of Milan and its environs.

3. Various machines for raising water.

4. A canal with sluices and weirs, and details of same.

5. Plan for excavating and embanking a canal, with long MS. details.

6. Coloured sketch for delivery of water from the canal of S. Cristoforo.

7. Sketch map of the Red Sea and the Mediterranean with MS. notes as to their respective levels.

8. Construction of military bridges, with various details.

9. Military bridge with details of knots; sketches of *balestre*; fishtraps.

10. Details of windlasses, with varieties of toothing, and palls. A stone-thrower of unusual size.

11. Rough sketch, and finished drawing of a stone-throwing machine worked by a tread-wheel.

12. Machine for raising heavy bodies, such as a stone column. Device for flinging down scaling ladders raised against a wall.

13. Numerous details of machinery for transferring vertical and horizontal motion. Machine of uncertain use, possibly a scheme for a *mitrailleuse*.

14. Machine for cloth-dressing, and details of same.

15. Machine for cutting marble, with numerous details and notes.

16. Projects for aërial machines; parachute; lamps; turning-lathe.

17. Machine to regulate the shape of iron bars to be used for cannon.

18. Designs for artificial wings, with MS. explanations.

19. Drawings referring to experiments on attrition.

20. Machine for throwing silk.

21. Details of clockwork, with new kind of escapement.

22. Hydrographic map of the Loire and its affluents; kneeling female; male head; geometric measurements.

23. Balestra, or stone-thrower, mounted on wheeled carriage.

24. Sketches of the equestrian statue of Sforza, and case for transporting same.

IN THE LOUVRE, PARIS.

Among the more important are—

Head of a Young Man, in profile, wearing a leather cap. A highly-finished pen-and-ink drawing, washed with ink; engraved by M. Caylus.

Head of a Child, profile, and slightly turned to the left, in pencil, and heightened with white on pale green paper. This has served as a study for the Infant Jesus in "La Vierge aux Rochers."

Head of a Young Man, in profile, turned towards the right, with a crown of oak-leaves wreathed among his hair; finished with silver point and black lead pencil on prepared paper.

Head of an Aged Man, three-quarters, and turning towards the left. In red chalk; engraved by Caylus.

The Bust of a Young Man, three-quarters, turned towards the right; with luxuriously abundant hair. In red chalk.

Head of a Woman, nearly full face, with glance directed towards the left. Above, to the right, a profile of a young man. In silver point, on paper tinted with pale blue.

Bust of a Woman, full face, looking towards the right. Drapery surrounds the head, and forms, in its fall, a knot on either side. In silver point, washed and heightened with white on sea-green tinted paper.

Study of Drapery, enveloping the lower part of the body of a person in a sitting posture. Painted in black and white on fine canvas.

Portrait of a Young Woman, life-sized, seen to the bust. The head is in profile, and turned towards the right; the hair is waved, and falls upon the shoulders. The bust, in three-quarters, is covered with a shining robe with large sleeves; the right hand reposes on the left arm. This sketch, which has been executed with great care by the master himself, is drawn in black lead and red chalk, heightened by touches of pastel. It was formerly in the Calderara Pino Gallery at Milan, and also in the Vallardi Collection, and was acquired at a public sale in 1860, for 4200 francs.

Study of the Virgin, for the picture of the Holy Family, representing the Virgin seated on the knees of St. Anne, in the

Louvre. Drawn in black lead, and washed with Indian ink, and heightened with white on paper slightly tinted with bister. Octagon in form.

A beautiful drawing, which, however, appears to have been entirely retouched by the hand of some modern master. It was in the collection of Sir Thomas Lawrence, and numbered 182 in the Catalogue of the sale of that belonging to the King of Holland, but was afterwards obtained through Mr. Samuel Woodburn, at the price of 750 francs.

IN THE ROYAL GALLERY, FLORENCE,

there is a large collection, most of which have been photographed by Alinari. Among them are—

A Dragon attacking a Lion.

Portrait of a Man with curling hair, profile.

Female Head with jewelled head-dress, profile.

A Mother and Child with a Cat.

Female Head, in profile, looking to right.

Portrait of a Man wearing a cap, profile.

Study for Drapery of a kneeling figure.

Female Head, full face. Head of an Old Man, full face.

Study for Drapery of a seated figure.

Study of the Head of Mona Lisa.

Study for Drapery of a standing figure.

Head of a Man crowned with laurel, profile.

Female Head, three-quarter face.

Study for La Belle Ferronnière. Study of a Hand and Forearm:

Head of a Man, full face, with Leonardo's handwriting.

Three grotesque Heads of Old Persons.

Anatomical Studies, five sheets (one, David slaying the Lion).

Two Knights on Horseback and four Foot Soldiers.

IN THE ALBERTINA GALLERY, VIENNA.

The Visitation. Head of Christ.

Head of St. Anne. Head of the Virgin.

Ascension of Mary Magdalene. Head of a Monk.

Head of an Old Man. Portrait of Savonarola.

Caricatures (two sheets). Study of Two Horses.

Study of Drapery. Seven Studies of Heads.

IN THE ACADEMY OF THE FINE ARTS, VENICE.

There are thirty-three drawings by Leonardo in this collection: among the principal subjects we find—

A portrait of Leonardo, with a large beard.

A Head of Christ (small), bowed down and crowned with thorns.

A Sketch for the St. Anne of the Louvre, very charming.

Three Dancing Figures, after the antique.

A sheet of caricatures, among which may be traced those of Francis I., Savonarola, and some Florentine Poets.

Studies of the Infant Jesus, smiling at His Mother, while He is caressing a Lamb.

Sheets of Figures showing the proportion of the human body.

A sheet of Flowers, drawn from nature, and highly finished.

A rough sketch representing cavaliers fighting with foot soldiers, among whom are some skeletons—probably studies for the cartoon of the " Battle of Anghiari."

IN THE BRITISH MUSEUM.

Head of a Man in profile. Drawn with silver point on blue paper.

Head of a Man, full face. Highly-finished pen drawing on blue paper, heightened with white.

A Sheet containing three Caricature Heads.

Aged Men and Women, two drawings. Grotesques.

Study of a Virgin and Child and Cat and other compositions (three sheets).

A Group of Monsters with figure of a Man holding a shield.

Slight sketch of Horsemen.

A sheet representing various engines of war; with handwriting.

Head of a Man in profile. Red chalk drawing on white paper.

Nude Figure of a Young Man holding a staff.

Virgin and Child, the latter with His right hand raised as in benediction. Pen drawing, heightened with white, on green paper.

A Woman and Child and three profiles (two sheets).

Study of a Skull of a Horse.

IN THE ROYAL COLLECTION, WINDSOR CASTLE,

there are several portfolios of drawings by Leonardo, of which the following are the most noteworthy.

Leonardo's own Portrait.

Head of Woman, full-face.

Profile of a Youth.

Head of a Man with a malignant expression.

Study for the St. Anne.

A beautiful Youthful Head with a longing expression.

Study of a Male Head in red chalk.

A Profile Head of a Child.

A Male Head, with large and noble features.

A page of studies of numerous Profile Heads.

First outlines of a Virgin and Child and St. John.

Beautiful Male and Female Profiles (on reverse of above).

Four Caricatures, and a Head wreathed with oak-leaves.

A Young Girl in profile. On blue paper with silver point.

A Female Head, three-quarter face. Similar style to foregoing.

A Youth resting on a Spear, and pointing forward with one hand.

Part of a Male Figure, in red chalk.

Various Skulls, two entire and two divided.

A beautiful Youth in profile. Slight pen drawing.

A Knight in full gallop, an Archer, and a War Chariot.

A sheet of Elephants and Horsemen.

A Horseman in an animated attitude in full gallop. Probably a study for the Sforza Monument.

A sheet of studies of Oxen and Asses.

Studies of Horsemen, and a Man on foot below. Probably a study for the celebrated cartoon of the "Combat of Horsemen."

Neptune restraining his Sea-Horses

Two studies of Horses.

Sketch for the Monument of Francesco Sforza.

Studies of Horses.

Four drawings of St. George and the Dragon.

Various designs for the Sforza Monument.

Dogs and Cats Fighting.

Various Landscapes.

A Youthful Figure seated; a Prisoner in rags.

A sheet of studies containing two groups of the Virgin and Child and St. John, and two versions of St. John and the Lamb.

A sheet of studies of a Mother and Child, a Child with a Cat, two Children with Cats, and two Children embracing.

A drawing of a Hand.

Study for the foreshortened foot of Pomona in the picture by Francesco Melzi, at Berlin.

A sheet of excellent studies of Hands for the Mona Lisa.

Study for the Drapery of a Kneeling Figure.

Study of a Sleeve.

Various studies of Foliage.

Studies for the Coiffure of Leda.

Study of an old Camel.

A number of Men raising a ponderous Weight.

Two Heads, on tinted paper.

An Allegory.

Speaking of this magnificent collection of drawings, Herr Passavant says, "Three volumes of Original Drawings, a selection from which, entitled 'Imitations of Original Designs, by Leonardo da Vinci, in his Majesty's Collection,' was published by John Chamberlaine in 1796. . . . These drawings by Leonardo are sketched either in red or black chalk, or in pencil upon tinted paper. Some are drawn with the pen; but only a few in water colours or heightened with white. Among the portraits, his own, taken in profile, is the most interesting, drawn with red chalk, two-thirds the size of life. In Bartolozzi's print from this drawing the fine intellectual expression and fire of the eye is but feebly rendered. Generally speaking, his dotted engravings give no adequate idea of this kind of drawing. The other drawings represent a variety of subjects: figures, caricatures, horses, and other animals, with some fine anatomical studies of these latter; a small sketch, also, of an elephant battle, spiritedly drawn on red chalk; added to these, several designs for optics, hydraulics, and perspective; a foundry, with all kinds of military machines, and a drawing showing the effects of a bomb which is bursting in a tower; maps of the country, following the course of different rivers—one of the Arno, another of the Vallambrosa, and the country between Volterra and Livorno; the effects of an inundation, as drawn at the time from nature; sketches of mountains, plants, etc., which he introduced into his paintings; also the plan for some work, explained by sketches of the subject. Besides these, in this general workshop of the Muses, we also meet with MSS. of music, the meaning of each note given beneath in Leonardo's own hand. Lastly, a number of pen drawings of anatomical subjects, with an explanatory text, which, according to this master's usual method, is written from the right hand to the left. These sketches belong to 'A Treatise on Anatomy,' and formed one of the thirteen books which the Chevalier Melzi, the friend who accompanied him to France, compiled from his effects after his death. Three of these numbers fell into the possession of Pompeo Leoni, sculptor to the King of Spain, one of which, with a gilt inscription, 'Disegni di Leonardo da Vinci restaurati da Pompeo Leoni,' was probably purchased by the Earl of Arundel in 1636, at the time when this nobleman was ambassador from Charles I. to the Emperor Ferdinand II. of Austria. This book, and the portraits by Holbein, were found, upon the accession of George III., in Queen Caroline's room at Kensington Palace."

AT CHRIST CHURCH COLLEGE, OXFORD.

Virgin and Child; half-length, half-life size.
Two sheets of Allegories.
A sheet of studies for a Machine.
Horseman and Prostrate Figure.
Studies of Crossbows. (On reverse of above.)
Lodovico Sforza, a fine portrait. In black chalk, life size, but probably by a scholar of Leonardo's.

AT CHATSWORTH (Duke of Devonshire's).

Head of a Madonna. (Study for "La Vierge aux Rochers.")
Portrait of a Florentine Youth.

EARL OF WARWICK'S COLLECTION.

Study of a Head of the Virgin; in black chalk.

MR. MALCOLM, OF POLTALLOCK.

Head of a Warrior; silver point on prepared ground.

Study of a Head, resembling that of St. John in the Last Supper.

Head of a Man shutting his eyes, as if dazzled by a brilliant light.

A sheet of studies of Five Caricature Heads.

A LIST OF PAINTINGS AND DRAWINGS BY LEONARDO, MENTIONED BY DR. WAAGEN IN HIS "TREASURES OF ART IN GREAT BRITAIN."

In the British Museum.—A Collection of Original Drawings.

In the National Gallery.—Christ Disputing with the Doctors. (Probably by Luini.)

In the Royal Academy.—Cartoon. The Virgin seated in the lap of St. Anne.

The Last Supper. Copy by Marco Oggione

In Lord Ashburton's Collection.—The Virgin, Infant Saviour, and St. John, with attendant Angels. This beautiful composition was formerly in the apartments of the Escurial, and came to England in the Collection of General Sebastione.

In the Holford Collection.—A Study of the Head of the Virgin in "La Vierge aux Rochers." (Small size, in brown, on panel.) In this picture the features have the refined feeling which belongs to Leonardo alone.

At Gatton Park (The Countess of Warwick's).—La Vierge au bas-relief. Purchased by the late Lord Monson.

In Mr. Danby-Seymour's Collection.—Mona Lisa, a copy.

La Belle Ferronnière, a copy. (? by Beltraffio.)

In Mr. W. A. Mackinnon's Collection.—St. Catherine. (Ascribed to Leonardo, but probably by one of his pupils.)

In Earl Brownlow's Collection.—Mona Lisa, Replica of. A very delicate and beautiful example on panel.

At Hampton Court Palace.—Herodias' Daughter with the Head of St. John the Baptist.

The Royal Collection, Windsor Castle.—Three Volumes of Drawings, the most important of which are already noted (p. 233).

At Christ Church College, Oxford. (General Guise's Collection.)—A Collection of Seven Drawings, described on page 235.

At Basildon Park (James Morrison's, Esq.)—Flora. From the collection of Sir Thomas Baring.

At Charlton Park (Earl of Suffolk's).—La Vierge aux Rochers. (Most probably the original.)

At Stourhead House (Hoare Collection).—The Holy Family. Painted on parchment.

At Leigh Court (Sir W. Miles's).—Salvator Mundi.

At Thirlestaine House (Lord Northwick's).—The Virgin and Child (the Virgin standing). Ascribed to Domenico Ghirlandajo, but more like Leonardo.

At Chatsworth (Duke of Devonshire's).—Portrait of a Florentine Youth. (Most probably a portrait by Beltraffio.)

At Wooton Hall (Davenport-Bromley Collection).—The Virgin and Child, the latter holding a violet. Landscape with Lake of Como in background. (Called Luini, but most probably Leonardo.) From the Feschi Gallery.

At the Fitzwilliam Museum, Cambridge.—La Vierge au bas-relief, a copy. Two children playing on a greensward enamelled with flowers.

At Glendon Hall (Booth Collection).—A Lucretia.

At Holkham Hall (Earl of Leicester's).—MSS. entitled " Libro originale della natura, peso e moto delle acque, di Leonardo da Vinci, in tempo di Lodovico il Moro, nel condur che fece le acque del naviglio della Martesana dell' Adda a Milano."

At Lord Yarborough's.—St. Anne. Copy, probably by Salaino, of the picture in the Louvre.

In Lord Kinnaird's Collection.—La Columbine. Formerly in the Collection of the King of Holland.

PAINTINGS BY LEONARDO, OR ATTRIBUTED TO HIM, LENT TO
THE EXHIBITIONS OF THE WORKS OF THE OLD MASTERS,
AT THE ROYAL ACADEMY, BURLINGTON HOUSE.

In 1870.

	Belonging to
La Vierge aux Rochers ...	*Earl of Suffolk.*

In 1871.

Christ bearing His Cross ...	...	*Sir T. Proctor Beauchamp.*
Head of Christ (Crayon)	...	*Baroness North.*
St. Peter (Crayon) ...	...	*Baroness North.*

In 1872.

Virgin and Child ...	...	*Duke of Buccleuch.*
Portrait of a Young Man, said to be of the Achinta family		*Mr. W. Fuller Maitland.*

In 1876.

Portrait of a Lady holding a Vase	*Marquis of Lansdowne.*

In 1877.

Creator Mundi ...	...	...	*Sir William Miles.*

LONDON : PRINTED BY WILLIAM CLOWES AND SONS, LIMITED,
STAMFORD STREET AND CHARING CROSS.

CPSIA information can be obtained
at www.ICGtesting.com
Printed in the USA
LVHW082010280321
682767LV00034B/1435